CU00950129

Nick D:
Plays: 1

The Dead Monkey, The King of Prussia, The Body, Ting Tang Mine

The Dead Monkey: 'A cat-and-monkey game suspended ludicrously somewhere between Strindberg and Sam Shepard. Nick Darke's strange and quirky comedy . . . fully justifies the faith placed in him.' *Financial Times*
'Darke has something both hilarious and horrific to say about the decay of a marriage, and he compels the attention while doing so.' *Sunday Telegraph*
'Darke's play has found a metaphor of disturbing originality.' *Sunday Times*

The King of Prussia: 'A meaty play . . . seethes with life, wit and ideas. Darke gives shape to a Cornish identity that feels vital and real and has nothing to do with clay pipes and clotted cream. Like Cornwall's coves, it has many unexpected depths. The piece acts as a critique of capitalism. It also raises questions about the points where justice, conscience and the law part company.' *Financial Times*
'An unexpected delight . . . action-packed, racily written, dashes you round many a hairpin bend of plot, and glances irreverently at contemporary issues . . . a tonic, like a day at the seaside.' *Independent*
'A real gem, a classic of the genre.' *Observer*
'This much fun must be illegal.' *The Times*

The Body: 'The evening is full of surprises . . . The best moments in Nick Darke's play are extremely good – and not all good in the same way. The funniest sequences come in the first half, which has as a climax a hilarious scene . . . The second half of the play, which is more suspenseful, builds to a powerful climax . . . The most obvious debt is to Brecht. There are other reminiscences: of Auden and Isherwood's *The Dog Beneath the Skin*, of Tom Stoppard's *After Magritte*, and of T.S. Eliot's verse plays.' *Times Literary Supplement*

Ting Tang Mine: 'A lament for an industry and a way of life; but this should not suggest anything sentimental. The writing is rugged and muscular; lyrical but not ornate; vigorous but not folksy . . . oddball, quirkily parochial, and as authentic as a slice of rough bread.' *Sunday Times*
'Combines idiosyncratic earthiness with the clear didacticism of moral fable.' *Independent*

Nick Darke was born and raised in St Eval, Cornwall, the son of a farmer. He trained as an actor and worked at the Victoria Theatre, Stoke, throughout the 1970s. His first play, *Never Say Rabbit In A Boat*, about a group of Cornish farmers who invest in a fishing net, was performed at the Victoria Theatre in 1978, directed by Peter Cheeseman. He went on to write over twenty plays which have been produced by, amongst others, the Royal Shakespeare Company, Royal National Theatre, Royal Court, BBC radio and television. His work is translated and performed regularly throughout the world. He lives in the parish of his birth where he works as a lobster fisherman. He won the George Devine award in 1979 and is a Bard of the Gorseth Kernow.

NICK DARKE

Plays: 1

The Dead Monkey
The King of Prussia
The Body
Ting Tang Mine

introduced by the author

Methuen Drama

METHUEN DRAMA CONTEMPORARY DRAMATISTS

1 3 5 7 9 10 8 6 4 2

This collection first published in Great Britain 1999
by Methuen Publishing Ltd

The Dead Monkey first published in Great Britain in 1987
by Methuen London
in *Ting Tang Mine & Other Plays*
Copyright © 1987 by Nick Darke
The King of Prussia first published in Great Britain in this edition
Copyright © 1999 by Nick Darke
The Body first published in Great Britain in 1983 by Methuen London
Copyright © 1983 by Nick Darke
Ting Tang Mine first published in Great Britain in 1987
by Methuen London
in *Ting Tang Mine & Other Plays*
This revised version copyright © 1987, 1999 by Nick Darke
Collection and Introduction copyright © 1999 by Nick Darke

The right of the author to be identified as the author of this
work has been asserted by him in accordance with the Copyright,
Designs and Patents Act, 1988

A CIP catalogue record for this book
is available from the British Library

ISBN 0–413–73720–9

Typeset by Deltatype Ltd, Birkenhead, Merseyside
Printed and bound in Great Britain by
Cox & Wyman Ltd, Reading, Berkshire

Contents

To Jane, Henry and Jim

A Chronology
of first performances

Introduction

The first theatre I ever worked in (and the last, as an actor)
was the Victoria, Stoke. Like all the best theatres it was not
purpose-built but had metamorphosed several times from
duck pond through cinema via night club to playhouse. It is
at the time of writing, a car park. In the nine years I was
employed there as an actor I appeared in over eighty plays,
some of them written by living authors who visited regularly
and attended rehearsals. The Vic had two other unique
features. It stayed open 50 weeks of the year, employing a
permanent company, and it was in-the-round. The theatre
itself was nothing more than a box with black walls. Four
hundred seats surrounded a square stage about 20ft × 20ft.
The bottom row was three feet away from the actors and
once on there was nowhere to hide. The box was magical in
the sense that it changed its character and shape to become
the world of whatever story was being told on the night.
The nature of the stage and its proximity to the audience
meant that scenery could never be more than waist-height,
and moving furniture in a blackout was not an effective way
to change a set, so to create a realistic living room was
difficult but to launch a hot-air balloon or harpoon a whale
was no problem at all. Fluidity of action, jump-cuts from
location to location, short scenes, diversity of characters,
music as narrative were the bread and butter of the Vic and
I've fed on them ever since. Apart from *The Dead Monkey*,
which is set in a hut on a beach throughout, the plays in this
volume are classic Vic fare. They demand little more than a
magic box and half a dozen versatile actors to transport you
from the high seas to revolutionary France in the bat of an
eye. Load the plays with ornament and they tend to
collapse. Pace and fluidity are the watchwords, even
entrances and exits can be dispensed with if the performers
are kept onstage throughout, changing costume, picking up
props or sitting and sharing the action in a neutral zone
around the stage. The songs should lift and charge the

action, never slow it down or stop it. Underscoring is hard to achieve without marring clarity and focus. A sluggish or drab approach to staging should be avoided, they are after all comedies.

Few of the playwrights I met at the Vic offered me advice on how to become one but I learned by working with them that playwriting is a technical skill. Playwrights don't write plays, they create theatre. The playwright's tools are language, actors, action. To this end it is pointless offering help of a literary nature to novice playwrights, the best advice you can give is 'go and be an actor'. The most effective way to learn about structure and dialogue is to perform in a badly constructed play with appalling dialogue (there were a few of those at the Vic, not many, but enough). The secret of how to write plays lies in performing, not writing them. The authors of the best plays produced at the Vic had a clear, practical idea of exactly how they should be staged and the success of the production depended on how well we, the company, could explicate their singular vision.

The question most frequently asked about *The Dead Monkey* is did Dolores have sex with the simian or didn't she? When I'm asked this, invariably at the beginning of rehearsals by the actor playing Dolores, my reply is always along the lines of 'I'm not sure' or 'I don't know', 'She may have, or may not'. The director nods his or her head sagely and launches into a treatise about how the strength and mystery of the play is Dolores's ambiguity, her vicariousness, her ability to live a lie and believe it. Why else did she stay with Hank all those years? Why indeed, habit? But the real answer, although I never say it, is *yes*! Dolores fucked the monkey! Of course she did! Sex with a monkey is unthinkable, not of this world, but then, and here is the key, *neither is the play*. The audience is asked not to suspend its disbelief on this one but to leave it at home locked in a cupboard. Dive in at the deep end, take the story at face value, find the logic, create the world, transport us across the seas and far away to Dead Monkeyland. It's natural for

an actor to be cautious and the question is best answered
not by the author but by the process of discovery. As the
play is explored and probed uncertainty gives way to
conviction, so by the first night when the actors finally
beach themselves on the shores of their particular paradise
the conundrum is forgotten. However, some actors arrive at
the conclusion that she *didn't*. When this happens the play is
dominated by Hank. It becomes Hank's play. Hank is the
protagonist and Dolores the victim. The balance is upset
and Hank's despicable act at the end becomes not tragedy
but bathos. By fucking the monkey Dolores takes the
initiative, she *does* things. Her death at the hands of Hank is
caused by her actions as much as his. Tragedy is always
triggered by people who *do* things. Lady Macbeth was no
prevaricator, she didn't pretend. When she got up to go she
got up and went. Same with Dolores. If Dolores fucks the
monkey the land becomes remote, exotic and exciting, a
place where anything is possible, another world. If she
didn't commit the act we're back in good ole Wierdsville
California. *The Dead Monkey* belongs to Dolores, not Hank.

    The King of Prussia is a play about smugglers. Of course it
is. But every play set in the past must illuminate and
simplify the complexities of the present otherwise they're
not worth doing, so *The King of Prussia* is also about second-
home owners. Holiday homes are a blight on Cornwall
where they inflate the market and place housing beyond the
reach of local people. The arrival of their owners for a short
period in the summer is an invasion, they bring their
suburban values, habits, and worst of all aesthetics, impose
them onto the community, then retreat to their first homes
leaving behind a dead place with empty desolate houses.
Suzanne Stackhouse is Cornwall's proto-second-home
owner. In the words of John Carter, she 'd'come down ere,
play around, bugger off and leave we to pick up the bits.'
Her attitude towards the local people is arrogant and
superior. She is an out-and-out villain with not a single
redeeming feature. She is two-dimensional, predictable and
transparent. She rips through the place like a hurricane,

leaving a trail of devastation behind her. The only predictable thing about her is that she'll be back next year. Smuggling at that time made a vital contribution to the local economy and John Carter had a strong sense of responsibility towards the community which is not shared by the likes of Suzanne. In *The King of Prussia*, set in 1787, Eddy renounces smuggling to go fishing. In an earlier play of mine, *The Catch*, set in the present day, the central character abandons fishing to go smuggling.

The Body has songs, a chorus of farmers, a body covered in mud which talks, a rector who pretends he is a Chinaman and much more besides. The second act starts at the same time as the first but in a different place and it tells the same story from another perspective. As written it makes sense, just, but don't try to place the scenes in any sort of chronological order, you'll go insane. If I have a favourite play this is it. The first scene of the play is stolen from *Mann ist Mann* by Brecht who filched it from *Cannery Row* by Steinbeck who nicked it from who knows where. The play is popular with drama schools and university theatre societies, a campus classic. I assumed when the Cold War ended that the nuclear theme would lose its topical edge and make the play a period piece but I'm sorry to say it hasn't.

Ting Tang Mine is a parable of capitalism. Tin mining in Cornwall was a notoriously speculative, boom-and-bust operation. Fortunes were made and lost at the swing of a pick. Those who benefited most were the mineral lords, the landed gentry, who charged for the right to undermine their property. The mineral lords have been blamed for the collapse of the industry, it is claimed by some that they charged too much rent for their land and priced the ore out of the market. Cornwall's mines were honeypots for venture capitalists, gamblers and speculators who got rich on the backs of working people. Cornwall's last mine, South Crofty, shut down in 1998 ending thousands of years of continuous ore extraction. Those who raised the tin to grass, the miners, couldn't see the sense in the closure as it was, after all, showing a profit. There were potential buyers from all over the globe who showed interest, raised hopes then pulled out. An anxious time was had by all but in the end the pumps were switched off, the mine flooded and made defunct. As I watched and heard the story unfold I thought of writing a play about it but then I realised I already had. It's called *Ting Tang Mine*.

All of these plays (apart from *The Dead Monkey*, which comes from somewhere else) in one way or another concern the shifting fortunes of the small farming and fishing community where I was born and bred in Cornwall. At the time of writing there is no industry left here, only trade, a practice which predates the extraction of tin. However today's trade is not maritime but internal, the principal routes are not plied between Ireland or Phoenicia but down the M5 and up the A30. Tourism has replaced mining, fishing and agriculture as the area's principal earner. Like mining, tourism puts Cornwall at the mercy of speculators and fortune hunters and those who make the biggest buck are the landowners. Like mining, tourism defaces the landscape and offers little remuneration and less dignity to its workforce. Trade is usually what happens after a product has been manufactured, extracted, harvested or caught. Now that trade is all that is left, any sense of community and common purpose once provided by those activities is lost. Culture is debased and everything, including history, becomes a commodity.

Nick Darke
Porthcothan, 1999

The Dead Monkey

The Dead Monkey was first performed by the Royal Shakespeare Company at The Pit, Barbican, London, on 1 July 1986. The cast was as follows:

Vet	Antony O'Donnel
Dolores	Frances Barber
Hank	Bruce Alexander

Directed by Roger Michell
Music composed by Jeremy Sams
Designed by Chris Townsend

Act One

Scene One

The kitchen/diner of a small wood shack close by a beach in California. The furniture is cheap. There is a table, two chairs, and an easy chair. A large fridge. Against a wall there is a pile of magazines: Harpers and Queen. *There are copies of the magazine scattered on the floor, in strategic places. There is a bowl of oranges and an orange crusher. The kitchenette is partitioned off from the main room. There is a window in the partition, and a bead curtain in the door. The bedroom, off, is beyond the kitchenette.*

A dead monkey lies on the table. It is half covered with an Indian blanket. A woman, **Dolores,** *paces the floor. She is agitated. A* **Vet** *inspects the monkey with his stethoscope. He covers the monkey with the blanket and folds his stethoscope.*

Dolores   Is he dead?

Vet   Oh yes. He's dead.

Dolores   Oh God. Oh God.

Vet   He died of natural causes Mrs Wandaback. He was an old monkey.

Dolores   What shall I do?

Vet   With the monkey? You have several options. You could bury him, we have an animal cemetery in a pleasant corner of the zoo. Costya forty dollars. Or you could have him cremated, costya little more.

Dolores   What the hell's Hank gonna say? It'll break his heart.

Vet   Or you could eat him. Monkey flesh is considered a delicacy.

Dolores   . . . break his heart.

Vet   There's a lotta people consider it an honour for the monkey. To be eaten by ah. By Mom and Dad.

Dolores   I couldn't eat it.

Vet   It's a trying time for you Mrs Wandaback. If you just pay me my fee, $24.60, I'll sneak out and leave you to your bereavement . . .

Dolores   Yes. The fee.

She hunts in a shoulder bag which hangs over the back of a chair. She finds a couple of dollars. She then proceeds to find money all over the room, inside an empty cookie jar, amongst the oranges, amongst the magazines, in the fridge. Finally she amasses twenty-four dollars.

You've cleaned me out. Could I mail you the sixty cents? I'm expecting my husband, he brings home the bacon in this family . . .

Vet   That's fine . . .

Dolores   Such as it is.

Vet   We'll forget the sixty cents Mrs Wandaback.

Dolores   You're very kind. Could you reserve a place in the cemetery for the monkey? I'm sure Hank will wanna see him given a decent burial.

Vet   Popular choice Mrs Wandaback. It's a lovely, quiet little spot, right by the armadillo house. And for another $35 we provide a headstone of your choice. According to religion.

Dolores   Oh, that's nice. Hank will appreciate that.

Vet   What religion does your husband follow?

Dolores   He's an atheist but I know he will adopt something for this.

Vet   Have him come in and see the range before he makes a choice. I'd advise against Buddhism. Buddhas cost and they tend to get stolen.

Dolores   Thank you. You've been a great help.

Vet   I try to be. (*He starts to go.*) Oh . . .

Dolores   Yes?

Vet   Should you decide on another monkey, we have
plenty in stock, right by the dolphinarium.

Dolores   Thank you. I'll inform Hank of that.

The **Vet** *goes.* **Dolores** *fixes herself a drink, a dash of vodka
with the product of a crushed orange. She goes and uncovers the
monkey down to the neck.*

Dolores   Poor little monkey. I did all I could. Old
age. Well, that'll do for Hank. I sure dunno what he's
gonna say. When he left y'a week ago, you was jumpin
up and down, chattering away, playing ball with him in
the garden, scratching your underarms, a healthy
monkey. He'll just never believe you're dead. You were
always Hank's little monkey. I could never figure out
why, as soon as Hank left the house, you so completely
altered your personality. I had no idea it was within a
monkey's physiogomy to do that. But I guess it was
because he was your brother. I grew to love you in the
end. Sad as hell you're dead. Sad as hell. Christ I'm, so
sad. Goodbye little monkey. I love ya . . .

She covers him. A door slams out back. **Hank** *enters. He is a
big, rangy guy. He is awkwardly dressed in a salesman's suit. He
is tired and grimy. He walks straight to the easy chair and flops.*

Hank   Hullo sweet.

Dolores   Hullo Hank.

Hank *rises. He kisses* **Dolores** *full on the mouth. He is
horny. When he has finished with her,* **Dolores** *asks:*

How was your trip?

Hank   My trip? It was a journey through a whore's

soiled undergarments.

Dolores Gee I'm sorry to hear that Hank.

Hank No it was good.

Dolores You made a lotta sales?

Hank I sold all my stock. And more. But who the fuck to? Sharks. Leeches. Assholes. And what for Dolores? To pay off my company debts! Christ there are guys out there look at me and say he's so dumb that Hank he thinks a Mexican border pays rent.

Dolores Oh Hank honey, they don't.

Hank Plain as a lead pipe.

He vigorously squeezes oranges into the juicer.

You know what I think of the world Dolores? This thought revolves around my head when I'm gunning down the freeway. The centre of the world is a monkey's asshole. Every time the monkey shits the world contracts a little bit. Shits some more and the skin draws tighter across the globe. Pretty soon, this is before I hit the next state, the whole world is a vast pile of steaming monkey's shit. But the monkey is so fuckin greedy he starts eating himself and he shits himself through his own asshole. Then there is nothin left but monkey shit.

He's finished juicing and pours juice into the jug.

Hey! I forgot! How's the monkey?

Dolores Monkey's dead Hank.

Hank Shit! Dead? Shit! Where?

Dolores Right here Hank, on the table.

Hank *goes to the table. He uncovers the monkey.*

Hank Aw, hell. My little monkey!

Hank *falls on the monkey and weeps.*

Dolores I'm sorry Hank I'm real sorry.

Hank My little little monkey!

Dolores (*crying*) Broke my heart Hank, broke it right in two. I dunno what I'm gonna do without him.

Hank Aw, my little monkey! Oh God I was gonna play so many games, I bought a bat'n'ball for him, bought a big beach ball, I blew thirty-seven dollars in a kidstore . . .

Dolores Aww, Hank . . .

Hank . . . gotta sackfulla nuts out there . . . big walnuts . . .

Dolores Hank we . . .

Hank I think of him all the time I'm out there gunning down the freeway, can't wait to get back to my little monkey . . .

Dolores Can't you Hank?

Hank My li'l monkey!

Dolores I loved him too Hank, he was a companion to me when you was away . . .

Hank *recovers. He straightens up and reverently replaces the blanket over the monkey's head.*

Hank How d'e die Dolores?

Dolores Old age Hank.

Hank Old age. Well. Rest in peace.

Hank *returns to the juicer. He juices more oranges.*

Any ice in the icebox?

Dolores I'll fix you some ice Hank.

Hank Thank you Dolores. Mighty grateful.

Dolores *opens the fridge and gets out some ice. We notice the* *fridge is empty.* **Dolores** *finds a glass for* **Hank** *and places ice inside it.* **Hank** *fixes himself a long orange drink with a dash of vodka. He sits in the easy chair.* **Dolores** *sits in a dining chair.* **Hank** *stares into space.* **Dolores** *stares into space.*

Hank (*at length*)   We're living in the armpit of an opera singer's vest Dolores. This is what I'm thinkin when I'm gunning down the freeway. We hear all round us the cacophonous overtones of a gross, distorted drama. We sense the massive shiftings of a roaring body round a stage. What we experience is stinking perspiration and the darkest corners of a dying animal in its third and final act.

Dolores   Yes, Hank.

Hank   Yeah. It's occasions like this, when the monkey passes on, that I dream of when I'm gunning down the freeway.

Dolores   I know Hank.

Hank   Shit! Maybe I should ask for a new automobile.

Dolores (*hugging* **Hank**)   Oh Hank. I love you Hank. I love you so much!

Hank (*stroking her hair*)   Thanks Dolores.

Dolores   Hank. We've got each other now. No one else. No monkey . . .

Hank   That's correct, Dolores . . .

Dolores   Why don't we . . .

Hank   What?

Dolores   Monkey around? Make love? Right here, right now, on the kitchen floor.

Hank *surveys the kitchen floor. It is filthy and covered in magazines.*

Dolores   Maybe from the depths of our grief, might

come, something else?

Hank   Another monkey?

Dolores   He's up there looking down on us Hank. His spirit is with us. All around us. It'll never leave us. Maybe in ten years time we'll tell our children about the monkey and they'll say We know. We know he's here.

Hank   Say, that's a sweet thought Dolores.

Dolores   It is Hank. I don't have many lately.

Hank   What are we doin Dolores? Shit! I'm home two goddam nights! Then it's out again. Wisconsin! Wis-fuckin-consin!

Dolores   We're at a crossroads Hank.

Hank   I hate my job, my monkey's dead.

Dolores   I was speaking with Judd a lot when you was away this trip . . .

Hank   Judd?

Dolores   He says there's a job goin for ya anytime y'ask for it down at the junk lot . . .

Hank   I can't work for that jerk Dolores. You know that.

Dolores   Bring you closer to me . . .

Hank   Bring me a whole lot closer to Judd . . .

Dolores   Judd's changed. He's altered Hank, since college days . . .

Hank   How do you know?

Dolores   I'm round there most days when you're away. Susan's my buddy, you know that.

Hank   You leave the monkey?

Dolores   I left the monkey here Hank. I can't take

him round there Hank, they have fruit trees. A date palm.

Hank What is a jerk like that doin with a date palm?

Dolores What d'yexpect I should sequester myself with the monkey twenty-four hours a day?

Hank Maybe that's how he died. Pining for company.

Dolores I never stay long Hank. I stop enough to say to Judd and Susan how much I miss you and how much I wish you'd find a job near home. That's all.

Hank All the same . . .

Dolores He died of old age Hank. Please, let's not hand round blame . . .

Hank No. No Dolores, no. If I get the smallest hint that you might've neglected my monkey, imagine what these thoughts will grow into when I'm gunning down the freeway. Shit.

Dolores I know how much that monkey meant to you Hank. Why the first thing y'ever did when y'walked in here was Hi monkey! Hey monkey, see what I gotcha! Out the garden monkey! Let's play ball! Oh! By the way. Hullo Dolores . . .

Hank . . . Hey . . .

Dolores . . . let's fuck. Scram monkey while me and Dolores fuck a little. How often d'you dream about that on the freeway huh? Because as soon as that piece of whimsy's loosed up the canal it's out again. With hey monkey!

Hank Dolores! Dolores! This is serious!

Dolores Y'know the vet said he's gotta loada fresh monkeys in the zoo right by the dolphinarium but I don't want another monkey Hank, soon as he said it I said to myself shit no. Much as I love monkeys, Hank

ain't ever gonna sneak another monkey into this house.
From now on, I'm Hank's monkey.

Hank   C'mon Dolores. Let's monkey.

Dolores   I'm gonna withhold monkey from you Hank,
until you start out treating me like a monkey.

Hank   OK OK OK you wanna showdown I'll give ya
one . . .

He paces the room.

Dolores   I'm not after . . .

Hank   Look at this shithole! Look at it! No food in the
frigidaire! Basin fulla dishes! Magazines all over the
floor! Crap all over the floor!

Dolores   That's monkey crap!

Hank   Clean it up!

Dolores   I spend my life cleaning up monkey shit!
Soon as I've cleaned up one pile the goddam monkey
goes and dumps someplace else!

Hank *lifts a magazine off the floor.*

Hank   Look at this! Monkey shit underneath the
magazine!

Dolores   That's how I clear it up Hank! I drop a
magazine on it. The shit dries out and sticks to the
underside of the magazine. I pick up the magazine two
days later and the shit lifts clean off the floor.

Hank   Look at the magazines! *Harpers and Queen!* How
much does that costya!

Dolores   I don't even read the goddam magazines. I
buy em exclusively for the shit!

Hank   So why the fuck doncha buy summin cheaper!
Time magazine or *Third World Review!*

Dolores   The shit sticks best on glossies Hank! That's the stark facts of the world we live in . . .

Hank   C'mon Dolores. C'mon . . .

Dolores   It cost us so much money Hank . . .

Hank   The monkey?

Dolores   Think how much less a child would cost us. Disposable diapers. I tried diapers on the monkey once . . . I never told you. I thought you'd be offended.

Hank   What happened?

Dolores   He ate the diaper.

Hank   Coulda bin the diaper killed him.

Dolores   This is six years ago Hank.

Hank   Yeah, he was getting old.

Dolores   He was a sad old monkey Hank. Face it.

Hank   What we got t'eat?

Dolores   Oranges.

Hank   How come we never got food?

Dolores   Oranges are the only things the monkey wouldn't eat. I stock the frigidaire fulla food and first thing he'd do was open the door and clean it out.

Hank   Never did that when I was around . . .

Dolores   He was a whole different animal when you was around Hank. If I tried to stop him eating he'd damn near kill me. I put a chain around the frigidaire one time and he pulled it over.

Hank   Jeez . . .

Dolores   I kept all this from ya cus I love ya. And I know how much the monkey meant. And I know what you think about when you're gunning down the freeway.

All those thoughts that crop up inside your head.

Hank   Yeah. I'm gonna put in for a new automobile Dolores. I've decided. It's the purple. Gets through to the brain.

Dolores   Maybe something a little green. Green's relaxing.

Hank   There's a Chrysler.

Dolores   Go for it Hank. You deserve it.

Hank   Yeh. Chrysler. Any mail?

Dolores   Yes Hank. There's mail.

Hank   Let's see it.

Dolores *fetches* **Hank**'s *mail from under a pile of* Harpers. *It's all the same mail. About twenty letters from the bank.*

Hank   All from the bank.

Dolores   Yes Hank.

Hank *opens a couple of letters. Then he gives up. They contain returned cheques.*

Hank   They're returning any cheques now. No credit on the credit card. No cash. Nothin.

Dolores   I have nothing either Hank.

Hank   What we gonna eat tonight?

Dolores   Could eat the monkey Hank.

Hank   Eat the monkey?

Dolores   The vet said it's the greatest honour we could pay him.

Hank   How the hell d'ya eat a monkey?

Dolores   You have to skin it first.

Hank   How the hell do ya skin a monkey?

Dolores   You cut off its extremities, nail it to the door, slit it down the middle, and yank its skin off like a coat.

Hank   Where the hell d'y' learn all this?

Dolores   Could make an orange sauce to go with it, like duck.

Hank   We could take a walk along the beach and pick seakale to go with it.

Dolores   Oh seakale sets monkey flesh off real good . . .

Hank   It's what we stayed in California for, for Chrissakes. The seakale and the oranges.

Dolores   No other reason Hank. We have a banquet.

Hank   Oh Christ.

Dolores   Cost us forty dollars to bury it.

Hank   Forty dollars? Shit. Let's eat it.

Scene Two

Three hours later. The table is laid for two. Candles are lit. There is a strainer piled high with seakale and a dish of orange sauce. **Hank** *and* **Dolores** *sit at opposite ends of the table with a plate each of roast monkey.* **Hank** *takes a big spoonful of kale and holds it above the strainer before he places it on the plate. He helps himself to orange sauce.* **Dolores** *does the same.*

Dolores   You don't know how long I've waited for this Hank.

Hank   Y'know we haven't screwed on the beach for ten years?

Dolores   No. I know.

Hank *takes a mouthful. He is pleasantly surprised.*

Hank   Hell this is good!

Dolores   It's bin a lovely evening Hank.

Hank   We just left it all behind us didn't we? Takes one glorious screw on an empty beach, with the Pacific there, pounding away. I sang a song y'know?

Dolores   Beach Boys?

Hank   You got it.

Dolores   I thought that was what you were doing.

Hank   And now a candlelit dinner. All it takes ain't it? What we always said. Somehow we left it all behind.

Dolores   Just the two of us . . .

Hank   First time.

Dolores   First time ever. First time we ever really made love, alone, without the monkey.

Hank   He was always there, on the beach, wasn't he.

Dolores   I could never really forget him.

Hank   I just never thought, when he was alive y'know, out there in the sunshine, laughing, chattering, scratching his underarms, talking to me. He talked to me, his Daddy, my little monkey . . .

Dolores   He talked to me too Hank.

Hank   Yeah. I know that now.

Dolores   He talked to you through his mouth.

Hank   Used to pick the nits outa my hair . . .

Dolores   Me too Hank.

Hank   He used to play with me Dolores did you know that? With my . . .

Dolores   I know Hank. I know it . . .

Hank   I didn't like it much at first. Kinda disgusted me. But I thought hell it's natural. He thinks I'm his brother and that's what brother monkeys do. It's natural to a monkey. Let him fiddle around.

Dolores   He fiddled with me too Hank.

Hank   What?

Dolores   Oh yes. When you weren't here. He, he went a long way. He was very well-endowed Hank.

Hank   Sheeit . . .

Dolores   Did y'ever thinka that? When you was gunnin down the freeway?

Hank   You was two-timing me with a monkey?!

Dolores   C'mon Hank . . .

Hank   Let's have it Dolores, let's have the full story! I haven't heard the half of it have I Dolores, have I, huh! The god-dam half of it!

Dolores   Hank you're destroying the atmosphere . . .

Hank   Me! Destroying the atmosphere . . . You're a goddam cannibal! C'mon! Hit me! Give it to me straight!

Dolores   Well first off Hank that monkey ain't the first.

Hank   The first monkey?!

Dolores   The first shitkickin nitpickin underarm-scratching bullshit-chattering long-armed short-assed coarse-haired ape I've had the pleasure to do business with!

Hank   Business!?

Dolores   How the fuck else d'you think I've managed to finance your goddam pet! Am I dishin y'enough dirt Hank? Uh. Food for thought? Whilst gunning down the freeway?

Hank   Stop now Dolores! Stop! Tell me it isn't true!

Dolores   I loved that monkey Hank. First real honest male I ever came across. He didn't talk, that's the difference. That's the difference. No bullshit.

Hank   Did you used to bring em here? These men?

Dolores   Oh, Hank . . .

Hank   Did ya? Dolores! Did ya? You goddam bitch!

Dolores   You couldn't give a shit about me! The monkey!

Hank   DID YA?

Dolores   NO! I had em on the beach for fifteen dollars a poke!

Hank   On the beach! Fifteen dollars!

Dolores   Then I hit on it. The big one. I had the idea some a these fat executives in their big limos might pay through the nose to watch me do it with a monkey. I was right!

Hank   Did they come here? In my house!

Dolores   I did it in the limo! Hundred and fifty dollars! Once! Just once! Last night! Then the fuckin monkey went'n croaked on me, just when we was onto a good deal.

Hank   So that's what killed the monkey.

Dolores   Yeah. That's what did it. That's what finally took him off.

Hank   That poor little monkey. Poor, poor goddam monkey. Old age be fucked. He just couldn't take the big time.

Dolores   First time I ever did it on the beach Hank . . .

Hank   I'm not interested . . .

Dolores   First time, on the beach, for ten years. I was angry.

Hank   Dolores . . .

Dolores   . . . Angry with you, angry with the monkey, just angry I ever had to do this at all . . .

Hank   No more . . .

Dolores   I got a guy off the street. He had a woolly hat on he never took off.

Hank   Dolores!

Dolores   He forced his tongue down insida my throat, had a tongue like a dogfish. So I bit it. He yelped and withdrew . . .

Hank   I don't believe this . . .

Dolores   I said you wanna keep that thing on a lead . . .

Hank   You're crucifying me!

Dolores   He said it's bin in better mouths than yours . . . I said when you've cooked it in batter and served it up with french fries you can put it back . . .

Hank   Dolores, for Chrissakes!

Dolores   This hurting you Hank?

Hank   I'm not hearing this!

Dolores   This hurting you more'n your goddam monkey?!

Hank   I don't hear it!

Dolores   Well what do you wanna hear?!

Hank   I wanna hear what the fuck happened to the hundred and fifty dollars!

Dolores   Oh, Hank!

Hank   You got me doin cartwheels through a catflap here Dolores. I can't think straight.

Dolores   D'you think thinkin straight got me into all this? D'you think I could possibly have sex with a monkey in the back of a limo with a shithead lookin at me groaning with pleasure if I was thinking straight?

Hank   Maybe you should see a shrink.

Dolores   I don't need a shrink.

Hank   What happened to the hundred and fifty dollars?

Dolores   The monkey ate it Hank. Last thing he ever ate.

They both remember their food, which they have almost eaten, and study what's left.

Hank   Shit.

Dolores   Hank? Will you go see Judd?

Hank   Yeah. I'll go see Judd.

Scene Three

Two hours later. Night. **Dolores** *sits in the easy chair. She has her head back, staring at the ceiling.* **Hank** *arrives home. He is very drunk. He stands unsteadily over* **Dolores**. *She doesn't move.*

Hank   Hi Dol.

Dolores   See Judd?

Hank   I saw Judd.

Dolores   What he say?

Hank   We had a few beers.

Dolores   I can see that.

Hank   Talked over old times. Crazy y'know. Crazy.
When y'ole buddy, he's sitting there, in his chair, he
said to me y'know Hank, we're livin in the crutch of a
ballerina's tutu . . .

Dolores   He did?

Hank   He went on to tell me exactly the thoughts I'd
had whilst gunning down the freeway. He put it more
er . . .

Dolores   Elegiacally.

Hank   Yeah.

Dolores   Comes a sitting in a junkyard.

Hank   He always had this gift . . .

Dolores   What else you talk about?

Hank   I was saying, phyaw, shit. Crazy. Crazy y'know.
Crazy. Only takes two buddies sitting in a junklot.
Talkin over old times . . . This is it. Old times. Christ we
went through it with a toothcomb Dolores. Chicago,
high school, college, his dad, my dad, his ma, my ma,
the autos we had, the surfing, the monkey, Mexico . . .

Dolores   . . . covered a lotta ground.

Hank   Two buddies. Sitting in a junklot. Talkin over
old times. Rakin up the past. Dredgin it up. Spreading
the shit. Few beers. We was watchin the waves. There
was a pointbreak out there . . .

Dolores   Always was . . .

Hank   Shit the waves was, musta bin six foot. Perfect
shape. I said you still surf Judd? He said yeah. Still surf.
Just like that. Yeah. That hurt. That hurt me. How
could the bastard be so fuckin cruel?

Dolores Y'expect him to lie and say no?

Hank It was the least he could do!

Dolores You asked him!

Hank Yeah. Guess so.

He can't stand any more. He lies on the floor.

Dolores Say anything else?

Hank Wer reminisced. We raked up the past, no stone unturned Dol . . .

Dolores Yeah you said that . . .

Hank I'm making my point.

Dolores Well make it before you forget it.

Hank We ain't got nowhere Judd, er Dolores. We ain't got nothing. And it takes, it takes a, it takes a goddam history! History lesson to bring it on home to this little brain a mine, that the country is a monkey's asshole . . .

Dolores No more dime-store philosophy Hank . . .

Hank This ain't, this is the real thing . . .

Dolores New start Hank . . .

Hank This country . . .

Dolores No Hank!

Hank Hear me OUT! Blast ya! Hear what I have to say! This is important! To me!

Dolores Go ahead Hank.

Hank It . . . it's . . . just . . . I forgot.

Dolores Doesn't matter does it. What you think. It's what you do. Did ya talk about that? The future?

Hank Hell no Dolores. We was so wrapped up in the

past we clean forgot to talk about the future.

Dolores   So you never got round to talkin about workin for him.

Hank   The guy's a jerk Dolores.

Dolores   A jerk.

Hank   I can't work with a jerk. Honest. I can't.

Dolores   He ain't jerk enough for you to drink his beer.

Hank   Shit I take beer off any bastard. I have to.

Dolores   How come he's a jerk? So you can't work with the guy.

Hank   I didn't say I can't work with the guy.

Dolores   Sure you did . . .

Hank   Said I can't work with a jerk.

Dolores   You called him a jerk. So you can't work with the guy.

Hank   That's exactly what *I* said. You know me Dolores. I'd be impossible to live with.

He shuts his eyes. It's too much to shut them, so he opens them again. He sleeps with his eyes open, staring at the stars.

Dolores   Y'know I knew a guy once Hank.

Hank   Yeah?

Dolores   He was a great guy.

Hank   Yeah.

Dolores   He had a beat-up Oldsmobile, with a surfboard on top. Kinda surfboard you don't see no more. It was a nine-foot long board, with one fin. Kinda surfboard if ya put it on top of a beat-up Oldsmobile it turns a few heads, when he was gunning down Main

Street. Shit could he ride that board this guy. He was
poetry to watch. He could hang five, hang ten,
quasimodo, head dip, shoot the tube, he didn't talk
about it, he did it. He couldn't give a shit about the
world or the country or nothin. He'd bin to college but
he was no buck-chaser. And y'know what about this
guy? Y'know what it was that set him up above all the
thousand other guys just like him? For me? What did it
for me, was this guy had a monkey. A sweet, good-
natured, springy li'l monkey. Monkey went everywhere
with this guy. Slept with him, walked with him, ate with
him, talked with him. He surfed with him! I remember
when they held the world championships, right here on
this beach, Micky Pentz, from Hawaii, the world
champion and everybody's god, asked to surf with the
monkey for his sponsor, and he couldn't do it. He wiped
out and almost drowned the monkey. There was only
one guy who could hang five with a monkey on his
back, cus he was the only one guy in the whole fuckin
world who couldn't give a shit about anything else
except hanging five with a monkey on his back! Micky
Pentz tried it for his sponsor, earn hisself a few extra
bucks! He didn't do it for the monkey! And he wiped
out! There was only one guy Hank! Y'know who that
was Hank? Y'know who that was!

Hank No?

Dolores It was you Hank! It was you! Did you talk
with Judd about that? Did you talk about that? Did it
hurt too much to talk about that? Did you think about
it? Did you ever think about that when you was gunning
down the freeway Hank?

Hank We can get a fresh monkey . . .

Dolores I don't wanna fresh monkey! I wanna fresh
Hank!

Hank You want the old Hank. You ain't gonna get
the old Hank.

Dolores   I don't want the old Hank. I said, I wanna fresh Hank! A new Hank. A future Hank! But I want that little essence of the old Hank, somewhere in the new Hank! It's still there, somewhere Hank, but it's bin smothered with shit. Now I'm prepared to dig around a little bit Hank and find it, but I need you here with me. Cus right now I see you three days a month then you're off again down the freeway and filling your head with shit. So if you go off again in two days' time to Wisconsin, you take me with you, or you leave me behind. But I won't be here when you get back.

Silence. **Dolores** *puts her head back and stares at the ceiling.*

Dolores   You throw up tonight Hank?

Hank *is asleep. She kicks him from where she sits.*

Dolores   Hank!

Hank *wakes up.*

Dolores   You were asleep?

Hank   Guess so.

Dolores   When did you fall asleep?

Hank   Hell I dunno. Right about the last time you mentioned the monkey.

Dolores   When was that Hank?

Hank *grunts.*

Dolores   You throw up tonight Hank?

Hank   Uh?

Dolores   You throw up tonight?

Hank   I think I'm about to. The stars are spinning round.

Dolores   We're inside Hank.

Hank   Then I'm about to.

He gets up and runs out back. **Dolores** *sets her head back and stares at the ceiling.*

Scene Four

Next day. Morning. **Hank** *is on the phone. He's reached the end of a conversation. He slams the phone down and whoops for joy.*

Hank Hey Dolores! Dolores! Hear this!

Dolores*'s voice comes from out back. It's indecipherable.*

Hank Come out here! Come right out here!

Dolores *enters. She is in a dressing-gown.*

Hank This is the big one honey! This is where our fortunes change! They got me selling bibles in Nebraska! Y'know the last guy who did that? George Nitscratchski? He cleared twenny-four hundred dollars in three days! They love me. They love me. Someone in that pool loves me! They only ever give that pitch to a man who's earned it right? Dolores, this is it!

Dolores When do they want ya?

Hank Right now. Jeff Lonsdale, sent him up there for er, Harvest Thanksgiving, that's a big time for bibles, right? He's had a heart attack. Whizzkid, he was only twenny-six, needs a replacement right away or they miss the, the . . .

Dolores So you're going now huh?

Hank This minute. Seeya honey. Back in one month a rich man . . .

Dolores I won't be here Hank . . .

Hank Yeah yeah OK, OK. Seeya.

Dolores You won't Hank.

Hank I'll get a sub from the pool right? Three

hundred dollars. Send it down to you . . .

Dolores It'll pay for my fare.

Hank Where the fuck to? C'mon Dolores they want me now . . .

Dolores Then go.

Hank You're screwing me up! Fuck what is this?! You're screwin me up!

Dolores Goodbye Hank . . .

Hank My finest hour! You're screwin it up!

Dolores I'm not Hank . . .

Hank You're shittin on me! You don't want the money? You don't wannit!? Christ, you're perverse! You're a crazy bitch! You be here right! You be here when I get back! You be here when I get back or I'll never see y'again! I'll walk out on ya!

Dolores You walk out here now and you walk out on me cus I won't be here when you get back to walk out on! And yes, you will never see me again. Ever ever.

Hank Goodbye Dolores!

He walks out into the garden. He stops.

Shit. C'mon c'mon c'mon c'mon . . .

Dolores C'mon Hank. It's my ultimatum I'm afraid.

Hank I can't . . .

Dolores Take me with you . . .

Hank I can't take you with me. No women no pets, y'know the rules.

Dolores Goodbye Hank.

Hank *comes back. He holds* **Dolores**.

Hank You be here huh? You be here please? Please

honey, you be here? Please?

He drops to his knees and holds her round the waist, sobbing.

Dolores I will not.

Hank I forgived ya for all that with the monkey. I
forgived ya for all that with the monkey. I forgived ya
didn't I?

Dolores There was nothing to forgive.

Hank Start out again, fresh start, new hopes, big
money Dolores. Shit we spoke all that. Two days, non-
stop, great, heroic talk . . .

Dolores All for nothing Hank, if you go through that
gate.

Hank I gotta go through the gate. I got to!

Dolores Go Hank. Look at me. Look at my face.

Hank *looks up at* **Dolores**'*s face with tear-filled eyes.*
Dolores' *eyes are dry. She is cool.*

Dolores Look at my face. No tears. No nothing. I
don't care Hank. It's your choice. Go or stay, I don't
mind. But I don't care either way, I don't care.

Hank Y'ain't cryin?

Dolores I ain't cryin.

Hank You don't care?

Dolores It's what I said. I don't care. One day we
might meet again, in a limousine. Green Chrysler
perhaps. You'll be fat and successful, and I'll be laid out
in the back, screwin a monkey.

Hank Shit no.

Dolores You know what I'll be seeing? With my eyes
shut? A lovely guy, hanging five, with a monkey on his
back. He's the guy who'll make me cry. He's the guy

who'll make me care. Not you Hank.

Hank   I don't know what you're talkin about . . .

Dolores   You don't Hank, cus you were asleep.

Hank   Who the fuck is this guy, while I was asleep?

Dolores   It was you Hank.

Hank *rises.*

Hank (*indignant*)   While I was asleep?!

Dolores   You weren't asleep for all of it Hank. But you weren't listening, or you didn't comprehend, or whatever, it doesn't matter does it.

Hank's *bag is waiting for him. He picks it up and heads for the garden gate. The* **Vet** *appears through the gate. He carries a hutch. It is heavy with the weight of an animal. Unseen.*

Vet   Hi there.

Hank   Who the hell's this?

Dolores   Oh! Hullo. This is the, er, vet Hank.

Vet   Mrs Wandaback. Mr Wandaback, I'm glad to find you home.

Hank   Yeah I'm glad to find me home. (*To* **Dolores**.) He don't look like a vet to me.

Vet   Mr Wandaback I'm a vet. Believe me I'm a vet. And I'm a vet with glad tidings for you people here today.

Dolores   We owe him some money Hank. Sixty cents.

Hank   Here . . .

Vet   No. Mr Wandaback let me say first how sorry I was to be the one who had to proclaim your monkey dead. But I've found in the past if an animal's dead there's no point saying otherwise.

Hank   I can understand that.

Vet   Thank you sir.

Hank   You're welcome.

Vet   Sir I got to thinking after I left this household
how poignant was the reaction of your good wife. Most
times, when an animal grows old like yours, particularly
a monkey, there is a sense of relief. With Mrs
Wandaback it was different. Here was real devotion.
How truly sad she seemed. How selfless. How she
thought of you and how you would take it. How bereft
you would be. Got to thinking here was a couple who
worshipped their pet. Who cared for their pet like a
child. No sooner had I arrived back at the zoo, when I
was called upon to administer to a birth. What my job's
all about Mr Wandaback. Birth and death. And what's
in between. Disease. But never has the juxtaposition
between birth and death been so vivid. Never have I left
a scene so heavy with grief, and after a short journey in
my car, why as you know, you take a right outa here,
straight down Main Street, left at the bank, and there's
the zoo, right between the high school and the DA's
office. I hopped from my car and was overwhelmed with
all the joyous grunts and moans of, of motherhood. I
gazed down at the helpless, newborn litter, and one little
fellow turned his blind eyes at me and made the soft,
mewling cry which is the hallmark of all animals at that
point in their lives when the world is an innocent place,
devoid of evil. And I thought to myself, you gorgeous
little beasty. You defenceless, wise pathetic little
goobydoobywoobynoonoo. You deserve better than a
zoo. I'll try you out on the Wandabacks. They will take
you to their bosom. They will feed you, and nurture
you, and, and love, yes love you. I've brought it with
me. In its very own little hutch. Please, please, take it,
please.

Hank   What is it?

Dolores (*in tears*)   It's a goobydoobywoobynoonoo Hank. Weren't you listening?

Vet   Oh no Mrs Wandaback. Bless you. That's my personal way of talking to animals, it seems to get results. No this is a, a very rare breed of, now don't be put off, it's nothing like the kind you eat. It's a Macedonian Curly Pig. Take a look.

Hank *and* **Dolores** *look inside the hutch.*

Dolores   Oh. It's beautiful.

Hank   Little whopper.

Vet   They don't grow a whole lot.

Hank   Is it a boar or a girl?

Vet   It's a, a, er, boar.

Hank   That's good.

Dolores   A little boar. Oh, Hank.

Hank   Whaddathey eat?

Vet   Oh, er anything. Anything at all you care to throw at em. Except pork.

Hank   Respond to training?

Vet   Oh yes. Train 'em. They have a very high intelligence rating. There's some states accept 'em as dogs in their canine shows . . .

Dolores   Oh . . .

Vet   You can do em up real nice, train their curls to go one way with rollers? I saw one with a pearl bracelet through its nose and Eiffel Tower earrings. Won a big rosette in the poodle section.

Dolores   Oh, Hank . . .

Hank   Certainly tugs at my heartstrings Dolores . . .

Dolores Mine too Hank. Mine too.

Hank You ah, you reckon I could take it surfing with me?

Dolores (*ecstatic*) Oh! Hank!

Hank If I made a backpouch for it, slung it on my back.

Vet See no reason why not. They take to water. They're like ducks in water. Quite amphibious.

Hank Like a dog on land, like a duck in water. Could call it Dogduck.

Dolores Dogduck.

Vet Dolores, Hank, and Dogduck.

Hank *bends and takes a look in the hutch.*

Hank Dogduck. Hey Dogduck. (*Whistles.*) Here boy, Dogduck. Dogduck . . . Hey he knows his name. Dogduck. He's a bright boy. Ch'choo . . .

Dolores *joins* **Hank** *at the hutch.*

Dolores Dogduck? Hey, Dogduck? Good firm teeth Hank he's got.

Hank What is he snarling or grinning?

Dolores Oh he's smiling Hank you can see that. He's so sweet.

Hank Hey Dogduck. Responded that time y'see that?

Dolores We could manicure his, his tusks Hank, make them less sharp . . .

The **Vet** *heaves a sigh of relief and starts to slope off, leaving* **Hank** *and* **Dolores** *cooing over Dogduck. They continue cooing over Dogduck as the lights fade.*

Act Two

Scene One

Six months later. The room is cleared and brighter. Effort has been made to make the place more nest-like. A Malibu board stands outside.

Dolores *is slumped downstage in the easy chair. She wears beachwear, she is wet and dedraggled. The* **Vet** *stands by the table, he is wet through and dripping. Around the table, on the chairs and the floor, are candelabra, cutlery, glasses and mats, hastily removed from the table in the crisis.*

Hank *lies unconscious on the table. He is covered to the waist with the Indian blanket. His chest is exposed and the* **Vet** *examines him with his stethoscope. The* **Vet** *ceases his examination, and after opening* **Hank**'s *mouth and peering down his throat, walks down to* **Dolores**.

Dolores Is he dead?

Vet Hell no. He's gonna be dandy.

Dolores You're a very brave man.

Vet Please, no.

Dolores You risked your life. You charged into the sea and dragged him unconscious through the boiling surf. You laid him on the sand and resuscitated him, God knows how . . .

Vet Mouth-to-mouth. Never pleasant.

Dolores You literally grasped him back from the jaws of hell. I don't know how to repay you.

Vet Bless you Mrs Wandaback, I'll overlook the fee.

Dolores What about Dogduck?

Vet Leave Dogduck to me. He'll be capering on the

beach. Your husband has had a traumatic time. He
needs rest, attention, love and understanding.

Dolores   What should I do when he comes through?

Vet   Do you know anything about seaweed Mrs
Wandaback?

Dolores   We practically live off the soup.

Vet   First thing you do with a drowning victim is check
his oesophagus and trachea for debris, such as weed,
which might impair his breathing. You ah, you're
familiar with the dark brown, slimy stuff I'm sure, with
the little pods full of air? Ones we used to squeeze
between our fingernails when we was kids and pop!

Dolores   Oh of course! I know the ones! We did that
a whole lot! It was fun.

Vet   I still do it.

Dolores   So do I, when no one's looking.

Vet   I did it to your husband's tonsils.

Dolores   O my God.

Vet   They're a touch inflamed that's all. He may feel a
little hoarse. Hot milk.

Dolores   I'll warm some.

Vet   Lace it with honey.

Dolores   I'm sure he'd love Dogduck to be here when
he . . .

Vet   I'll go after him now . . .

Dolores   I hope you find him, for Hank's sake.

Vet   I surely will.

Dolores   Hank loves him so much.

Vet   I can see that.

Dolores   You can?

Vet   I felt privileged when he invited me along today, to such a touching event. I'm only sad it had to end like it did.

Dolores   I just dunno what I woulda done if he'd, if he'd drowned.

Vet   They are tenacious beasts, and natural swimmers.

Dolores   No I . . . oh . . .

She buries her head in her hands. **Hank** *grunts and stirs.*
Dolores *rushes to him and smothers him.*

Dolores   Hank! Oh Hank!

Hank   Dolores. That you?

Dolores   It's me Hank.

Hank   What the fuck happened?

Dolores   You wiped out Hank! You wiped out!

Hank   Dogduck?

Vet   Dogduck's gonna be fine Mr Wandaback.

Hank *grips his throat.*

Hank   Uygh! My throat!

Vet   Your lymphatic tissue will be tender for a while Mr Wandaback. I was a touch zealous, in the heat of the moment. I waived the fee.

Hank   What the fuck did you do?

Dolores   He saved your life honey, that's what he did.

Vet   I'll, er . . .

Hank   Saved my life! I wiped out, that's all! It's when he grabbed me I lost consciousness!

Dolores   Oh Hank, it wasn't like that Sweetpea . . .

Hank   Dolores!

He chokes.

My throat! What the fuck did ya do to my throat!

Dolores   Hank!

Vet   He's traumatised!

Dolores   You took a bad wipe-out! We saw from the beach, we were there Hank! Now if the vet hadn't waded in and pulled y'out who knows how it woulda turned out Hank! For Chrissakes he saved your life!

Hank   What the fuck did he do to my throat!

Dolores   He pinched your goddam tonsils that's all!

Hank   I don't have any fuckin tonsils!

Vet (*sloping off*) I'd better dash . . .

Hank   Scram before I rip your tongue out!

Dolores (*to the* **Vet**)   Thank you so much. Thank you.

Vet   Remember. Love and understanding.

Dolores   Hot milk.

The **Vet** *goes.*

Hank   Feel like I gone ten rounds with the Boston Strangler . . .

Dolores   I'm supposed to give you love and understanding Hank, because you've had a traumatic experience.

Hank *chokes badly.* **Dolores** *panics.*

Dolores   O my God! Hank? Milk!

She runs towards the kitchenette. **Hank**, *choking, makes noises and points at his back.* **Dolores** *comes and hits him hard on the back.* **Hank** *throws his hands to his mouth and regurgitates violently. From the recesses of his mouth he withdraws a small* *sprig of seaweed.*

Hank   Gimme a glass of water.

Dolores *does this.* **Hank** *takes the glass and drops the seaweed in it.*

Hank   Evidence.

Dolores   Have you any idea what it costs for a qualified medical person to save your life here in California? He did it for nothing!

Hank   I wouldn't speak too soon if I were you, my throat is killing me.

Dolores   It's tender that's all. It'll clear up in time. Honeybunch?

Hank   Yeah. Guess so.

Dolores   Come on.

Hank   OK. Dolores?

Dolores   Yes Hank?

Hank   I'm sorry.

Dolores   That's fine.

Hank   I'm sorry I fucked up. Hell I'm so sorry. I'm sorry Dolores I'm so sorry I fouled up.

Dolores   Hank. Sweetpea. You are older than you once were.

Dolores *caresses* **Hank**.

Hank   It's bin a wonderful six months Dolores.

Dolores   Yes Hank.

Hank   The days on the beach. You, me and the pig. They were golden days weren't they?

Dolores   Yes.

Hank All the hours we spent planning for today. The day, the date, the hour, the minute when I would rise again with Dogduck on my back, slung in a backpouch riding a perfect perfect six foot pointbreak up to fuckin heaven! The motto, remember the motto you dreamed up?

Dolores Old surfers never die.

Hank Old surfers never die . . . they drown!

Dolores Oh Hank . . .

Hank I'm sorry kid . . .

Dolores Please don't be melancholy . . .

Hank *is in tears.*

Dolores I'll fix you some milk.

Dolores *goes to the kitchenette and puts the milk on.* **Hank** *struggles off the table, wrapped in the Indian blanket. He feels his throat and hobbles to the fridge. The fridge is empty except for one can of beer. He takes the beer, shuts the fridge and hobbles to the easy chair. He sits and opens the beer. He drinks and places the can on the floor.*

Hank Dolores.

Dolores (*in the kitchenette*) What is it honey?

Hank I love you Dolores.

Dolores I love you too.

Hank Ya. Good.

He takes a drink of beer while **Dolores** *is tinkering in the kitchenette.*

Hank What are you doin?

Dolores Oh, tinkering.

Hank In the kitchenette?

Dolores   Heating some milk.

Hank   Why don't we monkey around uh?

Dolores   You want to?

Hank   Heck I'm hot if you are.

Dolores   I'l lie back and let you do it to me Hank.

Dolores *has entered from the kitchenette and is re-setting the table.*

Hank   I love you Dolores.

Dolores   I'll get into it as we progress.

Hank   Doesn't it make you feel horny? Fact that I'm horny.

Dolores   Oh sure it does Hank.

Hank   Then why lie back and let me do it?

Dolores   I said, I'd get into it.

Hank   If you're already horny Dolores, what's keeping you?

Dolores   You're splitting hairs Hank.

Hank   I don't think so.

Dolores   All right. You lie back and I'll go on top.

Hank   I'm happy on top.

Dolores   I'd prefer to go on top.

Hank   Why's that?

Dolores   Whichever you like Hank.

Hank   Because if you lie back and I go on top my gut hangs down is that it?

Dolores   Hank. You don't have a gut.

Hank   I have a gut. Don't kid me I don't have a gut.

Dolores   It may take a little longer for me to get into it if I lie back. It might have to do with your non-existent gut, or the paint on the ceiling which is flaking . . .

Hank   There.

Dolores   Whatever Hank, perhaps I'm just the kinda girl who likes to fuck on top.

Hank   You fucked every whichway in the past, when I didn't have a gut.

Dolores   Why don't we just forget it?

Hank   It was on the agenda!

Dolores *has poured hot milk into a jug and brought it round to* **Hank**.

Dolores   You don't want this.

Hank   I don't?

Dolores   You got yourself a beer.

Hank   Then I won't have the milk.

Dolores   You're supposed to drink the milk.

Hank   You just told me I didn't want it.

Dolores   With beer? I've heard of mixing your drinks Hank.

Hank   You have the beer. It's our last beer. I'll drink the milk.

Dolores   I don't want the beer. I don't drink beer. I'm watching my weight.

Hank   What is that supposed to mean?

Dolores   Means I don't want the beer Hank.

Hank   Means you're beating me round the head with my gut.

Dolores   I'm not beating you round the head with your gut Hank. You are.

Hank   Well your jugs are in great shape if that's any consolation.

Dolores   I don't recall I was seeking any.

Hank   I was?

Dolores   No Hank. No. Thank you for paying me the compliment about my breasts.

Hank   And your butt has never looked better.

Dolores   My butt is spreading. I had to let out my beachwear.

Hank   That's exactly what I mean. I always thought you had a too-slender butt. It's a well-proportioned butt now. The cheeks jostle when you walk. That's how I like it.

Dolores   Then perhaps I should lie on my stomach.

Hank   I'm not the problem.

Dolores   I never said I was. I said I was happy to lay back and let you do it Hank.

Hank   Well for fucksake then let's!

Dolores   No! I'm sorry Hank. I'm not in the mood.

Dolores *takes the milk back to the kitchenette.* **Hank** *drinks his beer. The* **Vet** *enters.*

Vet   Am I interrupting anything?

Hank   No!

Dolores   Is it Dogduck?

Vet   Yes.

Hank   What?

Vet   He stayed in the sea some time after our

evacuation of the beach. Then he came out of the water
and frolicked on the sand. He was sportsome and I
couldn't catch him. Do you know Mrs Operkl?

Hank   Yes! We know Mrs Operkl.

Vet   She was walking her dog down the far end of the
beach. A big dalmatian, named Spotty. Dogduck
scampered up to Spotty and rolled on his back, begging
for his tummy to be tickled and licked. Spotty severed
his spinal cord, dislocating the odontoid peg and
punctured the trachea, with his teeth.

Hank   Say that again?

Vet   Spotty bit off Dogduck's head.

This sinks deep in **Hank**.

Dolores   Is he dead?

Hank   Awwwww, SHIT!

Vet   He was snorting and slavering with glee right up
to the last Mrs Wandaback. He died a happy pig.

Hank   Dead! Dead!

Dolores   Don't blame yourself Hank.

Hank   Who the fuck does she think she is she can
allow her dog to do a thing like that!

Dolores   Dogs do this Hank, they're a . . .

Hank   What the hell kinda beach is it you can't allow
an innocent pig to run around without having his fuckin
head bit off!

Dolores   Hank, please, don't get heated . . .

Hank   These fuckin widows they retire down there on
their ole man's life insurance and they haven't bin here
five minutes they think they own the fuckin place!

Dolores   This is not the case Hank.

Hank   I won't have it!

Dolores   Neither will I Hank, now wrap up!

Hank   I held down a rotten fuckin job for fifteen years Dolores and I have citizen's rights like any other bastard!

Dolores   No you don't Hank.

Hank   And if I say my pig can caper down a beach there ain't no fuckin Operkl in the whole of the United States gonna deny me that right!

Dolores   *She* didn't bite his head off Hank, her *dog* did!

Hank   I will not be intimidated!

Dolores   Nobody's intimidating you!

Hank   Operkl's intimidating me!

Dolores   Her dog bit your pig's head off, that's all!

Hank   That's not intimidation?!

Dolores   No!

Vet   It's a species typical posture . . .

Hank   Who's next Dolores? Who's safe on that beach now?

Vet   The dog is being treated in our psychiatric unit, right by the elephant compound.

Hank   Dogduck one day, me the next, that's the way I see it Dolores, and that is intimidation!

Vet   We identify the stimuli, then we desensitise him and counter-condition his responses.

Dolores   (*indicating* **Hank**)   Whose, his?

Vet   The dog's to pigs.

Hank   Shoot him! For Chrissakes shoot him!

Vet   That is a premature reaction if I may say so Mr Wandaback . . .

Hank   Premature?

Dolores   It's prehistoric!

Hank   Whose fuckin side are you on!

Vet   Counter-conditioning is a long and expensive process, but Mrs Operkl can afford it and the results can be astonishing. Everyone is rewarded, Mrs Operkl, her dog, me, and of course, pigs.

Hank   Those who still have a head!

Dolores   Hank!

Hank   And I haven't noticed you so fuckin sorry to see the back of it!

Dolores   Back of what?

Hank   His head!

Dolores   That's right! That's right! That's right Hank I hated him!

Hank   You hated him?

Dolores   Dogduck was not the answer Hank.

Hank   You, you gave him everything.

Dolores   I don't need reminding of that.

Hank   You hated him?

Dolores   I despised him.

Hank   You devoted six months of your life to him.

Dolores   Not to him Hank, to you.

Hank   Spent your last nickel on him.

Dolores   You did. Prime steaks, sweet potatoes, he ate more'n the goddam monkey!

Hank   Gave him a little bell to hang round his neck at Thanksgiving . . .

Dolores   Tinkle tinkle drove me up the goddam wall!

Hank   You was up all night knitting him a lounge-coat!

Dolores   Which he never wore!

Hank   Yes he did Dolores he wore it round the house with his bootees.

Dolores   He wore the Easter bonnet with his bootees Hank whilst unpicking the lounge-coat with his tusks!

Hank   You hated him? You hated him? You hated him?

Dolores   Yes. Hank. I hated him.

Hank   Aw shit! How can you say that?

Dolores   Because I'm through with lying. We've had six months of lies Hank. You can't change back to what you were. You are what you are now and I . . . I despise it.

Hank   Despite what?

Dolores   You Hank.

Hank   Me too?

Dolores   Yes. You too.

Hank   Aw hell!

Dolores   I force myself to like it and *I* change. *I* become dishonest. Then we're both liars Hank. Trying to kid each other we're telling the truth. We know we're not telling the truth but we believe each other's lies. After that it's meltdown. We lie and we lie and we lie and we lie and we go down and down and down. Then we patch up and up and up and we look down the chasm and all the patches are there, bulging with lies.

There's nothing there any more Hank.

Hank *is stunned.*

Hank (*to the* **Vet**)   I gave up my job for this! I could've had Nebraska now! I could be a wealthy man! I gave it all up for this! And I went out there, struggling with the ocean for the day I surfed with Dogduck on my back and all the time she was sitting here on her fat butt hating him!

Dolores   My FAT BUTT!

Hank   And despising me!

Dolores   I've done everything I can . . .

Hank   You've done everything, you've done nothin! The only thing you done is lay out in the back of a limousine and . . .

Dolores (*screams*)   No!!!!

Hank   . . . get fucked by a monkey!

Silence. **Dolores** *turns to ice. The* **Vet** *colours.*

Dolores   How can you say that? In front of a vet!

Hank   Did he go on top? Did his fuckin gut hang down?

Dolores   That's disgusting. That is truly disgusting.

Hank   The great advantage of an aging monkey. They manage to keep a concave gut.

Vet   Mrs Wandaback? Is it true? I have to know.

Dolores   Yes. It is true.

Vet   In the back of a limo?

Dolores   Yes.

Vet   By day? Or night?

Dolores   It was dark. I had my eyes shut.

Vet   Was the courtesy light on?

Dolores   How in hell should I know!

Vet   It's astounding.

Dolores   It's disgusting!

Vet   Mrs Wandaback I can't tell you how excited I am by these revelations. Intimacy with a monkey. We've been trying to achieve this for years! Your rapport with animals is, is unique. Did you know the Macedonian Curly Pig had been known to disembowel cattle? The MCP is one of the most alienation-sensitive creatures known to vets, and yet you, whilst apparently hating Dogduck, managed to bring him up a docile, fun-loving creature who wore an Easter bonnet, bootees, and unpicked a woollen lounge-coat with his tusks! Mrs Wandaback . . .

Hank   Hey mister willya get the hell outa here before I bite your goddam head off!

Vet   Sir I have to speak with your wife.

Dolores   Let him have his say Hank, now you've told him.

Vet   Mrs Wandaback, under article three of the constitution of our zoo we are required to maintain a comprehensive remedial unit. Ours operates on a range of fronts from basic animal psychotherapy at forty dollars an hour right up to the very frontiers of neurological research which is funded by the Pentagon. The spearhead of our programme right now is an in-depth study of species-typical behaviourisms which is being conducted by me and Artie Kake, the giraffe steward. Mrs Wandaback, we want you on our team. Come and join us? I mentioned we received generous patronage from the military, we could pay you in telephone numbers.

Dolores   To fuck monkeys?

Vet   Oh no! Bless you, no. Just to be there. Just to sit with unsettled animals, and be one of them.

Dolores *says nothing.* **Hank** *scowls.*

Vet   Think it over. But remember you are a very remarkable person. You should consider the benefits you could bring to the animal kingdom, the whole human race, and perhaps above all, me and Artie Kake.

The **Vet** *goes. After a while,* **Dolores** *speaks.*

Dolores   I'll never forgive you for this.

Hank   You put me there. You drove me to it.

Dolores   I did no such thing. I told the truth. That's all. I told the truth.

Hank   You gonna take this job?

Dolores   Of course I will.

Hank   And leave me?

Dolores   Who knows where your jealousy and envy will stop? You bring out our dirtiest linen and wash it in front of a vet.

Hank   You gonna leave me here? On my own? All day?

Dolores   It'll get me out of the house Hank. Could be the one hope I have left to preserve my sanity.

Hank   That's the first thing you'll lose working with a guy like that! He's a lunatic! He can't tell an airpod from a fuckin tonsil! Who the fuck ever psychoanalysed a dog?! It's no accident he works in a zoo Dolores, what beats me is they let him out!

Dolores   Do you think I don't know a nutcase when I see one Hank?

Hank   What's more he's a jerk.

Dolores   Oh that too.

Hank   Then don't take the job.

Dolores   Oh no Hank. I'll take the job. I'll grab the job by the neck and rattle its bones, you see if I don't.

Scene Two

Several days later. The shack is empty. **Hank** *enters, running. He wears shorts, T-shirt, a towel round his neck, and running pumps. He puts his hands on the table ledge and leans forward, panting. He takes the towel from round his neck and wipes his face and neck. He straightens up and feels his gut for firmness. He looks down at his gut and takes a fold of flesh in his hands and squeezes it. He flings his hands in the air and places them round the back of his head. Legs apart, he bends sharply to touch his knee with the opposite elbow. Hits the table with his elbow. Yelps with pain and hugs his elbow. Removes his pumps and stockings. Leaps onto the table. He shoves cutlery, etc., to one end of the table with his bare foot. Kneels at the other end of the table and faces out. Paddles furiously with his arms down either side of the table. Grunts as he's doing this. Suddenly jumps to his feet and establishes a surfing stance. Surfs the table. Checks his gut from time to time as he twists and bends his body. Checks his watch. Starts 'walking the board'. Walks up to the front edge of the table and hangs five toes over the edge of the table. Twists and leaps in the air. Lands on a fork. Yelps, grabs his foot, hopping on the other. Falls off the table. He sits on the floor nursing his elbow, foot and butt.*

Hank   SHIT!

Dolores *enters. She carries two brown bags of groceries. She is dressed smartly in expensive clothes. She walks to the table. Sets the groceries down in the space* **Hank** *cleared for his surfing. Takes a glossy magazine from one bag and crosses to the easy chair. Kicks off her shoes and reads the magazine.*

Hank *rises painfully to his feet. Curls his injured foot and walks with a limp. He unpacks the groceries from the bags. They contain expensive items of food. Two steaks, wrapped,* **Hank** *leaves on the table, along with a clove of garlic. He limps to the fridge with beer, wine, champagne and oranges. He takes a huge bunch of grapes and cookies into the kitchenette.*

Dolores *reads her magazine.* **Hank** *emerges, limping, from the kitchenette. He carries the grapes, washed, in a bowl. He sets the bowl down beside* **Dolores**. **Dolores** *reads and eats grapes, absently.* **Hank** *carries more groceries through to the kitchenette.* **Dolores** *reads and eats grapes.* **Hank** *limps from the kitchenette with a chopping board, garlic crusher and steak hammer. Unwraps the steaks and crushes the garlic. Rubs the garlic into the steaks. Beats the steaks mercilessly with the hammer. Exhausted, he sits back.* **Dolores** *reads and eats grapes.* **Hank** *engages her in disjointed conversation.*

Hank   You're late back from work.

Dolores (*reading*)   Yes.

Hank   Where you bin?

Dolores   I called by on Susan.

Hank *stands and grabs a steak in each hand. Slides them off the chopping board and dangles them by his sides. Limps out with them to the kitchenette.* **Dolores** *reads and eats grapes.* **Hank** *emerges from the kitchenette wearing an apron. The apron is tied tight at the back.* **Hank** *wipes his hands on the apron, over his gut. This draws attention to his shape again.*

Hank   What did you do today? At the zoo?

Hank *finds a mirror hanging on the wall and removes it. Sets it up on a chair so he can see his body-profile. As he speaks he* *checks his stance, with the apron on.* **Dolores** *eats grapes and reads as she speaks.*

Dolores I sat up a tree talking to a giraffe.

Hank Say anything interesting?

Dolores I didn't mention your name Hank, if that's what you mean.

Hank Was he eating?

Dolores Yes.

Hank Wanna be careful they don't bite your head off. They got vicious teeth.

Dolores This giraffe doesn't have any.

Hank A giraffe with no teeth?

Dolores He's a radiation victim. Military stuff.

Hank *has discovered his gut protrudes less the looser the apron is tied. He experiments with stance-related string tensions.*

Dolores We had an airforce colonel visit the unit today. He was impressed with our progress. Gonna designate us more funds. Means I get a raise.

Dolores *has eaten her last grape.* **Hank** *heads for the kitchenette.*

Dolores He gave up eating.

Hank That's terminal.

Hank *is in the kitchenette.* **Dolores** *reads and picks grape skin from her teeth.*

Dolores The only way they could get it eating again was to put me up a tree along with it. Artie Kake, the steward, he's a nice guy, he said he'd resigned himself to him never eating again until I came along.

Hank *emerges from the kitchenette, limping.*

Hank   This was the giraffe.

Dolores   Yes.

Hank   The airforce colonel. He had all his teeth.

Dolores   Far as I could make out.

Hank *returns to the kitchenette.* **Dolores** *rises and stretches. She walks round the room, barefoot. She sees the mirror and checks her appearance in it. She likes what she sees. She adjusts her new dress. She turns and looks over her shoulder into the mirror. She stretches the back of the dress over her butt.*

Hank *emerges from the kitchenette and sees this. He holds a bowl full of salad.* **Dolores** *runs her hand down the profile of her butt. She stretches the dress tight round her butt.* **Hank** *swallows hard, feels his gut, and pushes it back.* **Dolores** *turns and repeats her performance with her breasts.* **Hank** *stuffs his mouth with lettuce. He slams the bowl down on the table and limps back to the kitchenette.* **Dolores** *eats a leaf of lettuce and returns to her chair.*

Dolores   The vet was treating Spotty today. Mrs Operkl's dog? Had an hour's psychoanalysis. Y'know what she dresses him in?

Hank (*in the kitchenette*)   What.

Dolores   Two small pairs of designer jeans and a T-shirt which says 'Nuke em'. Artie said I should keep away from Spotty. Which is why I was sent up a tree. I caught a glimpse of him from up the tree. He's so ugly.

Hank *emerges from the kitchenette with two steaks, cooked, on plates. He places them on the table.*

Hank   You see much of this Artie?

Dolores   He's my boss.

Hank   How old is he?

Dolores *rises and walks to the table.*

Dolores   Twenny-five? I dunno. He's young.

Hank *and* **Dolores** *sit at the table.*

Hank   Is he married?

Dolores   No.

They eat their steaks. **Hanks** *has recourse to nurse his foot occasionally, under the table.* **Dolores** *speaks as she eats.*

Dolores   Me and Susan are growing apart. She can't handle my newfound wealth. It was OK when I was the underdog but now I'm successful she's gone bitchy. She seldom smiles these days. You remember how she was always so jolly? I took her a bunch of flowers yesterday and they were not on display when I called by this afternoon. I poked around in their trash when I left and there were the flowers, underneath the skeleton of last night's fish. I went out of my way to choose their favourite brand so it's not as if they find em offensive, or consider them to be unlucky like the peacock feathers they threw out after Judd's mom and dad were killed in their car smash. I'm gonna tackle Susan head on over this. I'm gonna ask her what happened to the flowers? And if she says they wilted or attracted hornets or some such excuse like that I'll say I saw em in the garbage and it's plain to me they never reached display because the night I called by with the flowers you were cookin fish and were about to eat it when I left and the flowers were beneath the fish remains in the trash the next day when I departed and that proves they were thrown out before you ever sat down to eat your goddam fish! Of course, I run the risk of Susan askin what the hell were you doin pokin your snout into our garbage? Then I will blurt out an accusation of hardened attitudes towards me and she will deny it. She'll proclaim her affection for me is strong as ever and I'm imagining things and Judd will sit in the corner smoking his pipe and reading his mail-order catalogue while we have

a row, hating all the shouting and embarrassed by
Susan's displays of naked emotion. Susan will throw the
mincer at me. Or worse, hit me in the eye and I will
storm outa the house kickin over their trash on my way
to the car. That'll be another buddy down the pan. My
best buddy.

She continues eating. **Hank** *is ahead of her. He finishes and
pushes his plate to one side. He takes his foot from under the table
and lifts it up. Places his foot on the table next to* **Dolores**'
plate.

Hank   Take a look at my foot.

Dolores *takes a look at* **Hank**'*s foot.*

Dolores   So what.

Hank   See anything?

Dolores *takes a mouthful of steak and scrutinises* **Hank**'*s foot,
chewing.*

Dolores   I don't see anything.

Hank   I trod on a fork.

Dolores *takes another look at* **Hank**'*s foot.*

Dolores   Shoulda picked it up. It's called housework.

Hank   The fork was on the table.

Dolores *takes a final look at* **Hank**'*s foot.*

Dolores   I don't see anything.

Hank   It's painful.

Hank *removes his foot from the table. He rubs the sole and
replaces it under the table.* **Dolores** *continues eating.*

Dolores   What were you doing on the table?

Hank   Surfing.

Dolores *inspects the table, runs her fingers under the rim.*

Dolores It's bone dry.

Hank I was practising.

Dolores I think it's too early for you to go surfing.

Hank I didn't.

Dolores If you were thinking of it.

Hank I wasn't.

Dolores If you incapacitate yourself practising on the lounge table I don't think the Pacific Ocean is quite the place for you.

Hank I agree.

Dolores Good.

Dolores *has finished her steak. She pushes her plate ahead of her and wipes her mouth.*

Dolores That was nice. Thank you.

Hank *takes the plates through to the kitchenette.* **Dolores** *re-hangs the mirror on the wall. She crosses to the easy chair and replaces her shoes. She goes to the mirror and fusses with her hair.*

Hank *emerges from the kitchenette. He crosses to the easy chair. He sits.* **Dolores** *heads for the door.*

Hank Where you goin?

Dolores Out.

Hank Where?

Dolores See Susan.

Hank Why?

Dolores Confront her over this flower business.

Hank Why?

Dolores Because it's bugging me.

Hank Can't it wait?

Dolores No.

Hank Till tomorrow?

Dolores No.

Hank Oh.

Dolores I'll drive over.

Hank Right.

Dolores I won't be an hour.

Hank No.

Dolores Good.

She goes. **Hank** *picks his injured foot up and places it across his knee. He inspects the foot closely.*

Scene Three

Later that evening. **Hank** *sits in the easy chair.* **Dolores** *arrives.* **Dolores** *is drunk.*

Dolores So what have you bin saying to Judd?

Hank Haven't seen him.

Dolores Bull's *shit.*

Hank I waved at him whilst running on the beach a day or two back. He was out there with his metal detector.

Dolores You did more than wave.

Hank Yeah I said hi, maybe.

Dolores You stopped off in the junklot, exhausted, for a rest.

Hank I had run five miles, non-stop, across sand.

Dolores You had breath enough to tell Judd and

Susan about my antics with the monkey.

Hank *is silent.*

Dolores   Well it did the trick. They were of course deeply sympathetic for poor Hank whose wife is nothin more than a monkey-fuckin tramp. Come round any time Hank and sit with us in the junklot. Move in if needs be, when the whore brings her monkeys round. You're contemptuous.

Hank   Musta slipped out in conversation.

Dolores   It didn't work buster. I put em straight.

Hank   You're drunk.

Dolores   I had some wine.

Hank   So who's contemptuous.

Dolores   Oh Saint Peter here's never bin drunk. Don't twist it.

Hank   I ain't twistin.

Dolores   I gotta mind to stop your allowance.

Hank   I wouldn't do that if I were you.

Dolores   Why not.

Hank   I might just have to sell my story to Hollywood.

Dolores   I'll get there first.

Hank   They wouldn't believe you.

Dolores   Well Judd and Susan believe me, that's all I care about. They're back on my team.

Hank   What did you tell em?

Dolores   Let's just say they understand my motives. Let's just say that. Let's just say I managed to fill in a few gaps you left out whilst catching your breath no doubt, let's leave it at that. Let's just say I managed to convince them their *gut reaction* was a wrong one. Let's leave it there shall we? Let's say that.

Hank   What did you say?

Dolores   I told em what a shit you've bin to me these fifteen years. I told em what a fuckin shit you've bin. What a snivelling fuckin shit you've bin. (*Kicks off her shoes.*) What a snivelling wretched buddy-poaching shit you are. (*Walking round the room.*) Told em what a lazy, self-centred shit you are, (*Goes to the fridge and takes out champagne.*) what an asshole, what an impossible asshole you are, (*Going to kitchenette.*) told em what it's like to live with a pathetic, failed asshole, (*Emerges from kitchenette with a glass, crosses to table.*) told em what it's like to live with an asshole-shitting monster, cleaning up after him for fifteen shit-stained years. (*Uncorks champagne and pours herself a glass.*) Tole em the lengths I had to go to make ends meet with this shit and his asshole monkey. (*She sits at table and drinks champagne.*) How's your foot?

Hank   Better.

Dolores   I told em you've taken to surfin on tables. They found that pathetically funny.

Hank   They would.

Dolores   Yes I told em you three-sixtied on a fork! We burst out laughing on that one. (*She laughs.*) We pissed ourselves over that one! I told em you was limpin round the place with your apron on, maimed by a fuckin fork whilst surfin on a table! (*She laughs.*) They both found that extremely amusing. Even Judd took his pipe out and split his face on that one!

Hank   Only reason he smokes a pipe is so folks can distinguish his face from his ass.

Dolores   Judd is very handsome.

Hank   Handsome.

Dolores   Yes.

Hank   That's a new one.

Dolores   He's in fine physical shape. Surfs like a dolphin.

Hank   With his pipe in his mouth.

Dolores   I've always said to Susan she's a very lucky girl to have someone like Judd. I said so tonight.

Hank   I'm sure Judd appreciated that.

Dolores   Oh he tweaked my nipple and stroked my ass like he always does when Susan grinds the coffee.

Hank   You're lucky she didn't have to pick the beans.

Dolores   You're contemptuous.

Hank   I heard she makes him fuck with his pipe in his mouth for fear she might kiss his ass.

Hank *laughs.*

Dolores   That isn't funny.

Hank *laughs some more.*

Hank   I find it funny. I find it very funny indeed. That's fuckin hilarious!

Dolores *throws her champagne over* **Hank**. *He drips with it.* **Dolores** *screams:*

Dolores   It isn't funny!

Hank   Funniest fuckin thing I've heard all year!

Dolores   Well it's my duty to tell em that. Y'know? As their friend. As their best friend. As Judd and Susan's very best friend, and longest friend, it's my duty to tell em what you say, that you make obscene remarks about em behind their backs!

Hank   You tell em.

Dolores   I will tell em.

Hank   Tell em whatever you like.

Dolores   I will . . .

Hank   I don't give a fuck . . .

Dolores   I might just go and tell em now . . .

Hank   You go ahead. I'll finish the champagne.

Dolores   I'll take it with me.

Hank *rises and crosses to the table. He picks up the champagne bottle and drinks from the neck.* **Dolores** *tries to snatch it back.* **Hank** *grabs it from her, pulling her over. She loses her balance and falls to the floor.* **Hank** *kicks her.* **Dolores** *screams and gets up. She kicks* **Hank** *back on the shin.* **Hank** *grunts and shakes the champagne, squirts her in the face with it.* **Dolores** *screams and flails at* **Hank** *with her arms.* **Hank** *strides to the back of the room and breaks the bottle across the fridge. He turns with the broken neck in his hand.* **Dolores** *stops still, suddenly sober.*

Hank   Sober now?

Dolores   Yes.

Hank *tosses the bottle neck onto the floor.*

Hank   Clean it up.

Hank *crosses to the easy chair.* **Dolores** *makes her way to the kitchenette. She returns with a dustpan and brush.* **Hank** *sits.* **Dolores** *sets about sweeping up the broken glass.* **Hank** *reads her magazine.*

Hank   The shit they write in these magazines. The absolute garbage they fill em with. You gotta be a moron from zonko-land to read this.

He reads it. **Hank** *speaks as* **Dolores** *sweeps.*

Hank   Fancy crap. Waste of talent. Where does all the talent go to these days? The military and the magazines.

Where's all the great artists? They're designing F18s and stuffing magazines with junk. There's too much military and too many magazines. These magazines are the religious paintings of the Medicis. Fill the people's heads with shit so the military can go fuck over defenceless countries with impunity cus all the people back here are sitting home with their heads stuck in a magazine. The more brain-destroying the magazine the more gungho the military becomes. The more gungho the military, the more piss goes in the magazines. So when the balloon goes up and the bomb drops they won't ever know it happened cus they all willa died long ago from the trash they read in magazines.

Dolores *has finished sweeping up.*

Hank   Finished?

Dolores   Yes.

Hank   Take your clothes off.

Dolores   What?

Hank   I'm gonna 'make love' to you tonight.

Dolores   You're not gonna touch me.

Hank   I'm gonna tweak your nipple and stroke your ass like Judd.

Dolores   You're not gonna touch me.

Hank   You like I should break another bottle and grind it in your fuckin face?

Dolores   You're not gonna touch me.

Hank *rises and goes to the kitchenette.*

Dolores   You're not gonna touch me tonight or any night.

Hank *emerges from the kitchenette with the neck of the champagne bottle. He positions himself between* **Dolores** *and* *the door.*

Hank   Take your fuckin clothes off.

Dolores *starts to undress.*

Scene Four

One hour later. **Dolores** *sits alone, in the easy chair, wrapped in a sheet. It is dark. The room is lit by moonlight only.* **Hank** *enters. He stands in the doorway to the bedroom.*

Hank   Shoulda done it on the beach . . . shoulda gone to the beach . . . if we'd gone to the beach . . . took the blanket on the beach . . . remember that? When we used to do it on the beach? . . . First summer . . . used to feel horny all day long, had to wait till dusk then we'd get under the blanket and do it right there, on the beach . . . with the people walkin past and all and we never gave a goddam, remember that? . . . Dol? . . . if we'd, gone on the beach . . . like when we did it on the beach . . . Dol? . . . Dolores? . . . you awake?

He crosses to the easy chair.

Dolores   Go away.

Hank *kneels on the floor beside her.*

Hank   Dolores . . .

Dolores   Don't come near me.

Hank   I'm sorry Dol, I'm sorry, I'm so sorry. I didn't want it to be like this, I didn't want it . . .

Dolores   Go away . . .

Hank *rises.*

Hank   . . . I'm so sorry . . .

Dolores   Don't speak.

Hank   I'm so fuckin unhappy Dolores . . .

Dolores   Leave me alone.

Hank   Listen to me . . .

Dolores   Don't speak.

Hank   I'm so fuckin unhappy.

Dolores   Go away.

Hank   What did I do?

Dolores   Leave me alone.

Hank   Tell me.

Dolores *rises and runs into the bedroom.* **Hank** *sits in the easy chair.*

Hank   Aw shit. Aww, shit. What have I done?

Silence. Dawn breaks. The sun rises. **Hank** *sits in the easy chair, staring into space. A door slams out back.* **Hank** *rises. He goes to the fridge. He removes three oranges from the fridge. Slams the door shut. He takes the oranges to the crusher and crushes them. Drinks the result back in one. Returns to the fridge and takes out another three oranges. Slams the fridge door and crushes the oranges.*

Dolores *emerges from the bedroom. She is dressed in a very short skirt and tight pullover. She looks sexually provocative.*

Hank *finishes crushing his oranges. He walks to the table with his juice. Sits at the table.*

Dolores *finds her bag and extracts a vanity case from it. Sits at the table and lays out her make-up. She stands and applies make-up with the aid of a hand mirror. She makes up tarty.*

Hank *finishes his drink and crosses to the fridge. He opens the fridge door and extracts three more oranges. As he passes* **Dolores** *to the crusher he speaks:*

Hank   You gonna climb up a tree dressed like that?

Dolores   Yes.

Hank   Artie Kake gonna be underneath?

Dolores   I hope so.

Hank   Huh.

He crushes the oranges.

Dolores   I want you to go to Mexico and get us a divorce.

Hank   I don't want no divorce.

Dolores   It's the last night I ever spend with you.

Hank   Gonna shack up with Artie.

Dolores   That's none of your business.

Hank   It's my business.

Dolores   Send me my divorce papers at the zoo.

Hank   Care of the snake pit.

Dolores *goes to fridge and grabs herself a yoghurt. She goes to the kitchenette and finds herself a spoon.*

Hank *has finished crushing his oranges.* **Dolores** *sits at the table.* **Hank** *sits at the table.* **Dolores** *peels off the top of her yoghurt and licks the underside of the top. She eats one spoonful of yoghurt and places the spoon beside the carton. She continues with her make-up.*

Dolores   I'll give you the bus fare.

Hank   I don't want it.

Dolores   I'm already askin myself what it was made me stick with you fifteen years six months and thirteen days. Takes people decades to do that y'know? To look back on a past lover and find not one single trace of what it was attracted em together. Years it takes em. I'm already lookin at you and searching for what it was. It's gone. I've lost it. After one ugly, pointless, disgusting, fruitless, sleepless night. It was there, before last night. Right away in the distance. Through the mists, there was something there. Now there's nothin.

Hank *is eating* **Dolores**' *yoghurt.*

Dolores   I'd be thankful if you'd put that down.

Dolores *is packing her make-up away.* **Hank** *flicks a spoonful of yoghurt across her face.*

Dolores   That was a childish gesture. That was a childish, pointless gesture.

Hank   How many times did you get up like this when I was out on the road uh?

Dolores *heads for the kitchenette.*

Hank   How many times? How many times did I walk down that fuckin path? And you'd be in here, tartin up like a fuckin tramp!

Dolores *emerges from the kitchenette with a towel, she's wiping the yoghurt carefully from her face.*

Hank   Answer me that! How many fuckin times?

Hank *rises and snatches the towel from* **Dolores**.

Hank   How many times?

Dolores   Give that back!

Dolores *snatches back the towel. They have one end each. She tugs at it.* **Hank** *doesn't let go.*

Hank   Bust my fuckin ass for you! This is all I get! Fuckin killed myself for you! Fuckin bitch! This is all I get!

Dolores *hits* **Hank** *on the side of the face.* **Hank** *lets go of the towel. He punches* **Dolores** *in the face.*

Hank   Fifteen fuckin years! This is all I get!

He hits her again. Blackout.

Scene Five

Dolores *lies on the table. The yoghurt is beside her. The* **Vet** *inspects* **Dolores** *closely.* **Dolores** *is covered from ankles to waist with the Indian blanket.* **Hank** *is hunched in a corner. He looks mean and fiddles nervously with a wooden spatula.*

Vet   You did all this with your bare hands.

Hank   Yes.

Vet   She took some blows.

Hank   What have I done.

Vet   You broke her neck. Multiple abrasions around her face, widespread econymoses across her upper torso, intra-cranial haemorrhage, ruptured her spleen, cerebral contusions, you ah, you must be in pretty good shape.

Hank   Is she dead?

Vet   Oh yes. She's dead.

Hank   She can't be dead.

Vet   I'm no doctor, but believe me if your wife was an elephant she'd be dead.

The **Vet** *covers* **Dolores** *with the blanket.* **Hank** *snaps the spatula in two. The* **Vet** *hears this and glances at* **Hank***. He picks the yoghurt off the table. He sniffs it.*

Vet   This fresh?

Hank *nods. The* **Vet** *wipes the spoon with his shirt. He takes the yoghurt to the easy chair and sits. He eats as he speaks.*

Vet   I missed breakfast. I generally breakfast in the canteen. Right by the bat house. But I got your call this morning before I even made it to the bat house and I came straight over. Feelin kinda peckish. I guess I shoulda taken breakfast before I set off. I plan breakfast according to the animals I'm treating that day. I take a squint at the duty list on my way to the canteen past the bat house and if there's a carnivore under my name I eat kidneys and bacon. If there's an omnivore on my round I take a tomato with it. And when I have the good fortune to be called out to castrate a chicken, I get an egg. Good ole English breakfast.

He has finished his yoghurt. He stands and places the empty carton delicately back where he found it. He walks to the door.

Your wife had a remarkable gift with animals. We'll miss her at the zoo. Her contribution to Artie's giraffe programme was colossal. I'll sneak out now, and leave you to your bereavement.

The **Vet** *sidles out.* **Hank** *stands and walks to the table. He uncovers* **Dolores** *down to the neck. He speaks to* **Dolores**.

Hank   My poor little monkey. My poor, darlin little monkey, I don't know what the hell I'm gonna do without ya. I flicked yoghurt in your face, that was stupid wasn't it? Y'know you once said, after the monkey died you said if we ever had children and we told em we had a monkey they'd say We know. He's up there lookin down on us. I said that's a sweet thought. If you're up there lookin down Dolores for Chrissakes I dunno what I've done I'm so sorry, I wish to fuck I was up there with ya lookin down on me, if we was both up there lookin down we'd be happy wouldn't we? We'd get along real fine. Are you up there Dolores? Where are you! For fucksake! (*He falls across* **Dolores**.) Come back! Come back here! (*Shaking her.*) DOLORES come back! Please, come back. DOLORES *come back for Chrissakes!* DOLORES! DOLORES!

He slides her off the table and holds her tight, in the centre of the floor, crying her name and swinging her from side to side. The atmosphere changes. Music. They dance.

Dolores   Hey, I know you, you're the guy who surfs with a monkey on his back . . .

Hank   That's right.

Dolores   What's your name?

Hank   Hank. Hank Wandaback.

Dolores   I'm Dolores.

Hank   That's a sweet name.

Dolores   I hate it.

They dance.

Where's the monkey?

Hank   Right outside, playin in the garden.

Dolores   Introduce me?

Hank   Maybe we should get to know each other first.

They dance. **Hank** *smiles. The lights fade.*

The King of Prussia

The King of Prussia was first performed by Kneehigh Theatre Company at the Acorn Theatre, Penzance, on 8 December 1995. It subsequently toured, opening at the Donmar Warehouse, London, on 4 March 1996. The cast was as follows:

John Carter	Tristan Sturrock
Harry Carter/John Stackhouse	Giles King
Bessie Bussoe	Bec Applebee
Suzanne Stackhouse	Mary Woodvine
John Knill/Charlie Carter	Charles Barnecut
Edward Carter	Carl Grose

Other parts were played by the cast

Directed by Mike Shepherd
Designed by Bill Mitchell
Music by Jim Carey

The play runs without an interval

1787. Dawn. The deck of a schooner is revealed as the sun rises and slowly burns off the mist. A solitary deckhand sings unaccompanied a quiet, haunting song:

> Dawn breaks and no day was finer,
> Our schooner lies anchored
> Fresh home from China.
> Stood out four miles
> Due west of the Lizard,
> The crew, ocean-weary,
> Yearns for the shore

Lookout   Lugger! English! Two miles to larb'd! Gathering on us with all sail before!

Captain   That's our man. The King of Prussia.

Supercargo   Open the hatches! Prepare to discharge!

John Carter *is received on deck by the* **Captain**.

Carter   Where y'from?

Captain   China.

Carter   I don't want tea.

The hatchtop is replaced.

Did ye pick up any liquor on your voyage home?

Captain   A few ton.

Carter   Let's feel the strength of it.

He watches the **Captain** *give orders to the* **Supercargo**.

Carter   This is me brother's job but e's in gaol so I'm doin is job on toppa my job which is two jobs too many don't ya think? What's your price?

Captain   Five pounds?

Carter   Jack?

Captain   Nantz.

Carter   Bugger five. Three.

Captain   Three?

Carter   I wouldn't give ya five for jack. I'd consider four for geneva but nantz? Three's generous. In fact you've talked me out of three. Two or nothing. Geneva three. Four the jack. What did we agree, one?

Captain   Two . . .

Carter   That was geneva. And three pound for jack.

Captain   Four pound the jack . . .

Carter   So you have jack!

Captain   Yes!

A barrel is brought.

Carter   At two.

Captain   Two?

Carter   Thass better. Two for the jack.

Captain   Three.

Carter   You offered me two! I heard you say it. Come along Cap'm I'm a busy man willya shit or get off the pot?

Captain *hands a measure of brandy to* **Carter**.

Carter   Whass this, nantz?

Captain   Jack.

Carter (*studying the contents of the measure*)   It ain't geneva.

Captain   No.

Carter   That we do know.

Carter *drains the liquor and hands the measure back.*

Pound a tub.

Captain You said two!

Carter Thass for jack.

Captain This is jack.

Carter It ain't geneva so we'm down to jack and nantz.

Captain Nantz?

Carter I arn't so sure either Cap'm. Could be nantz could be jack. Now I'm prepared to take the risk and pay y'a pound a tub for what might turn out on closer inspection not to be geneva not to be jack but nantz.

Captain A pound!

Carter Good! Thass more like it. (*He shakes the* **Captain**'s *hand.*) Have y'never dealt with a free-trader before Cap'm?

Captain No sir.

Carter First thing you gotta learn is a free-trader's an honest man cus e d'break the law. And if you break the law you gotta be honest. If I offer you a pound then a pound is a fair price.

Captain How many d'ye want?

Carter Four hundred and eighty.

Captain Break bulk there!

Carter Fast and steady mind.

They watch the unloading.

See the gannets fishin Cap'm. There's always one oo range high and wide. Huntin while the others dive. Thass me.

Lookout (*off*) Ship! Weather bow!

The **Captain** *looks through his telescope.* **Carter** *crouches against the bulwark.*

Carter   How many ports?

Captain   Eight.

Carter   'Colour's is bulwarks?

Captain   Yellow and black.

Carter   Dark gaff tops'l?

Captain   Yes.

Carter   Jib?

Captain   White.

Carter   Tis the Revenue.

Captain   Bearing down fast.

Carter   I gotta brother imprisoned in France, a two undred tonner in pound and to cap it all ere come that bastard John Knill.

Knill   God dammit John Carter!

Carter   E dun't patrol Mount's Bay whass the bastard doin ere?

Knill   In the flesh!

Carter   (*yelling*)   Gittome to St Ives!

Knill   We got the bugger this time!

Carter   E's the only Revenue officer I can't deal with.

Knill   What a stroke of luck!

Carter   Haul off the land a league Cap'm. Outside the limit. Then let him fetch up and kiss me ass!

He gives a shrill whistle to his boat as he disappears over the gunwale.

Porthleah Farm. **Bessie Bussoe** *bangs hard on the door, opens it and yells through:*

Bessie   Charlie! Edward! Wake up! (*Noises from within.*) Your brother's gone sea with the Revenue up is ass I'm goin down point to head em off with a six-pounder!

Acton Castle. **John Stackhouse** *sits at his microscope. His wife* **Suzanne** *sits near by, sewing. In the distance, a cannon is fired.* **Stackhouse** *looks up.* **Suzanne** *stands and walks to the window.* **Stackhouse** *adjusts his microscope.*

Suzanne   Cannonfire.

Cudden Point. **Bessie Bussoe** *primes, aims and fires a cannon.* **Charlie** *and* **Eddy Carter** *join her.* **Charlie** *drinks a mug of tea,* **Eddy** *is still dressing, having just woken up.*

Charlie   First time I set eyes on John Wesley was 1746 March month.

Bessie   Where was that Charlie?

Charlie   Preachin down St Ives.

Eddy   Gwennap.

Charlie   St Ives.

Eddy   Gwennap.

Charlie   I was there.

Eddy   Pascoe Walters ad a 'pocalyptic vision.

The cannon is fired.

Stackhouse *adjusts his microscope.*

Bessie   Which 'pocalyptic vision are you talkin about Edward?

Eddy   The one e ad at Gwennap.

Charlie   St Ives.

Bessie   Was it the dogs?

Eddy   Yeah. Dogs.

Bessie   Thass Gwennap.

Eddy   E never ad dogs at St Ives.

Charlie   Bugger did! I was standin next to im!

Eddy   That was Gwennap.

Bessie   Too bad e's dead you could've asked im.

Charlie   E stood up in St Ives halfway through John Wesley and yelled the dogs the dogs the devil's dogs the dogs of hell are comin.

Bessie   Thass the dogs all right.

Eddy   That was Gwennap.

Charlie   Say Gwennap once more I'll 'it ya.

Eddy   Gwennap.

Charlie   You wad'n there ya wad'n born!

Eddy   Mother said twas Gwennap.

Charlie   God damme what did Mother knaw!

Bessie   Too bad she's dead she woulda told ya.

Mother (*from beyond*)   Twas Gwennap!

Bessie *fires the cannon.*

Stackhouse   Dammit!

Bessie *holds up her hand.*

Suzanne   They've stopped.

John Carter *arrives with a half anker of brandy on his shoulder.*

Carter   That bastard Knill. Thank Christ you opened fire on the bugger. (*To* **Charlie**.) G'back down and tell Richards soon as she's light we're crossin to France.

Charlie   Today?

Carter   I gotta get Harry outa jail for the Cawsand job. (*To* **Bessie**.) Got the papers?

Bessie   Yep.

Carter   Tis no damn good without im.

Exit **Charlie**.

Bessie   E's sure as hell to send men across the land.

Carter   Oo?

Bessie   Knill.

Carter   I got ten ton a jack down there.

Bessie   Can't store it in the cave.

Eddy   Not with Knill on the rampage.

Carter (*yelling*)   Charlie!

Bessie   Thass the first place they're gonna search.

Carter   Where we gonna put it?

Enter **Charlie**.

Bessie   'Bout the castle?

Carter   What about it?

Charlie (*to* **Carter**)   What?

Carter   Hold fire.

Eddy   Reckon they'd take it?

They look up at the castle.

Stackhouse *adjusts microscope.*

Bessie   Whass e like?

Charlie   Who?

Eddy   Matey in the castle.

Carter Stackhouse.

Bessie You pay im rent.

Carter Not if I can help it.

Charlie Id'n ere is e?

Eddy I seen im fishin.

Bessie E go fishin?

Eddy E d'pick seaweed.

Carter Seaweed?

Stackhouse *adjusts his microscope. Near by is a rack of fresh seaweed. He selects a specimen of weed and dissects it with a sharp knife on a board. He lays a particle of weed onto a glass plate and slides it under the microscope.* **Stackhouse** *works with intense concentration, bent over the lens making notes and sketches in a pad, holding weed to the light, experimenting with positions for the microscope, trying on a hat with a wide brim to shield the light from the lens, focusing, altering the plate position and the specimens for study.* **Suzanne** *sits on the opposite side of the room doing her needlepoint.*

Bessie *climbs on* **Carter***'s back and looks in through the window.*

Bessie Place is fulla seaweed.

Eddy Told ya.

Suzanne You're becoming a fanatic.

Bessie She says e's a fanatic.

Stackhouse Nonsense.

Carter Whass that, Bible Christian?

Eddy Botanist.

Suzanne A man possessed.

Stackhouse Don't be absurd.

Suzanne   All the signs are there.

Stackhouse   Name them.

Bessie   She's namin signs.

Eddy   Thas 'pocalyptic.

Suzanne   The castle for one. Why build it here? Miles from anywhere? On a cliff. Why? Seaweed. The lead-lined tanks you installed in the cellar. What are they for? Seaweed. For what purpose did you hire a gang of sixteen men for three months to dig a tunnel from the basement to the sea? Seaweed.

Bessie   Tis all seaweed.

Eddy   'Pocalyptic botanist.

Suzanne   And now this what's-it-called?

Stackhouse   Microscope.

Bessie   Microscope.

Suzanne   What does it do? Magnify doesn't it, minute particles of seaweed. This – what d'you call it?

Eddy   Microscope?

Bessie   Sh!

Suzanne   Microscope is the final straw. I've hardly seen you since you brought it here. What am I to do? Walk. Walk walk walk.

Stackhouse   Swim?

Suzanne   And swim.

Bessie *climbs off* **Carter**'s *back.*

Bessie   All she do is walk and swim.

Eddy   Swim?

Carter   I don't like it.

Eddy   Too 'pocalyptic.

Carter   Come on.

He starts to go.

Bessie   But there's a tunnel from the basement to the sea.

Suzanne   I warn you husband. There are things going on around here. The local people break the law. Systematically. All the time. And I might join them. I've thought of that y'know. For want of something to do. I am so bloody bored. How would you like a criminal for a wife? What if I were caught and sent to trial and found guilty and imprisoned? Would you notice? With your eye down that damned what's-it-called?

*Enter **Agnes** the maid.*

Agnes   The Kinga Prussia!

*Enter **Carter**, **Bessie** and **Eddy**. They stand awkwardly.*

Suzanne   Where's the king?

Carter   I'm the king.

Suzanne   Who's the captain?

Carter   What captain?

Suzanne   Captain Carter?

Carter   E's in France.

Suzanne   Isn't he the king?

Carter   No.

Bessie   E's the captain.

Carter   I'm the king.

Suzanne   You know my husband?

Carter   I pay im rent.

Stackhouse (*over microscope*)   Good.

Suzanne   Who's this?

Carter   Edward.

Suzanne   Prince?

Eddy   Eh?

Bessie   I'm Bessie.

Carter   She own the wink.

Bessie   Over Porthleah.

Suzanne   What is a wink?

Eddy   Dun't she knaw what a wink is?

Bessie   Drinkin parlour.

Carter   We was runnin in er monthly stock of jack this mornin. Thass legitimate duty-paid jack purchased from the bonded warehouse in Penzance when we got mistook for a notorious gang of free-traders and chased by the Revenue. We fear for the jack to be frank cus they're comin at us over the land.

Bessie   We need a place to put the jack.

Carter   With your permission.

They await a reply.

Suzanne   What is jack?

Eddy (*astonished*)   Eh?

Carter   Cognac brandy ma'am.

Eddy   Dun't she knaw nothin?

Carter   Show er the jack.

Bessie *pours a tot.*

Suzanne   I know what you're up to Mr Carter.

Eddy (*to* **Bessie**)   Bet she dun't.

Suzanne   I've observed your activities.

Eddy (*worried*)   Eh?

Suzanne   And I must say I'm keen to get involved.

Carter   Tis a hard school Mrs Stackhouse.

Eddy   Damn ard.

Carter   We're not askin you to get involved.

Eddy   God forbid.

Carter   That wasn't our intention.

Eddy   Not at all.

Carter   All we're askin for is use of that tunnel and the loan of a corner of your castle for a day or two.

Eddy   Thass all we're askin.

Carter   Nothin more.

Eddy   Id'n askin nothin more'n that.

Suzanne (*tasting brandy*)   O! This is good cognac. (*Tastes again.*) Beautiful. Distilled over coal by Dubouche ... from wine grown in Grande Champagne ... on the south bank of the Charente ... where the soil is pure chalk. (*Taps the barrel and smells the wood.*) The finest white oak grown in the forest of Limousin. (*She drinks more, closes her eyes and groans in ecstasy.*) O! Exquisite.

A shudder passes through her whole body.

Eddy   It's hit blood.

She drinks more and sways.

Carter   Mrs Stackhouse?

Suzanne   I could find a buyer for this.

Eddy   A buyer?

Suzanne   A good price.

Eddy   Good price?

Carter   I don't need buyers.

Suzanne   Got much?

Carter   Not much.

Suzanne   How much?

Carter   Don't tell er.

Eddy   Four undred and eighty half anker tubs at eight'n alf gallons to the anker's nine ton three undredweight and sixty-five pounds imperial.

Carter   Yeah. Thass approximate.

Suzanne   What did you pay?

Carter   Don't tell er.

Eddy   Pound a tub.

Suzanne   What's your price?

Carter   Don't tell er.

Eddy   Twenty-five shillin.

Suzanne   I could sell it for six.

Eddy   Pounds?

Carter   Huh?

Bessie   Where?

Suzanne   Bath.

Carter   Bath?

Eddy   Where the 'ell's Bath?

Bessie   Thass –

Suzanne   Two thousand four hundred pounds profit.

Eddy   Eh?!

Eddy *and* **Bessie** *look at* **Carter** *expectantly.*

Carter   This stuff's promised.

Suzanne   All of it?

Carter   Every last damn drop. I got people to supply.
Valued customers. I can't let em down. I ave a five-
shillin mark-up and no more. Thass my rule. Six bob if
y'live beyond St Columb. I'm an honest man. The
people I sell to can't afford nothin more. If it wad'n for
me they'd go without.

Suzanne   You should always sell at the best possible
price.

Eddy   I agree.

Carter   I'm the boss round ere.

Suzanne   What d'you pay your men?

Carter   That's between me and them.

Eddy   Two shillin.

Suzanne   A week's wage for a night's work.

Carter   Pay em well they do a good job.

Suzanne   How many can you call on?

Carter   Plenty enough.

Eddy   Thirty-three able-bodied.

Carter   Eh?

Bessie   Thass all Wendron bar Shadrack Vincent oo
got the wap.

Carter   Whass bitten Shadrack?

Bessie   I went to is farm and spoke to is wife.

Carter   What did she say?

Bessie   I said is Shadrack on for tonight?

Mrs Vincent   I doubt it.

Bessie   I said why?

Mrs Vincent   Not after last time.

Bessie   What appened last time?

Mrs Vincent   You gib'm a lame orse.

Carter   God dammit!

Mrs Vincent   E abandoned it out on Tredinnick Moor and carried undred pounda Congo tea fower mile to Ladock on is back and never gotta penny extra.

Carter   I promised im another shillin! Went clean out me mind.

Bessie   I gived er two on the spot.

Carter   Reckon it appeased er?

Bessie   Ard to say.

Carter   Didn she smile or nothin?

Mrs Vincent *keeps a straight face.*

Bessie   There's no bugger bears a grudge like Shadrack.

Carter   I want im back for the Cawsand job.

Suzanne   What's the Cawsand job?

Carter   Don't tell er.

Eddy   Job up Cawsand.

Carter   And I dun't wanna see Knill in Mount's Bay no more.

Suzanne   Who is Knill?

Carter   Dun't tell er.

Eddy   E's Revenue.

Suzanne   I shall look into that.

Carter   Eh?

Suzanne   My brother is a vice-admiral.

Carter   Knill's Revenue e in't Navy.

Eddy   They d'cross-fertilise.

Carter   You've said enough.

Suzanne   If I have to I shall talk to Knill myself.

Carter   Aw no y'can't do that.

Suzanne   Why not?

Eddy   Bin tried.

Carter   E wun't be bribed.

Suzanne   Care to wager?

Carter   I'll bet you a pound.

Eddy   Ten.

Bessie   What?

Suzanne   Make it a hundred.

Bessie   No!

Eddy   Yeah!

Carter   Done.

Eddy   E's untouchable!

Carter   E's too pompous.

Eddy   Too full of is own importance.

Carter   Too unctuous.

Eddy   E strut about St Ives like a pig with a sore ass.

Carter   (*affecting a Lemon Street accent*)   'Look at me I'm

John Knill.'

Eddy (*strutting*)   'I love my king.'

Carter (*exaggerated strut*)   'I am a devoted servant of my country.'

Bessie (*extreme strut*)   'I wear the uniform of an officer with pride.'

Carter (*outlandish pose*)   'I arrest you in the name of King George.'

Eddy (*outrageous strut*)   'My uniform is King George.'

Carter (*uncontrollable strut*)   'I *am* King George!

Enter **Agnes**.

Agnes   Mister John Knill!

Carter *and* **Eddy** *and* **Bessie** *vanish behind curtains.*

Enter **John Knill**.

Knill   Good morning ma'am. Please excuse my state of agitation. I galloped all the way from Marazion.

Suzanne   Would you care for a brandy?

Knill   Thank you Mrs Stackhouse I do not drink.

He watches **Suzanne** *pour herself a large tot and chuck it back.*

Knill   I've come ere to report a serious breach of law which has took place this mornin right under your forgive the expression – noses. You are aware all goods which are freighted into this country from foreign parts are required to pass through Customs where they are assessed for duty. Non-payment, the avoidance thereof – to put it bluntly forgiving your presence ma'am the bloody-minded arrogant detestable practice of cheating King George is a crime! Our poor demented monarch dammit e needs all the money he can get! I love my king. I am a devoted servant to my country. (*Wipes a tear*

from his eye.) I wear the uniform of an officer with pride.
There he was John Carter bold as brass beyond the
limit violating Revenue laws before my eyes! And I was
impotent to apprehend im! You shoulda seen the brandy
they was unloading outa that schooner! Four undred and
eighty half-anker tubs! Thass near ten ton! The duty
runs into hundreds of pounds! It breaks my heart the
loss to the Exchequer! And then to fire upon us with
cannon from the cliff. You must have heard it!

Suzanne Thunder, surely.

Knill No ma'am! That was cannon! My men was
under oars! Ad to row for their life! They ad balls
whistling around their ears!

He shudders and sobs.

Madam. The ringleader is a tenant of your husband's.

Suzanne A tenant?

Knill In the agriculture way.

Suzanne (*shocked*) Surely not?

Knill Mr John Carter.

Suzanne No!

Knill E's anchored up below this very castle!

Suzanne Well!

Knill E live not three undred yards across the cliff!
You breathe the same air as this monster. Be careful of
him Mrs Stackhouse. He's a dangerous, dishonest man.

A grunt from behind the curtain. **Knill** *assumes it to be*
Stackhouse.

Knill O yes. Take my advice. Have no dealings with
the Carter brothers beyond the acceptance of rent.

Suzanne Dealings?

Knill   He might try to implicate you in his activities.

Suzanne   Out of the question!

Knill   Mrs Stackhouse. He made an attempt to bribe *me* once.

Suzanne   Did he succeed?

Knill   Certainly not! *I* am an honest man.

A roar from behind the curtain. **John Carter** *strides out.*

Carter   So am I!

Knill   You! . . . Mrs Stackhouse!

Carter (*advancing on* **Knill**)   Two buggers called me dishonest today and that's two too many don't you think?

Knill   I arrest you in the name of King George.

Carter   Do ya fuck.

He lands a haymaker in **Knill**'s *face.* **Knill** *goes out like a light and collapses onto* **Carter**'s *shoulder.*

Carter (*heading for the door*)   Chuck the bugger off the cliff.

Exit **Carter** *plus* **Knill**. **Bessie** *emerges from behind the curtain.*

Bessie   Mrs Stackhouse! (**Suzanne** *turns.*) We gotta store this jack.

Exit **Bessie** *and* **Suzanne**.

Eddy *watches* **Stackhouse** *at work.* **Eddy** *opens his jacket and takes out a shrivelled seaweed plant. He lays it on the cutting block.* **Stackhouse** *looks up at* **Eddy**, *then down at the weed.*

Stackhouse   Palmaria palmata.

Eddy   Yep.

Stackhouse   Common enough.

Eddy   Take a closer look.

Stackhouse *squints at the specimen and shrugs.*

Eddy   The bugger's in fructification.

Stackhouse   So he is!

Eddy   See they granules?

Stackhouse   Astounding!

Eddy   Thass the seeds.

Stackhouse   You think so?

Eddy   I'm certain.

Stackhouse   Never be sure of anything until you have studied the internal structure.

He rushes it to the microscope.

Eddy   Pascoe Walters ad a 'pocalyptic vision up St Germans and twas weed. They was watchin John Wesley and Pascoe clutched is throat wi both 'ands and yelled the weed the weed tis chokin me the weed and e fell to is knees all red in the face. It took three men to prize is fingers off is own throat. E ad this vision of skullin is punt through thick kelp and e can't work the oar so e d'get stuck and the kelp grows out the water up the oar smothers the punt and twines round Pascoe and sucks out is blood and e's petrified into rock all bar is *nose.* Which is condemned for ever to sniff the stench of rotten kelp.

Stackhouse (*studying seaweed*)   I have never seen palmatus in such a mature stage of fructification.

Eddy   If you come across a rock six foot high covered in kelp with a nose stickin out. Thass Pascoe.

Stackhouse   Where did you find it?

Eddy   Arn't sayin.

Stackhouse   Whyever not?

Eddy   Cus I charge.

Stackhouse   How much?

Eddy   Thruppence?

Stackhouse   Here's a shilling.

Eddy   Climb down cove – this is low water mind –
and on the far side between the cliff and the rock which
d'break on the end of Ennys at half tide there's a drang.
Thass where the weed is. There's a lobster down there.
(**Stackhouse** *has donned a coat, picked up a bag and gone.*) I
seed is feelers but I can't catch'n. E's a cautious beast.
Black as night. Big as a buildin. I glimpsed is crusher
once. Size of your foot. It was low water on a big out
and it d'make a pool there and I took 'ook wi'me and a
net and splashed the water on the edge so e think the
tide is comin in. This brings im forth cus e's ungry.
Then you get behind im quick with the 'ook and slip
the net in under and yank im out. But e kicked with is
tail before I ad a chance to get the 'ook in behind and
the bastard put up such a cloud I couldn't see the 'ole
or nothin. Time the sand settled there wad'n a sign of
im. Not a feeler. Not a trace. Tis like e was never there.
Like e was a . . . a vision. Hellish fish you.

Eddy *stands on the cliff watching* **Bessie** *trussing* **Knill,** *who
is still unconscious and wrapped in a canvas shroud so just his
head shows.*

Carter   Oo got the papers?

Bessie *hands him papers.* **Eddy** *assists* **Bessie.**

Carter (*shuffling through papers*)   Bessie's in charge when
I'm away.

Eddy   Is when you're not.

Carter   Eh?

Bessie   They'm only valid in peacetime so if they go to war, scat.

Carter (*looking through papers*)   Maritime passes for me and Harry. Ownership bonds for the cutter. And a certificate from the Governor of Guernsey authorising Harry's immediate release.

Bessie   I only got three of they left.

Carter   Three?

Bessie   And they don't come cheap so tell your brothers to stay outa jail.

Carter (*takes a scrap of paper from his pocket and shows it to* **Bessie**)   This ere is the list of customers who're expecting a delivery of jack. (*Indicates on list.*) Mrs Winnit only take a quarter anker so you'll ave to break a keg. The rector of St Germans like is in a big stug so the faithful think tis pilchards. (*Hands list to* **Bessie**.) Get Wendron to deliver this tomorrer night. No later. I can't abide to let me customers down. This is no time at all to be goin to France.

Eddy   Ask 'Arry where Pascoe Walters ad is dogs vision.

Carter   Gwennap.

Eddy (*triumphant*)   Hah!

They've hitched **Knill** *to a block and tackle which is connected to a yard-arm on a sheerlegs over the cliff.*

Carter   Ready?

Bessie   Yep.

Carter *slaps* **Knill** *awake.*

Carter   Knill!

Knill *wakes and struggles.*

Carter   We're gonna pay ya fifty pound a year to leave us alone and quit patrollin Mount's Bay. That a deal?

Knill   No!

Carter   Hoist him up.

Bessie (*hoisting* **Knill** *up to the yard-arm*)   Harry ab'm missed one John Wesley. E was there when the bugger read the Book a Revelation from start to finish without the aid of a Bible.

Eddy (*hoisting*)   I knaw all the words to the Book a Revelation.

Bessie   But not in the order they'm written down in the Bible.

Eddy   Yeah. Thass the trick.

Carter   C'mon Knill. Undred.

Knill   You'll never buy me Carter!

Carter   Swing im out.

Knill *is swung out over the cliff and dropped a few feet. He screams.*

Eddy   Thass the one with lobsters in. Revelation.

Bessie   There id'n no lobsters in Revelation.

Eddy   Bloody are. .

Carter   Undred and fifty Knill. I pay cash Lady Day on the nail.

Knill   Go ta hell!

Carter   Drop!

With a scream **Knill** *is dropped down the cliff.*

Carter   Stop!

Bessie   There id'n a lobster any place in the Bible.

Eddy *and* **Bessie** *haul on the rope and* **Knill**'s *descent is checked. He can be heard screaming way below.*

Eddy   They'm all over the bloody Bible.

Carter   Leave im hang three days.

Eddy   There's lobsters in the Flood.

Carter (*looking over cliff*)   Then haul him up.

Eddy   Plague.

Bessie   Thass locusts.

Carter   Three days and three nights. That's how long I stood it when Rattery's bunch put me over St Agnes Head. If e dun't capitulate after that e's a better man than I am so let im go. Thass fair. You gotta be fair. Tis a tough business. There's men tradin now woulda put a pistol to is ead and ad done with it.

Eddy   Mullion crowd, they would.

Carter   And I can't gainsay that life would be easier with im dead. Cus it would. There's no denyin it.

Eddy   Pellew boys shot Wellard.

Carter   A dead Knill wun't say one thing and do another.

Eddy   Henry Cuttance.

Carter   A dead Knill wun't take our money with a smile and cut a leg off.

Eddy   More or less every bugger I know.

Carter   A dead Knill understands that if the law's unjust you have every right to break it. A dead Knill is an attractive proposition.

Eddy *offers him a knife.*

Carter   What's this?

Eddy   Part the rope.

Carter *smacks him sharp across the face.*

Carter   Kill im? For what? A few tonna jack? Ya can't take a man's life just cus the bugger disagree with ya. You gotta change is attitude to your way a thinkin by reason and persuasion. You're gettin too big for your boots. All this 'pocalyptic shit's makin y'insubordinate. The only way we can succeed is if you do what I say. That go for all of ya. Without question.

Enter **Charlie**.

Charlie   Boat's ready.

Carter   I'm to France.

Eddy   'Bout the jack?

Carter   What jack?

Eddy   Jack in the castle.

Carter   I gave er a list.

Eddy   Take it to Bath.

Carter   No ya don't!

Charlie   Bath?

Bessie   We need the money.

Charlie   Where's Bath?

Eddy   Far side a Fraddon.

Carter   That jack is promised.

Bessie   We're flat broke.

Carter   We got the Cawsand job.

Bessie   We can't go on sellin cheap and payin out on transport.

Carter   That's what we do it for.

Bessie   It don't add up.

Carter   It will after Cawsand.

Bessie   We'm up to our ears in debt.

Carter   I got to go to France.

Bessie   You go to France. I go to Bath.

Carter (*to* **Eddy**)   Tomorrer I want you to take the lugger –

Eddy   Goin fishin tomorrer.

Carter   No you're not! Sail to Jersey and seek out Monsieur Martell. Take on ten ton a jack and ask for credit. I'll pay im on me way back from France. Discharge it in the cave and make damn sure she dun't see it.

Eddy   Oo, Bessie?

Carter   Suzanne Stackhouse. Then you can send this lot to Bath.

Exit **Carter**.

Night. **Bessie** *addresses the* **Men** *of Wendron.*

Bessie   Kinga Prussia's gone to France and e's left me in charge. There's ten ton a jack to shift. We ad a scat with the Revenue so we gotta get ridda this stuff fast and out the county.

Man 1   Where?

Bessie   Bath.

Man 2   Thass too far!

Bessie   Your brother sailed to New York last week.

Man 2   E didn't cross Bodmin Moor to get there!

Man 3   Whass the road like after Camelford?

Man 1   There id'n one.

Bessie   Patchy. There's a good stretch round Okehampton.

Man 2   You be better off crossin to Padsta and sailin it up the Bristol Channel.

Man 1   Padsta? I'll go to Bath.

Man 2   How much ya payin us?

Bessie   Pound.

Man 1   There and back?

Bessie   Yep!

Man 3   Thass a four undred mile round trip.

Man 2   Take us two weeks.

Bessie   And I'm payin you five weeks' wages.

Man 3   No you're not.

Man 1   Five nights' wages.

Bessie   That depends which way you look at it.

Man 1   I know which way I look at it.

Man 2   I'll do it for a guinea.

Man 1   I'll do it for two!

Bessie   Two?!

Mrs Vincent   What's your horses like?

Bessie   Oo's that?

Man 2   Shadrack's missis!

Bessie   Shadrack with ya?

Mrs Vincent   E might be.

Bessie   Let's see im.

Mrs Vincent   Show us your orses first.

Bessie   Boys are greasin em.

Man 2   Expectin trouble?

Bessie   I told ya the Revenue's –

Mrs Vincent   Rosudgeon's crawlin with em.

Bessie   Whass Keneggy like?

Man 1   Clear.

Bessie   Go Keneggy way.

Man 3   I will for two guineas.

Bessie   You would'n be askin John Carter for two guineas!

Man 1   E'd be givin us three.

Bessie   You'll get one!

Mrs Vincent   Let's see your orses!

Dawn. **Knill** *swings in the breeze.*

Song
>   The Carters chose it well,
>   The place to hang John Knill.
>   This man, not predisposed to love,
>   Found himself swung out above
>   The very same secluded cove
>   Where lovely Suzanne Stackhouse goes
>   Once a day to bathe unclothed.

Knill (*writhing in his shroud*)   Mrs Stackhouse. O, Mrs Stackhouse!

Song
>   Once a day for half a week
>   John Knill gets a bird's-eye peek
>   Of a naked body quite exquisite
>   Whose beauty grows with every visit.

Enter **Bessie** *and* **Eddie**.

Song
So come the day of liberation
The boys expect capitulation.
Hoisted early, before she came –

Knill   God dammit put me down again!

Eddy   Eh?

Knill   Hell d'ya think your doin?

Bessie   E bin angin there three day an e wants more!

Knill   Drop me down this minute!

Eddy   We've never ad this.

Bessie   E's lost is mind.

Knill   I command you in the name of King George
put me over that cliff!

Eddy   Bugger's ad a 'pocalyptic vision!

Bessie   Unlash im and scat.

They untie the writhing **Knill** *and run.*

Eddy (*as he goes*)   Wad'n a lobster was it?

Knill   More beautiful than that!

Eddy (*perplexed*)   Eh?

Exit **Eddy**.

Knill (*to himself*)   O Mrs Stackhouse . . . Mrs
Stackhouse . . .

Knill *crawls to the edge of the cliff. He leans over.*

Where are you? My beauty? My beloved!

Enter **Suzanne**, *fully clothed with a towel across her shoulder.*

Suzanne   Mr Knill?

Knill   O!

Knill *attempts to rise but his legs buckle under him.*

Suzanne   Let me see.

She kneels and attends to **Knill***'s legs.*

Turn over.

Knill *lies on his stomach.*

Suzanne   You've lost circulation.

She ties a kerchief round her face then slaps his thighs hard and fast all over.

Don't be coy Mr Knill.

She massages the blood back into his legs.

My father's a surgeon and I trained as a nurse. I've dressed the wounded on three battlefields so I've seen all there is to see. Turn over.

Suzanne *expertly manhandles him onto his back and massages his calf muscles, his feet in her lap.*

How did this happen?

Knill   Those detestable Carters trussed me up and slung me over the cliff.

Suzanne   Where?

Knill   Here.

Suzanne   There?

Knill   I was suspended three days.

Suzanne   Face up? Or down?

Knill (*barely a whisper*)   Down.

Suzanne   Then you saw.

Knill   Yes.

Suzanne   Everything?

Knill   I am so vile!

Suzanne   Don't blame yourself Mr Knill.

Knill   Twas Carter put me there!

Suzanne   What would you give to see him gone?

Knill   My life!

Suzanne   O come Mr Knill.

Knill   The shame!

Suzanne   To view a woman naked?

Knill   The dishonour!

Suzanne   For whom?

Knill   Yourself.

Suzanne   There's none.

Knill   I shoulda called down to ya. Attracted your attention. But I didn't. Once you looked up when a peregrine caught your eye and his flight took im my way but e swooped to seaward and I . . . I thanked God. I offered a prayer of gratitude to my maker for givin me more . . . more . . .

Suzanne   Pleasure?

Knill (*breaking down*)   O wretched wretched man! I am so depraved!

Suzanne (*going to comfort him*)   Mr Knill –

Knill (*recoiling*)   Don't touch me again! I can't bear it!

Suzanne   There is no reason for being like this.

Knill   Forgive me!

Suzanne   You are forgiven! I forgive you.

Knill   Thank you ma'am. Thank you.

Suzanne   I will not be informing your superiors –

Knill (*shrieks*)   No!

Suzanne   I said I will *not*.

Knill   O thank you thank you thank you.

Suzanne   The matter will go no further.

Knill   No further.

Suzanne   I will do my utmost to ensure that my brother for instance, who is a vice-admiral, hears nothing of it.

Knill (*shudders*)   Vice-admiral?

Suzanne   The secret is safe.

Knill   Vice-admiral.

Suzanne   Why who even knows you were here?

Knill   Carter!

Suzanne   O yes. Well now he's in France. I know people in St Malo. I could arrange for him to be detained.

Knill   Carter?

Suzanne   Indefinitely.

Knill   In prison?

Suzanne   But there's the question of a boat.

Knill   How d'you mean?

Suzanne   I have a few friends in Bath whom I had intended to supply with cognac –

Knill   Uncustomed cognac?

Suzanne   Judges, physicians, a baronet or two, minor royalty –

Knill   Royalty?

Suzanne   A distant cousin.

Knill   Of King George?

Suzanne   And myself.

Knill (*awestruck*)   O! Mrs Stackhouse! (*Rising to his feet and attempting to bow.*) I ad no idea –

His legs buckle and he collapses.

Suzanne   Shall I go on?

Knill   Please do. Say whatever you like. Your . . . your . . . Highness . . .

Suzanne   Naturally I'd rely on Carter to run it for me. But with him in prison I'd be looking for another ship. A safe ship. A ship that could smuggle liquor without the slightest risk of detection. Given my sensitive connections –

Knill   Need a ship that is above suspicion.

Suzanne   The obvious choice is a Revenue cutter.

Knill   Y'mean my boat?

Suzanne   O Mr Knill.

Knill   The *Busy*?

Suzanne   You can't be offering –

Knill   No! I thought you meant –

Suzanne   But now you suggest it –

Knill   I didn't –

Suzanne   But you couldn't!

Knill   I know!

Suzanne   You? Cheat King George?

Knill   I can't bear to think of it.

Suzanne   Of course there's an answer to that.

Knill   It's out of the question!

Suzanne   A theory put to me by my brother.

Knill   The vice-admiral?

Suzanne   Yes.

Knill   The vice-admiral.

Suzanne   Shall I tell you?

Knill   I suppose you better.

Suzanne   We put all the draw-back we save into a fund and leave it to the king when we die. That way we'll not have cheated him. Merely delayed paying.

Knill   O, God elp me.

Suzanne   Once a week Mr Knill. That's all I ask.

She helps him to his feet.

(*Offering him her arm to lean on.*) And Carter gone for ever.

St Malo. A prison cell. **Harry Carter** *stands at the window with his back to the door. He works with a backstaff, shooting at the sun.*

Song
Here sits a man denied liberty,
A sailor who's accustomed
To roaming the seas.
Here sits a man innocent of crime,
Locked in a prison cell
Biding his time.

Enter **Carter**.

Carter   Brother.

The door shuts behind **Carter**.

Harry   That you John?

Carter   Gather up your stuff.

He impatiently watches **Harry** *slowly and meticulously fold his clothes and pile his books.*

Carter   Got the Stackhouse party workin with us.

Harry   Thass good.

Carter   Too damn good.

Harry   How's that?

Carter   I bought ten ton off the China ship.

Harry   What?

Carter   Jack.

Harry   What price?

Carter   Pound.

Harry   That's good goin.

Carter   She's took it to Bath and flogged it for six.

Harry *stops what he's doing to reflect on this.*

Harry   Who?

Carter   Stackhouse party.

Harry *resumes his packing.*

Carter   Tis all gone for profit. And I tellya somethin else. She a be pushin for less pay for the farmers. We'll have a riot on our hands. And all that goodwill built up over years gone for nothin. (*He knocks on the door to be let out.*) Guard! See what she gotta learn is there's a network of folk who's dependent on each other. And they all give and take. And the minute there's one oo start to get greedy then the whole damned network's busted. Guard! (*He bangs hard on the locked door.*) Why d'e lock the door? Guard! Whass the French for guard? Whass the boy's name out there?

Harry   Albert.

Carter (*shouts*)   Albert! Where be to! Venez-y!

He rattles the door but it's locked.

Harry   Got all the papers?

Carter   You ready?

Harry *has packed his bag and slung it over his shoulder. He looks around to check he's left nothing behind.*

Carter   Guard! Oy! Come ere! Hell's e to. (*Yells.*) Guaaaard!

His voice echoes down an empty corridor. **Harry** *whistles a short low whistle. The* **Guard** *immediately appears. The* **Guard** *and* **Harry** *speak French.*

Guard   Qu'est-ce que vous voulez Henri?

Harry   Tu vas nous libérer Albert?

Guard   Non.

Carter   What d'e say?

Harry   Pourquoi non?

Carter   No? E say no?

Guard   Je dois observer la consigne.

Carter   What d'e say? Show im this!

Carter *waves the Governor's letter at the* **Guard**.

Harry   Mon frère tient une lettre d'élargement.

He passes the letter through to the **Guard**, *who glances at it and hands it back.*

Guard   Cela s'applique à la paix.

Carter   Whassamatter with it?

Harry   Que signifie cela?

Guard   Elle n'est pas valable maintenant que nous sommes entrés en guerre.

Harry   Depuis quand allons-nous en guerre?

Guard   Depuis une demie.

Carter   What the fuck is goin on?!

Harry   E says since war was declared tis no longer valid.

Carter   War?

Guard   Vous attendrez ici jusqu'à ce qu'on vous transporte à la prison à Josselin.

Carter   How long we bin at war?

Harry   Half an hour.

Carter *sits heavily onto the bench.*

Carter   How long's it gonna last?

Harry   How long was the last one.

Carter   Thirty bloody years! Thirty years! I be an old man!

Harry   You'll be fifty-eight.

Carter   I'll be dead. So will you be cus I willa killed ya.

Harry   You gotta find something to occupy yourself. Like Cain, oo built a city in is mind.

Carter   Built a city did e?

Harry   Yes. Cain did.

Carter *concentrates.* **Harry** *unpacks his bag, meticulously laying out his belongings on the floor.*

Carter   She's done this. Stackhouse. She got war declared.

Harry   Build a city.

Carter   O yeah. You bet your life. God elp the

business now. I knew I couldn't trust er. She's got me out the way. Whatever possessed you in God's name brother to put into St Malo with no papers?

Harry   I'm learning how to navigate.

Carter   Where from? One enda the cell to the other? (*At door.*) Guard!

Harry   Don't harass im. E's the only friend we got.

Carter *slumps in the corner.*

Harry   Approaching Plymouth Sound from the Westward give Penlee Point a berth of half a mile. Bring the red obelisk on the Hoe in line with Plymouth New Church. Keep that mark on till Cawsand's open. Steer east until the New Church appears between the red beacon and the western end of the Citadel.

Carter   Aw God Jesus Christ Al-buggerin-mighty in hellfire and damnation.

Harry   Please brother. Quit the profanity.

Carter   Wanna cut me 'ands off while you'm at it?

Harry   I don't allow profane words on deck.

Carter   We in't on the bloody deck. Thanks to you we'm locked up in a cell!

Harry   Out of consideration for your brother and fellow prisoner. Please.

Carter   I can't even swear.

Harry   Build a city.

Carter   Fuck that.

Harry   Start with the people.

They sit silent on the floor at either end of the cell. **Harry** *opens his bible and reads.*

Kiddleywink. Lobster-pot on table. **Eddy** *bends a seven-fathom backrope to the becket and attaches a float to the other end.* **Charlie** *watches him.*

Charlie   What is it?

Eddy   Lobster trap.

Charlie   How d'ya catch em?

Eddy   They go in the neck.

Charlie *peers down the neck into the pot.*

Charlie   Why?

Eddy   Bait.

Charlie   Where d'e get it?

Eddy   Mousehole.

Charlie   Oo off?

Eddy   Boy Cuttance.

Charlie   Fishin now is a?

Eddy   E does a bit.

Charlie   I wouldn go sea with im.

Eddy   Arn't goin sea wid'n.

Charlie   E'll ave ya pressed.

Eddy   No e wun't.

Charlie   In the Navy quick as smoke.

Eddy   Wun't get me in the Navy.

Charlie   How many lobsters y'gonna catch?

Eddy   Enough.

Charlie   For what?

Eddy   Sell.

Charlie   Quit freightin?

Eddy   Ope to.

Charlie   'Arry wun't be appy.

Eddy   E'll manage.

Carter   Where did Pascoe Walters ave is dogs vision?

Harry   The dogs. (*Thinking.*) The dogs . . . the dogs . . .

Carter   Gwennap.

Harry   No. It was giant crabs at Gwennap. Dogs was St Ives.

Enter **Bessie**. *She has a bag with bonds, notes, cheques etc.*

Bessie (*referring to pot*)   Whass that?

Charlie   Lobster trap.

Bessie   Off the table.

Eddy *removes the pot.*

Eddy   Got the money?

Bessie   Yep.

Charlie   Bath money?

Eddy   'Bout the Guernsey jack?

Bessie (*emptying bag over table*)   Tis all there.

Eddy *and* **Charlie** *pick up the notes and coins.*

Bessie   Puddem back!

They drop the money. She hoards it to her.

We're gonna settle these debts.

She opens a ledger.

Charlie   All of em?

Bessie (*to* **Eddy**)   Bring the slate. (*To* **Charlie**.) Pour the brandy.

Eddy *rummages for the slate.* **Charlie** *goes to liquor cabinet.*

Charlie   Jack or nantz?

Bessie   Nantz.

Eddy   Jack.

Bessie   Nantz.

Eddy   Geneva.

Bessie   No gin.

Charlie   Why no gin?

Eddy   Jack thun.

Bessie   You'll ave the nantz!

Eddy   Dun't like nantz.

Charlie   I'll ave the jack.

Eddy   Whass wrong with geneva?

Bessie   I can sell gin. I can sell jack. The nantz I can't give away.

Eddy   Tis disgusting thass why.

Bessie *pours three nantzes. The boys drink with disgust.*

Bessie   Charlie count the money and Edward write down the debts as I shout em.

They bend to their tasks. **Charlie** *counts out notes, cheques and coins.* **Eddy** *sits with the slate and chalk.* **Bessie** *flattens crumpled bonds and slips, and turns back the pages of the ledger to where the last paid debt was underlined.*

Carter   How long we bin ere?

Harry   I bin ere eight month three weeks six days you bin ere six days.

Carter   They're gonna be askin where we're to.

Harry   No they're not.

Bessie   Two years' rent undred and sempty-fower pound.

Carter   Oo's gonna tell em?

Harry   I got a message out.

Carter   How?

Harry *whistles and* **Albert** *appears at the door.*

Albert   Oui?

Harry *meticulously folds a note written on crisp new parchment and hands it to* **Albert**. *They converse a few muttered words of French then* **Albert** *disappears.*

Carter   You reckon that got ome?

Bessie   Dionesius Williams of Sennen sixteen pound for a flocka sheep.

Harry   E got word to Monsieur Dot oo told Madame oo teach at the school to give it to Mother Confessor first thing Monday morning.

Carter   A nun?

Harry   She ad breakfast Wednesday with Mademoiselle Renard who carried the news to the horse fair at Landernau Friday. There's a dealer called Henri oo rode like fire to fetch up at Brest by dawn Sunday to get to Monsieur Lerue before e go into church.

Bessie   Macculloch of Gulval three undred and twenty-six pound nineteen and eight.

Harry   Monsieur Lerue run an open boat from Brest to Porthleven every Sunday after church and it take im fifteen hours with a followin wind.

Bessie   Bobo George of Mullion thirty-three pound eighteen and tuppence for powder.

Carter   What time d'church end Sunday in Brest?

Harry   Two o'clock.

Carter   That late?

Harry   Monsieur Lerue is a Catholic.

Carter   Can ya trust im?

Harry   The news willa reached Porthleven by five o'clock this mornin.

Bessie   Christopher Pollard of Madron two undred and sixty pound for five bullocks.

Carter   Who d'this Catholic know in Porthleven?

Harry   There's a baker called Giddy.

Bessie   Martha Blewett for untaxed salt sempteen and six.

Carter   I know Giddy.

Harry   You knaw is cousin Eddy Giddy the JP from St Erth. This Giddy, Gilbert –

Carter   Gilbert Giddy –

Harry   . . . sells Lerue a fresh loaf at five thirty on the dot.

Carter   Gilbert Giddy's got the message.

Harry   Now we got to wait three hours before Mrs Hicks buys er yeast buns.

Carter   Dun't she bake er own?

Harry   Mrs Hicks is blind.

Carter   Which Mrs Hicks is this?

Harry   Widow of John Hicks of Tolponds.

Bessie   John Hicks of Tolponds –

Charlie   E's dead.

Bessie   Is a?

Eddy   How much d'we owe im?

Bessie   Thruppence.

Charlie   Strike it off.

Harry   She willa told Melchisedeck Kinsman –

Carter   . . . who at eight thirty give er a lift on is orse to High Lanes.

Harry   You got it.

Carter   There they met Jack Brenton who was driving his cows to Calvarry when he was overtook by Dr Ball on his way to visiting Mrs Day at Pentreath. Whass the time?

Bessie   Whass the time?

Harry *stares through the window.* **Charlie** *checks through in the parlour.*

Harry   Town clock says

Harry *and* **Charlie**   Ten twenty-eight.

Bessie   Eighty-one pound Doctor Ball for remedial work on left leg.

Eddy   Whose left leg is that?

Charlie   Harry's.

Bessie   And sixteen and sixpence to Jack Brenton for milk.

Harry   How we gonna get across the parish border?

Bessie   Add it all up thun.

Eddy *adds up.* **Charlie** *still counts the money.*

Carter   Mrs Day, once she got er medication has the strength to go and visit er usband's grave.

Harry 'Course, e was a Rosudgeon man.

Carter And if Shadrack's missis is feedin er chickens –

Bessie How much?

Charlie Eight undred and ninety-five pound and one penny.

Carter Take er fifteen minutes to walk from er chickens to the wink.

Harry Assuming Bessie's in –

Bessie Whass the debt?

Eddy Eight undred and ninety-four pound nineteen shillin and eleven pence.

Carter There should be a knock on the door round about –

Harry *stares through the window.*

Bessie So we'm in credit to the tune of –

Charlie (*bangs a coin on the table*) Thruppence.

The town hall clock strikes the half-hour.

Harry Now.

A sharp knock on the kiddleywink door. **Bessie**, **Charlie** *and* **Eddy** *stand.*

Bessie Oo is it!

Enter **Mrs Vincent**.

Eddy Shadrack's missis.

Mrs Vincent Got summin for ya.

She hands **Bessie Harry**'*s note, which by now is crumpled, dirty and tattered round the edges.* **Bessie** *reads the note.*

Bessie We'll ave to sell up.

Eddy What's appened?

Bessie   Cancel Cawsand.

Eddy   Eh?

Bessie   Our free-tradin days are over.

Eddy   Hell.

Bessie   Your brothers are good as dead.

Eddy (*smiling*)   Better go fishin.

Punt. **Bessie** *at the oars.* **Eddy** *hauls his pot.*

Song
I arn't sure if there's a god,
E never showed isself to me.
But I shall keep an open mind
So long as lobsters swim the sea.

It might be Neptune or Poseidon,
I don't care what name e's got
So long as I can stand beside'n
When I'm haulin up that pot.

The pot comes to the surface. It contains a lobster.

Bessie (*on seeing the lobster*)   Christ. Y'got one.

Eddy   'Course I got one.

Bessie   You got one.

Eddy   Yeah!

Bessie   Gonna sell it?

Eddy   'Course I'm gonna sell it.

Bessie   Where y'gonna sell it?

Stackhouse *sits at his microscope, his straw hat on his head.
Enter* **Eddy**. *He carries a bulging satchel.* **Eddy** *coughs. Then
he coughs louder.*

Stackhouse (*without looking up*)   That you my love?

Eddy   Eh? Tis Edward.

Stackhouse   Ah.

Stackhouse *takes off his hat.* **Eddy** *opens his satchel and withdraws a lobster.*

Stackhouse   Magnificent.

He takes the fish and admires it.

Eddy   Wanna buy im?

Stackhouse   Where did you catch it?

Eddy   Arn't sayin.

Stackhouse   How much?

Eddy   You tell me.

Stackhouse   Shilling.

Eddy   Two shillin.

Stackhouse   Very well.

Eddy   Per pound.

Stackhouse   What does it weigh?

Eddy   Three pound.

Stackhouse   Six shillings.

Eddy   That sound reasonable.

Stackhouse   Let me first put it into one of my tanks down below in the cellar and then I shall find (*Tapping his pockets.*) the money. Wait here!

Exit **Stackhouse** *with lobster.*

Eddy, *pleased with the transaction, walks around the place picking up this and that, feeling increasingly at home. He sits at the microscope. He peers into the lens. He can't see much so he puts on the hat. This time when he looks he gets a fright and jerks his head back. Then he looks again into the lens and is hooked.*

Enter **Suzanne**. *She carries letters tied in a scroll.*

Suzanne   John Knill is here.

Eddy *keeps the hat on and stays hunched over the microscope.*

Suzanne   I shall receive him in this room. I can't bear to be alone with him.

Eddy *grunts.*

Suzanne   I hate that bloody instrument. Can't you see what it's doing? Your work used to be a source of wonderment to me. Now I am an intruder into your world of magnification. An unwelcome stranger.

Knill *enters, unseen by* **Suzanne**, *and stands in the doorway.*

Suzanne   You don't look up when I come into the room. You don't respond when I talk to you. You are not even aware of my existence. I might as well not be here. I could be in Bath. All you care about is what you can see on your damned little glass plate. I despise it.

Knill *coughs.* **Suzanne** *swings round.*

Suzanne   Have you got the jack?

Knill   Yes. Ma'am.

Suzanne   Down below?

Knill   Eighteen ton.

Suzanne   Well done.

Knill   All discharged. My first run completed!

Eddy *almost chokes on the microscope.*

Suzanne   Have you brought me a sample?

Knill *opens a flask and wipes the neck with a silk handkerchief while* **Suzanne** *unscrolls the letters and starts to read. He proffers her the flask.*

Suzanne (*drinks*)   Hm.

She puts the flask on the table.

(*To* **Eddy**.) Taste that.

Eddy *knocks the brandy back in one.*

Suzanne (*reading the letters*) D'you know what these are?

Knill No ma'am.

Suzanne (*reading*) Letters of exchange. My brother intercepted them.

Knill The vice-admiral?

Suzanne The Navy has ordered a prisoner exchange.

Knill O dear.

Suzanne (*reading*) John and Henry Carter for two extremely high-ranking French noblemen who are at present residing in Bodmin Gaol.

Knill Dear O dear.

Suzanne Now we are at war the Admiralty is keen to get the Carters back. (*Waves the orders.*) The interception of these has bought us time. But we must ensure the French authorities are made aware of the danger the Carters represent to the Republic.

Knill How . . . we gonna do that?

Suzanne It's a matter of great urgency Mr Knill.

Knill O I can see –

Suzanne You say you have discharged all the jack?

Knill (*uncertain*) Ye-es?

Suzanne Then I think you should turn your ship around and sail straight to Brest. There hire a horse and ride with all speed to (*Referring to letters.*) Josselin where the Carters are gaoled. Inform the prison governor that for the good of la République they should be executed immediately.

Knill (*feeling his neck, rubbing it hard*)   O Mrs Stackhouse. I . . . I couldn't do that. No dear. Tis impossible. I got duties to perform.

Suzanne   None so crucial as this!

Knill   Tis a damned dangerous job! They're putting every bugger on the block – forgive my profanity –

Suzanne   I'm so sorry Mr Knill. I assumed you were prepared to risk a little for my sake. I was given that impression.

Knill   Oo by?

Suzanne (*thrusting the letters at* **Eddy**)   Read that.

Eddy *grabs the letters and stuffs them in his shirt.* **Suzanne** *circles* **Knill**.

Suzanne   Imagine the Carters dead.

Knill *swallows hard.*

Suzanne   You and I Mr Knill. Alone. Working together –

Knill   Together – alone.

Suzanne   In two years we'll be running the biggest smuggling ring in Europe.

Knill   Mrs Stackhouse. I've hung off a cliff and seen you naked and thought of nothin since.

Eddy *has a discreet seizure.*

Knill   If one short gallop will keep us close for ever then I can't restrain myself. I am after all a man. I shall go to France.

Suzanne   I'll see you to your ship.

Exit **Suzanne** *and* **Knill** *out the front.* **Eddy** *stands and watches them go. Enter* **Stackhouse** *from the back.*

Stackhouse (*finding money*)   Here.

Eddy   Gotta go.

Stackhouse   Your payment.

Eddy   Forget it.

Stackhouse   What?

Eddy *makes for the door: he sees* **Suzanne** *approach. He turns and walks back into the room.*

Stackhouse *(holding out money)*   Ah.

Eddy   No.

Stackhouse   What?

Eddy   Shuddup!

Stackhouse   Eh?

He watches **Eddy** *hide behind the curtain. Enter* **Suzanne**.

Suzanne   Did you hear what he said?

Stackhouse *(gazing at the curtain)*   What?

Suzanne   I've seen you naked and thought of nothing since.

Stackhouse   Who – ?

Suzanne   I can't restrain myself I'm a man.

Stackhouse   Y'mean – ?

Suzanne   John Knill!

Stackhouse   What?

Suzanne   Didn't you see him?

Stackhouse   No.

Suzanne   He was here.

Stackhouse   Where?

Suzanne   In this room.

Stackhouse   No I was –

Suzanne   Give me the letters.

Stackhouse   The what?

Suzanne   The letters I gave you.

Stackhouse   What letters?

Suzanne   The letters of exchange!

Stackhouse   I don't know what you're talking about!

Suzanne *picks up the microscope.*

Stackhouse   What are you doing. Put it down!
Suzanne put that down!

She dashes the microscope against the floor. **Stackhouse** *is
speechless.*

Suzanne   Now perhaps you will pay attention to what
I am telling you. John Knill was in this room saying
lurid, suggestive, disgusting things to your wife –
attempting to seduce me with you, my husband, sitting
not five feet away.

Stackhouse *is on the floor wailing, attempting to salvage his
beloved instrument.*

Stackhouse   I was in the cellar with a lobster! That's
not John Knill! It's Edward Carter! He's there! Behind
the curtain!

Suzanne *runs to the curtain.*

Suzanne   He's not.

Stackhouse   Then he's escaped.

Kiddleywink. **Bessie** *holds up an advertisement and reads it to*
Charlie.

Bessie   Announcement of a sale by auction at the Star
Inn Marazion of the lease for the premises situated at

Porthleah Cove –

The door bursts open and **Eddy** *stands on the threshold. His eyes are wide and his mouth open. He holds at arm's length the letters of exchange.*

Eddy   Touch that.

Bessie (*advancing towards him slowly*)   Why?

Eddy   Is it real?

Bessie *recoils.*

Eddy   I've just ad a 'pocalyptic vision.

Bessie   Where?

Eddy   Castle.

Bessie   How?

Eddy   Suzanne Stackhouse picked up the microscope, dashed it on the floor and screamed at er usband Knill seduced me.

Bessie *and* **Charlie**   Knill?

Eddy   But e wad'n there.

Bessie   Oo Knill?

Eddy   The usband.

Bessie   Where was e?

Eddy   In the cellar with a lobster.

Charlie   Oo was there?

Eddy   Me!

Bessie   E seduced *you?*

Eddy   Who?

Bessie   Knill.

Eddy   E's runnin er jack.

Bessie *and* **Charlie**   Knill?!

Bessie   It's gotta be a vision.

Charlie   There's no truth in this.

Eddy   Eighteen ton!

Bessie   Tis too damned apocalyptic.

Eddy   Touch the papers!

Bessie   You touch em.

Charlie   I arn't touchin nothing.

Eddy   Some bugger better touch em quick cus the boys are gonna die.

Bessie *gingerly touches the papers.*

Bessie   They'm solid.

Eddy   Read em.

Bessie (*takes letters*)   What are they?

Eddy   Exchange letters.

Charlie   What for?

Eddy   Harry and John.

Charlie   Oo with?

Eddy   French noblemen up Bodmin Gaol.

Bessie   Here. (*She hands one set of papers to* **Charlie**.) You go to Bodmin, get the two Frenchmen and meet us on the south quay in Brest Tuesday at dawn.

Exit **Charlie** *with one set of papers.*

Bessie   C'mon Edward.

Exit **Bessie** *and* **Eddy**.

Brest. **Knill** *walks the streets. All around him there are angry revolutionary* **Crowds**, *baying for blood and singing the Marseillaise.*

Knill (*offering money to passing* **Sans-Cullottes**)   I need a horse! Un cheval m'sieur! Goddamit id'n there no horses in France? I can't walk to Josselin! Eh mister! Give us orse!

Sans-Cullotte 1   Whass this money?

Knill   Je veux cheval!

Sans-Cullotte 1   Here's a wealthy man!

Sans-Cullotte 2   A counter-revolutionary!

Sans-Cullotte 1   An aristocrat!

Sans-Cullotte 2   Cut off his head!

Knill (*screams*)   NO!

Knill *is dragged off.*

Harry *and* **John Carter** *are reunited with* **Bessie**, **Eddy** *and* **Charlie** *outside the gaol.*

Knill *kneels with his head on the block, groaning. The blade is raised. Enter* **Eddy**, **Harry**, **Carter**, **Bessie**, **Charlie**.

Eddy   John Knill!

Carter   Hold hard.

Bessie   You're not gonna save im?

Eddy   Eh?

Harry   What?

Carter   Yep.

They all attempt to restrain him.

Bessie   Leave the bugger there to die!

Carter   Y'can't do that!

Eddy   Bloody can.

Carter   If you save a man's life e's yours. E belong to

you. Cus without you e'd be dead so that life is now
yours.

Eddy   No e ain't!

Suzanne   They did *what?*

Knill   Saved my life.

Suzanne   How?

Carter   Stop! (*Holding back the* **Crowd**.) Do you know
who this man is?

Crowd   No.

Carter   E's the King of Prussia!

Knill   Eh? Aw no!

Bessie   Whass e sayin now?

The **Crowd** *bays for blood.*

Carter   E deserve to die don't you think? Death to all
kings!

Roars of approval from the **Crowd**.

Carter (*to* **Knill**)   Come in with us or I'll leave ya to
die.

Knill   I can't!

Carter   Execute all monarchs!

Knill   O please!

Carter   Come in with us.

Knill   I dun't wanna die!

Carter   Yes or no?

Knill   Yes!

Carter (*yanking* **Knill** *to his feet by the hair*)   But wait!
Take a closer look! Observe! E's thin! Ave you ever seen
a king oo id'n fat? Look at is face! Hardly the face of a

complacent work-shy mollycoddled man! No! On my
life! This man's no king!

Sans-Culotte Oo is e?

Carter E's the greatest revolutionary of em all!

Knill Thass better.

Carter Because e calls imself a King!

Voice Vive la Révolution!

Another Voice Vive la République!

Another Voice Vive le roi de Prusse!

Carter If you call yourself a king there will be no
king! Cus we'm all kings! And if we'm all kings there's
no kings don't you think? Long live kings all! Death to
all kings!

Knill Death to all kings?

Carter Death to King George! (*To* **Knill**.) Say it.

Knill Please don't make me say it.

Carter Say it!

Knill I'm an officer of the crown!

Carter Ya wanna live?

Knill Death to King George!

A tumultuous roar. **Knill** *faints.*

Boat. **Harry** *at the helm.* **Knill** *lies out on deck. The others sit
around him.* **Carter**'s *in the bow, contemplative.*

Knill (*waking, barely audible*) Where am I?

Harry (*navigating, to himself*) 49 degrees 55 minutes
north by five degrees fifteen minutes west, heading 345
degrees, altering course to three twenty, five mile off
Lizard 'Ead . . .

Knill   Where?

Eddy (*looking over the gunwale, to himself*)   We'm over lobster grounds now.

Bessie   There's gotta be lobsters down there you.

Eddy   I can smell em.

Bessie   Good scuddy ground.

Eddy   Gotta be.

Knill   Eh.

Carter (*to himself*)   Turn left off Cathedral Close and walk east down Market Way. There you might encounter Mister Mynne oo live in a terrace of three-storied brick-built town houses off Union Street called North Parade –

Eddy   E's awake.

They all look down on **Knill**. *He peers up at each of their faces.*

Bessie   We eard you was freightin.

Knill   Oo told ya that?

Carter   Fact is we saved your life Knill.

Knill   You put me there.

Bessie   Suzanne Stackhouse did ya mean.

Eddy   Whass she like naked?

Carter (*smacking* **Eddy**)   You *filthy* little *shit*!

Bessie   We want you on our side.

Carter   You're with us now Knill.

Knill   O no –

Carter   The Stackhouse party's cruel as a Spaniard. She'll destroy us. You. Me. Edward. Harry. Bessie. Rosudgeon. Breague. Wendron. Penzance. Trura.

They'll be gone. Sit alone someplace and build a city in
your mind. When you got the thoroughfares all laid out
and the buildins and the sheds, people this city. Walk
past em in the street. Who are these people Mr Knill?
People you know or people you don't. People you love.
People you hate. People you're scared of. People who
owe ya money. People oo make ya laugh and weep. Or
strangers.

Eddy   From Bath.

Carter   Comin at ya from all angles in this city. They
force ya down a street where you don't wanna go. Up
an alley where you don't wanna go. Suddenly you're
lost. And there's undreds of em millin round ya. And a
blind's tied round your eyes and your head's forced
down on a block and the blade's raised high and the
executioner says die and the Kinga Prussia ain't there to
get ya back!

Knill   No!

Suzanne   The man's a criminal! A lunatic! An
extortionist! A despot! A traitor!

Knill   E saved my life!

Kiddleywink.

Bessie   What about the Cawsand job?

Carter (*to* **Harry**)   We got to do it brother.

Bessie   We got no money.

Carter   No choice.

Harry   Choice. Thass a word John Wesley use. We
got no choice e says. We got no choice between
profanity and the righteous path. Cus the righteous path
lead to 'eaven and they oo choose profanity will sure as
hell get burned.

Eddy   I've eard'n say that.

Carter   Mr Wesley don't discuss money do e.

Eddy   Portscatho. E said it there.

Carter   Mr Wesley got very little to say on the matter a money.

Eddy   Tis evil I've eard'n say that.

Carter   What I got to say about money is we got none and we gotta get some.

Harry   I'm prepared to accept that.

Carter   O. Are ya? Good.

Harry   Tis entirely my fault that we have no money. And for that reason I've come to an agreement with my conscience to make one final run.

Carter   Final?

Bessie   Agreement with what?

Carter   You gonna give up free-tradin?

Harry   Brother. Tis an abomination.

Bessie   Aw e's bin took bad.

Harry   That id'n me talkin.

Bessie   No tis Mr Wesley.

Eddy   It is I've eard'n say it.

Carter   Will you shuddup!

Bessie   Just what is it y'intend to do?

Harry   Devote meself to the circuit. Preachin.

Carter   If I'd known that I wouldna got y'outa jail!

Acton Castle. Enter **Knill**.

Suzanne   Well?

Knill   I spoke to Carter.

Suzanne   And?

Knill   They intend to do a run into Cawsand one day next week.

Suzanne   I thought as much.

Knill   God forgive me for what I've done.

Suzanne   Our Lord will thank you.

Knill   E wun't think much of why I did it.

Suzanne   It is a waste of His gifts to pour the finest cognac money can buy down the throats of sailors, whores and farmers who aren't bred to appreciate it. We are at war. In times of shortage give the best to those who need it most. And my royal cousin is desperate. But Monsieur Martell prefers to do business with the Tyrant King. The last of his vintage is destined for the mouths of peasants. That is not a crime Mr Knill. It is a sin. So I have instructed my brother the vice-admiral to take it by force.

Knill   Then what?

Suzanne   A man called Lobb will transport it to the Custom House in Saltash where you will stand guard –

Knill   Me?

Suzanne   . . . until reliable transport can be brought from Bath –

Knill   O no! I can't do that!

Suzanne   Why not?

Knill   There's a pirate called the *Black Prince* manned by Irish oo's causin havoc in the Bristol Channel.

Suzanne   No Mr Knill.

Knill   My superiors have given orders for all cutters to engage.

Suzanne   I saw to it.

Knill   I sail for Padstow tomorrow.

Suzanne   You are relieved of that duty.

Kiddleywink. Enter **Carter**.

Carter   We'm on. Tomorrer night.

Harry   Where's the freight?

Carter   Jersey.

Harry   How much?

Carter   Twenty-two ton.

Bessie   What price?

Carter   Three pound a tub.

Bessie   Three?

Carter   Thass on credit.

Harry   Jack or nantz?

Carter   Jack.

Bessie   Three pound a tub!

Carter   Gotta pilot?

Bessie   Jacob Steep.

Harry   Who's on the beach?

Bessie   Charlie's up Torpoint bookin Jimmy Babb
Ernest Binney Jack Rundell Amos Lobb sixteen men
from the parish of Maker and Shadrack with is
dungcart.

Harry   Strike off Lobb. I dun't want no Lobb on the
beach. (*To* **Carter**.) Where's your station?

Carter   I'll be up the Kingsand end.

Harry   I want a reliable man with a spout lantern on

Penlee Head.

Bessie   John Brodribb.

Harry   John.

Carter   Did that did ya?

Bessie   Yep.

Harry   'Bout the Revenue.

Carter   Taken care of –

Harry   Talk to Knill?

Carter   E's gone Padsta.

Harry   What for?

Carter   *Black Prince.*

Bessie   God elp im.

Eddy *stands.*

Eddy   I arn't goin.

Carter   Yes y'are.

Eddy   Goin fishin tomorrer.

Carter   No you're not.

Eddy   I dun't wanna go.

Carter   Why.

Bessie   Tis Knill.

Carter   Don't you think I've weighed it up? Don't you think I've used me judgement on this? Don't you think I know Mr Knill by now? Mr Knill belongs to us. We've bought him. We paid him the highest fuckin price there is and that's is life.

Eddy   The Navy's amassin up in Plymouth Sound.

Carter   They wun't trifle wi'we.

Eddy   Undreds of men o'war.

Carter   They can't be bothered wi'we.

Eddy   *Cumberland. Powerful. Bombay Castle. Carnatic. Andromeda.* Five-thousand cannon all primed and aimed at we!

Carter   We got orders of attack.

Eddy   *Impregnable*'s there. *Druid.*

Carter   We *are* the Navy.

Eddy   *Myrmidon.*

Carter   We're supposed to be there.

Eddy   In't supposed to be landin twenty ton a jack.

Carter   Deada night.

Eddy   Onto an open beach.

Carter   No moon.

Eddy   I dun't like it.

Carter   You dun't know . . .

Eddy   I dun't trust Knill.

Carter   E's with us now.

Eddy   Is e hell e's seen the Stackhouse woman naked.

Carter   So what?

Eddy   Oo would you rather be with?

Carter   What's that supposed to mean?

Eddy   E's incandescent with lust.

Carter   You are.

Eddy   Can't it wait till the Navy's gone?

Carter   We got no money!

Eddy   Oo's fault's that? Tid'n mine. I can make me own way wi'lobsters. I dun't need to go to Cawsand.

Carter *hits him hard across the head.*

Carter   You dare question my judgement!

Eddy   Gimme a beach station.

Carter   You'll go on the cutter.

Eddy   I wun't go on the cutter.

Harry   If e's goin I want im on the cutter.

Carter   See? E want y'on the cutter.

Harry   I'll pick y'up down cove four o'clock tomorrer and bring with ya Thomas Collins, John 'Owdler, David Stewart, Robert Kear, Will Bean, John Morris, and Philip Durant.

Exit **Harry**.

Eddy   I dun't want me name in a muster book just for the sake of a few ton a jack. Cus e think e can judge the mind of a tide-waiter. A gauger. Thass all Knill is a blasted lurker. You wad'n there when we pulled the bastard up over the cliff. You woulda seen oo's side e's on. E was beggin we to put'n back over so e could see er naked. You only lasted three days and three nights wi Rattery's bunch e was prepared to stay there all week!

Cutter.

Harry (*at the wheel, calls to* **Eddy**)   Bring the red obelisk on the Hoe in line with Plymouth New Church.

Eddy (*in the bow*)   Aw fuck. Looka that. There's the *Brunswick*. The *Norfolk. Carnatic. Orion.*

Harry   That done?

Eddy   E's on.

Harry   Drop anchor.

Kiddleywink. Night.

Carter   Bessie! Wake up! Bessie!

He pours himself a tumbler of water and breaks off a chunk of bread. He eats and drinks in great gulps.

Bessie!

He pours water from a jug over his face. Enter **Bessie**.

Carter   They got us. The bastards got us.

Bessie   Who?

Carter   Navy.

Bessie   How?

Carter   Harry's shot to shit.

Bessie   Shot?

He slumps into a corner. **Bessie** *opens a locker and takes out a jug of cognac. She pours a tot and hands it to* **Carter**.

Carter   Whass this, nantz?

Bessie   Jack.

He drinks.

What happened?

Carter   They anchored in the bay. We was on the beach. All prepared. 'Arry Rundle and the Torpoint boys, Maker, half St Germans, Brodribb on the cliff dark as pitch could see is lantern clear as day. Pilot boarded and 'Arry says coast clear? and Steep says there's no danger there's boats enough to discharge all your cargo so 'Arry says –

Harry (*to* **Eddy**)   Leave the jib with the trysail and mizzen set –

Carter   . . . and they open the hatches.

Activity on the deck. Hatches opened, lifting blocks and tackles lowered, etc.

Harry   There's boats rowing up from the shore.

Carter   Steep tells him thass our boats coming to take out the goods –

Bessie   Steep?

Carter   *Steep* tells im this. E's *our* man! And a voice shouts up –

Voice   D'you know these is two man o'wars' boats?!

Bessie   The bastard.

Harry (*yells*)   Cut the cable!

Eddy   They'm under the starn!

Harry   Close the hatches!

Eddy   E's shot off the trys'l tack! We can't move! They're boarding us over the starn!

Carter   The crew run below. 'Arry's left to fight a boardin party. Single-handed. A rating gets killed. And they came at 'Arry with their broadswords. Beating im about the head. E rambled forward and fell. E was left for dead on deck for two hours. Twice an officer felt his heart and thought him dead. Then the ship drifted. The tide was on the ebb and she went aground and made a great heel toward the shore. In the confusion 'Arry slides off the deck and down a rope. But e's took be a cramp in is bad leg. E sink like a stone and e go astern in deep water. E gived up hope a life and swallered water. But e found a rope and hauled on it. Made one end fast to the side. E touched bottom with is foot. E find another rope. So. E veers on one. And hauls upon tother. That brung im up under the bowsprit. And on the beach. I said to Charlie there look, oo's that? E said tis 'Arry. How d'you knaw? E said thass is greatcoat. You couldn't tell. Couldn't tell'n by is features. His head's in smithereens. His face is all atoms. There's blood. Everywhere.

Bessie   Where's e to?

Carter   Shadrack's dungcart. I rode ahead. Alerted Dr Ball. The cutter's breakin up on Cawsand beach. They locked the jack in the Saltash Custom House.

Bessie   What about Eddy?

Carter   . . . eh?

Bessie   Edward. Where is e?

Carter   God forgive me.

Bessie   E id'n dead?

Carter   Tis all my fault.

Bessie   Is e dead?

Carter   I'm an honest man.

Bessie   O no.

Carter   I take the blame.

Bessie   E's dead!

Carter   Worse!

Bessie   Pressed?

Carter   Yes!

Bessie   God in heaven!

Carter   Dun't admonish me Bessie.

Bessie   You stupid ignorant stubborn bastard!

Carter   I know what I done!

Acton Castle. Enter **Carter**.

Carter   Me brother Edward's bin took be the Navy. E's chained to the gundeck of the *Bombay Castle*. They sail east on convoy duty Monday. Thass a two-year

round trip. You told us once you gotta brother oo's a
vice-admiral –

Suzanne   Out of the question.

Carter   Mrs Stackhouse all my life I've called meself a
king. I've lived in the way I believe a king should but
no king bar Frederick ever did. Yes e went to war but e
ad courage. E was upright and proud. E never ad
occasion to beg any bugger in is life. Neither ave I. I've
come close. Damn close. And I know there's kings oo
beg for a pastime but I arn't one of em. Until today
that is. I'm beggin ya Mrs Stackhouse. Beggin.

Suzanne   Get out of here.

Carter (*on his knees*)   Please. Please release Edward!

Suzanne   Get out!

Kiddleywink.

Carter   I was on me ruddy knees! I was beggin er!
Y'ever seen me beg? I'll only beg for Edward. I wouldn
beg for no bugger else. Suzanne Stackhouse! I! The
Kinga Prussia! Was beggin er! I'll be beggin Knill next!

Bessie   I can't see ya beggin Knill.

A knock on the door. **Bessie** *checks through a crack.*

John Stackhouse!

Enter **Stackhouse**.

Stackhouse   I've brought instructions for Edward
Carter.

Bessie   Edward?

Stackhouse (*holding up a notebook*)   It's vital he peruse
this most carefully as it contains precise notes on how to
preserve specimens of plants and should be followed to
the letter. Particularly the section on fructating palmata.
In the glass case on my study table there is a Gelidium

sent to me by Withering and that is an example of how he should preserve the Gigartina stellata but he must *not touch* the cabinet as I've sealed it against air. Here's the key to the castle.

Bessie   Thank you.

Bessie *takes the key.*

Edward's gone mister.

Stackhouse   I told him to be here.

Carter   E won't be comin back.

Stackhouse   My wife and I leave for Bath today.

Carter   Too bad.

Stackhouse   That boy is *vital*! He said he'd be here. Without him I cannot finish the book.

Bessie   What book?

Stackhouse   A botanical description of marine plants with drawings from nature. There are certain algae which, it's maddening, fructate in my absence.

Bessie   You better get im back.

Stackhouse   I don't know where he is.

Bessie   Chained to the gundeck of the *Bombay Castle*.

Stackhouse   That's my brother-in-law's ship.

Carter   The vice-admiral?

Stackhouse   I knew this would happen.

Bessie   You better talk to your wife.

Stackhouse   That's impossible.

Bessie   Why?

Stackhouse   Because we're not on speaking terms.

Bessie   Since when?

Stackhouse   The day she destroyed my microscope.

Bessie   This often appen?

Stackhouse   No. It's the first. When we moved here for the summer I talked to her all the time, frequently through the night.

Bessie   So if you was er what would you do with the microscope?

Carter   Throw the fucker down a mineshaft.

Stackhouse   Well –

Bessie   What happens when you get to Bath? There's all your friends. They're gonna be sayin whass up wi you two in't you talkin? Are they ever gonna make up? Ere's two lovebirds when they left Bath you couldn't stop em talkin. They didn't sleep for talkin. All they ever did was talk. No time for naked bathin.

Stackhouse   Eh?

Bessie   What took place down there in Mount's Bay? Was they bewitched? Somebody gotta break the silence. Who? Which one? Shall we toss a coin?

Stackhouse   O no! That's not right.

Bessie   Why?

Stackhouse   I'm expecting an apology.

Bessie   For what?

Stackhouse   Breaking my microscope!

Bessie   They wun't buy that in Bath. Oo's the one who ignored is wife? Oo's the one oo spoke in monosyllables? Mr Stackhouse? Monosyllabic? That's not the chatterbox we waved goodbye to! Whatever appened? Ooever effected this transformation? Did one a they free-traders cut out is tongue? O no! Could it be the seaweed? Oo ever eard a dabberlocks renderin people speechless? I eard she filed for divorce. On what grounds? E was unfaithful. Oo with? Baroness Bladderwrack. Oo told ya that? Tis all over Bath!

Stackhouse   I'm beginning to see what you mean.

Bessie   Spin the coin!

She spins.

Stackhouse   Suzanne.

Suzanne   Yes?

Carter   Reckon that a work?

Bessie   E'll go straight ome now and apologise.

Stackhouse   I'm so sorry.

Bessie   They'll argue about oo started it –

Suzanne   It's my fault.

Stackhouse   No it's mine.

Bessie   And why –

Suzanne   I was bored.

Stackhouse   I was too obsessed.

Bessie   Then they'll make up.

Suzanne   I love you.

Stackhouse   I love you.

They embrace.

Bessie   At which point their personalities will completely alter.

Suzanne   O my God.

Stackhouse   What's the matter?

Suzanne   That poor boy!

'Bombay Castle'. Below decks.

Rating   Edward Carter!

Eddy (*from the depths*)   Yep.

The clatter of chains.

(*Standing and rubbing his wrists.*) Now what?

Rating   You're a free man.

Eddy   Aw. Thanks.

Kiddleywink. Enter **Eddy**.

Eddy (*to* **Bessie**)   Law's against Harry. There's a price on is head.

Bessie   How much?

Eddy   Three undred.

Carter   Good price.

Bessie   What for?

Eddy   They're sayin e killed that rating.

Carter   Did e?

Eddy   Did e bollocks.

Carter   You saw did ya?

Eddy   I was there remember?

Carter   You gotta thank me for gettin you out.

Eddy (*pouring himself a brandy*)   Get nothin outa me. (*Spits out brandy.*) Fuckin nantz.

Bessie   No jack.

Carter   I was on me knees beggin!

Eddy   I was on me back shackled to a cannon with Will Bean's ass in me face!

Carter *attacks* **Eddy**. **Bessie** *intervenes.*

Bessie   Leave im be!

Eddy   Thass all right Bessie.

Carter   E can look after isself.

Bessie   No e can't.

Eddy   Yes I can.

Bessie   Siddown John.

Eddy   Yeah. Siddown.

They watch **Carter** *to see if he obeys them. He casually walks to the cabinet, takes out a pistol, shot, powder and cleaning gear. He sits and cleans the pistol.*

Eddy   Do e know about us?

Bessie   No.

Eddy   You ab'm told im?

Bessie   I waited for you.

Eddy   Want me to?

Bessie   I'll tell im.

Eddy   I will.

Bessie   I better.

Eddy   No.

Bessie   Let me.

Eddy   I gotta say it.

Bessie   E'll kill ya.

Eddy   I'm is brother.

Bessie   Don't mean a thing.

Eddy   Ya can't take a man's life just cus the bugger disagree with ya. You gotta change is attitude to your

way a thinkin by reason and persuasion. (*To* **Carter**.)
Me and er are . . .

Bessie   Say it.

Eddy   Goin fishin.

Bessie   We are given up free-tradin.

They watch him carefully.

Carter (*cleaning pistol*)   You Bessie?

Bessie   Yep.

Carter   Why?

Bessie   We got these traps.

Eddy   Catchin lobsters.

Carter   Sellin em?

Bessie   Yes we are.

Eddy   What price?

Bessie   Two shillin a pound.

Eddy   Hah!

Carter   Oo to?

Bessie   Stackhouses.

Carter   When they'm ere.

Eddy   Give e a list?

Bessie   They've gived us names of gentry all over the
county.

Eddy   'Bout Shadrack?

Bessie   I spoke to is missis.

Mrs Vincent   E've fitted out is dungcart with a
leadlined tank.

Carter (*cleaning pistol*)   What about Mrs Winnit?

Thought about Mrs Winnit? Whass she gonna do? And the rector of St Germans. There's whole parishes depend on we. Wendron. Breague. Germoe. Thought about they?   .

Bessie They'll live.

Carter O they will.

Carter *rises and sticks the pistol in his belt. Exit* **Carter**. **Bessie** *continues sweeping.*

Eddy Where's 'Arry?

Bessie Upstairs.

Eddy Thass no good.

Bessie Castle's empty.

Eddy Stackhouse leave a key?

Bessie Yep.

Eddy We'll take im there.

Saltash. Outside the Custom House. **Knill** *addresses his troops.*

Knill (*agitated*) There's twenty-two ton a jack locked up in that warehouse and it belong to John Carter. These Carters are ruthless wily vicious people oo will do everything imaginable to get 'old a that brandy. They could attack any time day or night. You must be vigilant and if you see one of the buggers forgive my profanity shoot the bastard on sight and shoot to kill before e shoot you! O Suzanne my love why did you ave to tell your brother the vice-admiral to order is men to board that boat? And why post me to guard the stuff? I'm supposed to be in Padstow! She fixed it so I was ere when Carter came. What better way to rid the world of a tedious lovesick man? Well I'm ready for ya. O dear God. Forgive my lasciviousness. I beg you Lord tame my libido for heaven. Just gimme a little cloud to sit on and let not a naked angel of either persuasion

pass before me from here to eternity. O yes Lord. Take
me to your bosom. Let this be the day that I'm purged
of the vision of Suzanne Stackhouse naked once and for
all.

Something has touched the back of his head.

Ah. (*Strangely calm.*) Ere at last.

Carter *has materialised from nowhere and stands holding a
pistol to* **Knill**'s *head.*

Knill (*serene*)   Kill me now Carter.

Carter   Disperse your men.

Knill   You don't understand.

Carter   Open the warehouse.

Knill   I'm askin you.

Carter   I've come for me goods.

Knill   Tis a request for execution.

Carter *unhitches a bunch of keys from* **Knill**'s *belt and slings
them back to a confederate.*

Carter   That you Shadrack?

Mrs Vincent   Nope.

Carter   Oo is it?

Mrs Vincent   'Is missis.

Carter (*calling back*)   Take what's mine and nothin else!

Mrs Vincent (*off*)   Why?

Carter   Cus I'm an honest king. Arn't I Knill.

Knill   Lead me to the gutter and slaughter me sick
bullock that I am!

Carter   I warned y'about the Stackhouse party. They
d'come down ere play around bugger off and leave we
to pick up the bits. Now she's gone back to Bath so you

got all winter to forget about er Knill and forge a partnership with me.

Knill   For Godsake put a ball through me head!

Carter   We'm ard but we'm honest. We protect ya. And we share our wealth across the board. We treat you as an equal. 'Arry's gone to Wesley and Bessie's fishin so I need a good man at sea.

Knill   Please! Do your worst!

Carter   There's a schooner lyin four miles due west of the Lizard fresh home from China with sixty crates of Hyoon tea. I'll come with y'on this trip and show ya how to negotiate a fair price. Let's go.

Knill   I arn't shiftin till you've killed me!

Carter   What you do is set a figure in your own head and force him down to that with logic and confusion. There's three brands a tea. Hyoon, Bohea and Congo. So y'ask the Captain how's tea e says twenty pound you say Congo? E say Bohea cus they never got Congo. You say bugger twenty. Eighteen. I wouldn't give ya twenty for Congo. I'd consider nineteen for Hyoon but Bohea! Eighteen's generous. In fact you've talked me out of eighteen. Seventeen or nothing. Hyoon eighteen. Nineteen the Congo. Got'ny Congo?

Knill   Eh?

Carter   Good! That's a start. What did we agree sixteen?

Knill   Seventeen.

Carter   That was the Hyoon. And eighteen the Congo.

Knill   Nineteen the Congo.

Carter   So you have Congo.

Knill   No they never ave Congo.

Carter   Come along Captain I'm a busy man willya
shit or get off the pot.

Blackout.

Acton Castle. Cellar. The walls drip with damp. **Harry** *sits
next to a tank. He is wrapped in a blanket. His face is completely
bandaged. Footsteps echo down stone steps. Enter* **Eddy**.

Eddy   Right 'Arry?

Harry *inclines his head.*

Eddy   There's men in black coats up Helston brewin
mischief. Local people's all behind ya. They won't sell
you out. Tis the religious ones ya can't trust. The
'pocalyptic vision crowd. Buggers killed Pascoe. And you
intend to join em. Well keep away from Helston. In fact
Bessie's booked you a passage for America.

Enter **Bessie**.

Bessie   Right 'Arry? (*To* **Eddy**.) Shadrack's outside.

Eddy   There's twenty-three lobsters in the far tank.

Bessie *heads for a dark corner of the cellar. The tunnel doors
open throwing a shaft of daylight across the cellar floor. Enter*
Carter.

Carter   Right 'Arry? Sold the jack.

Eddy   Oo to?

Carter   Where's Bessie?

Bessie (*emerging from shadows*)   What d'ya want?

Carter   When you see the Stackhouse party give er
this.

He hands her a wad of money.

Eddy   What is it?

Bessie   Undred pound?

Eddy   What for?

Bessie   That bet.

Eddy   What bet?

Enter **Knill**.

Knill   Right 'Arry?

Eddy   She's forgot all about that!

Carter   She might. But I ain't. Cus I'm an honest man.

Knill   Where d'e want this tea?

Exit **Carter** *followed by* **Knill**. **Eddy** *lies down on the floor.*

Eddy   I ab'm slept for two days so when you'm ungry brother wake me up.

He falls asleep.

The Body

The Body was first performed by the Royal Shakespeare Company at The Pit, Barbican, London, on 22 April 1983. The cast was as follows:

The Villagers

The Farmers *of the parish*	Christopher Bowen, William Haden, Brian Parr
Grace Gross	Jenny Agutter
Kenneth Gross, *her husband*	Clive Wood
Mrs May	Brenda Peters
Alice	Lesley Sharp
Archie Gross, *Kenneth's father*	Christopher Benjamin
Gilbert *the policeman,* *Grace's brother*	David Shaw-Parker
The Body	Tom Mannion
The Rector	Derek Godfrey
Stanly, *Mrs May's husband*	Jimmy Gardner

The Americans

Walt	Pete Postlethwaite
The Lieutenant	John Bowe
Al	Niall Padden

Musicians
Timothy Hayes *Music Director/keyboards*
Jonathan Hess *saxophone/flute*
Peter Chapman *bass*
Tony McVey *drums*

Directed by Nick Hamm
Designed by Dermot Hayes
Music by Guy Woolfenden
Lighting by Michael Calf

Prologue

Three **Farmers** *of the parish address the audience.*

Farmers
  We, the farmers of this parish,
  Do admit
  The presence of
  American units
  On our airbase.
  We look out across
  Our meadows
  And count
  Nuclear weapons
  Amongst our sheep.
  We speak with one voice
  And keep our collective
  Mouth on the subject shut.
  We have no choice,
  We know that.
  And we gaze with mild disapproval
  Upon those who seek their removal.

One of our number, Kenneth, sat with his wife one morning, before breakfast.

Kenneth *removes himself from the* **Farmers**' *group and sits with his wife,* **Grace**. *She joints a bullock.*

Kenneth   Grace, I fancy mushrooms for breakfast.

Grace   Then pick some.

Kenneth   I think I might. That's what I was thinking.

Grace   Did you milk the cows?

Kenneth   Yes.

Grace   Feed the pigs?

Kenneth   Yes.

Grace   Count the sheep?

Kenneth   Yes.

Grace   Collect the eggs?

Kenneth   Yes.

Grace   Grease the combine?

Kenneth   I can't grease the combine Grace, not before breakfast, on an empty stomach.

Grace   Then don't leave it for me to do at the last minute. I can't reach the nipples. There's nipples on that combine was put in places a cockroach couldn reach.

Kenneth   My arms is too thick. Yours is thinner.

Grace   My bosom get in the way.

Kenneth   Then diet.

Grace   I aren't goin on a diet so you dun ave to grease the combine.

Kenneth   Good a reason as any.

Grace   And dun't forget the dance tomorrer night.

Kenneth   Tch!

Grace   Lookin forward to that.

Kenneth   The best field for pickin mushrooms on my farm backs on to the airforce base.

Grace   Be careful.

Kenneth   I tell you what I'll do. I'll keep my bedroom slippers on. It's a light dew and they won't get wet, and the Yanks will take me for what I am. A plain English farmer.

Grace   Don't bank on it.

Kenneth   I'll be as long as it takes me to pick a grain pan full of mushrooms.

Kenneth *goes.* **Grace** *sits. Music plays, then stops.* **Grace** *looks at her watch.*

Grace   He's late.

Music plays again. **Grace** *uncrosses her legs and re-crosses them the other way. Music stops. She looks at her watch.*

He's bin gone a day now. Twenty-four hours. I think I'm gettin worried. Soon be time to make inquiries. Start askin round a bit.

She goes. Music intro to **Farmers'** *song.*

Act One

*The **Farmers** of the parish, sing a song.*

Farmers
The farmers of this parish
Would dearly love to tell,
All about Mother May
A body and a – well,
Mother May went cocklin,
No, we haven't started right,
To get the yarn out viddy
We got to start the night
Before,
When Stanly stuck her bloomers
In the roof to stop the leak,
So she could take the bucket out
From underneath.
So now she got the *bucket*
To do with what she like,
And with the *bucket* in er and
She set sail on her bike.
Bike got a puncture
So she ayved'n in the ditch,
Decide to pick some cockles
From beneath the iron bridge.
Now *this* is where the story start,
With the cockles, and the *body*,
And Alice, and the iron bridge,
The bucket, and the . . .

Mrs May *and* **Alice** *walking, marche sur place.* **Mrs May**
muddy to the knee and carrying a bucket full of cockles.

Alice   Mornin Mrs May.

May   Mornin Alice.

Alice   Hear the larks?

May   Lovely.

Alice   You'm lookin rosy Mrs May.

May   Thank you.

Alice   Like you bin stridin against the wind.

May   Bin over the cliff.

Alice   You'm muddy half way to the knee.

May   Ah. Bin in the mud.

Alice   And you have in your hand a bucket.

May   There now.

Alice   Bin cocklin?

May   Observant Alice.

Alice   Bin under th'iron bridge?

May   Iron bridge Alice yes.

Alice   Iron bridge is it?

May   And I've found more'n cockles.

Alice   People often do, under th'iron bridge.

May   I was jabbin about with me toes in the mud, jabbin about for a cockle . . .

Alice   Ez . . .

May   And me foot oozed on summin soft.

Alice   Flesh.

May   I gived it a prod with me stick and it felt like Stanly's belly.

Alice   Twad'n Stanly . . .

May   An I put me 'and down, and twined me finger in a strand of seaweed.

Alice   Hair . . .

May   Twas a body, what I found beneath th'iron bridge.

Alice   Dead?

May   As a doormat.

Alice *stops to consider this and* **May** *stops also.*

Alice   Still there is e?

May   I ab'm brung the bugger 'ome in the bucket.

Alice   Just the one was it?

May   How many do e want?

Alice   Better inform an authority ad'n e?

May   I will do Alice, after I've ad me photograph took with it.

Alice   Ere come Archie Gross. Inform e.

May   I dun't inform Archie Gross a nothin. Me an e dun't mix.

Alice   Inform Gilbert. Policeman.

May   I will do Alice. But that there body belong to me. So dun't you go yakkin.

Archie Gross *walking marche sur place. He carries an empty bucket.*

Gross   Archie Gross, you're a lucky man. The sun's shinin and the larks are singin. You've an empty bucket in your 'and, danglin, by thy side, swingin for an back in time with a loose and easy gait, which is step by step drawin e closer to the cockle beds below the iron bridge. And there id'n nothin like a bucket fulla cockles in the world, bar a good eggy tart like Tysie make. Aw. Cloud loomin on the horizon, in the bulbous shape a Mrs May. She bring rain to me, she an me dun't conglomerate. Look like she bin cocklin, so thass summin I d'know 'bout er. Less she knaw bout me less

she can yack around the parish. And there's Alice with
er, sprig a blossom brought out be the rain.

They converge.

Mornin Mrs May.

May   So they say.

Gross *(raising his hat)*   Mornin Alice.

Alice   Mornin, Mr Gross.

Gross   Hear the larks?

Alice   Lovely.

Gross   Bin for a jaunt?

May   There and back. Whass that bucket?

Gross   Ohh, tis a bucket.

May   I noticed, you carry a bucket.

Gross   I could say the same about you.

May   But I'm on me way back. You'm on your way.

Gross   Ah. I'm er, goin to milk the cow.

May   Out here?

Gross   I have a cow, by name a Buttercup, who
wander.

May   I hope she yield a good gallon.

They pass.

Farmers *(sing)*
 So off they went
 To east and west
 With little said
 And love lost less.
 Mr Gross had told a fib,
 Proper little whopper.
 Mrs May and Alice went

To winkle out a copper.

Gilbert *stands at the station desk. A pile of dollar bills and a box of popcorn sit on the desk-top.* **Gilbert** *eats popcorn. He closes the book and buttons up his jacket.* **May** *strides in followed by* **Alice**.

Gilbert   Mornin Mrs May.

May   Now thun.

Gilbert   Mornin Alice.

Alice   Mmmmmmmmmmmmmmmm.

May   Gilbert.

Alice   Mmmmmmmmmmm.

May   Gilbert.

Gilbert   Goin dance tonight?

May   Got summin for e. Now listen ere boy . . .

Alice   What dance?

Gilbert   Parish 'all.

Alice   Dance tonight, is there?

May   Gilbert . . .

Gilbert   Goin?

May   Gilbert . . .

Alice   Mmmmmmm. Who's playin?

Gilbert   Manny Cockle and the Big Four Combo.

Alice   Ooh.

May   Gilbert!

Alice   You gonna take me?

Gilbert   Mmmmmmmmm.

May   Christ!

Alice   Cus I got to go now . . .

May   Alice will you stop yakkin maid!

Gilbert   Where to?

Alice   Eat me dinner.

May   Gilbert you on duty or no?

Gilbert   What e got for dinner?

May   GILBERT!

Alice   Eggy tart.

Alice *goes.*

May   *Now* thun!

Gilbert   Eh?

May   I found a dead body cocklin.

Gilbert   Whass a dead body doin cocklin.

May   *I* was cocklin, the body was dead.

Gilbert   Where to?

May   Iron bridge.

Gilbert   Under'n?

May   Ez you, under'n.

Gilbert   Hell. Whose body is it?

May   I dunnaw. E'm washed up more like. Up the estuary, out the sea.

Gilbert   Aw.

May   You comin or no?

Gilbert   I got ave me dinner.

May   Gaw damme boy twill be washed out again time you've ad your dinner!

Gilbert (*not enthusiastic*)   Come on thun.

They go.

Farmers (*sing*)
  Gilbert was reluctant,
  To say the very least,
  To go and dig up bodies
  Where bodies don't exist.
  But before we carry on with them,
  We've raced a bit ahead,
  We must return to Mr Gross,
  Who's *at* the cockle beds.

Archie Gross *cockling. He sits, removes his boots and rolls his trousers up. Checks the independence of his toes, walks a bit and whistles quietly to himself. Suddenly he plunges his foot into the mud, and feels for a cockle. Then he plunges his other foot, and he is cockling. He sings . . .*

Gross   There is nothing like a cockle . . . We are poor black cockles, who have lost our way . . . Old man cockle . . . Cockles in the night . . . Red cockles in the sunset . . . Once, I had a secret cockle . . . one two three o'clock four o'clock cockle, five six seven o'clock eight o'clock cockle I'm gonna rock, around, the cockle tonight . . .

His foot action turns into the twist and he is carried away. Then he stops, his face changes, and he feels very carefully with his toes. He's found the **Body**.

Gross   Hell.

He starts to edge his feet horizontally along the **Body**, *stopping at significant places. At last he gets to the head.*

Gross   Body.

He feels some more.

Dead. Damme. Now what. Shift'n. Handcart. Take'n church. Inform the rector.

Gross *goes off. He leaves the* **Body** *lying there. The* **Body** *is covered from head to toe with mud.*

Farmers *(sing)*
Now this is where our story start
To gather its momentum,
Mr Gross and handcart
Were there and back in no time.

Gross *comes back with a handcart. He lifts the* **Body** *on and off as they sing.*

The body lifted off the flats
And placed with haste
Upon the trap.
Mrs May, with rumblin gait,
Arrived with Gilbert,
A mite too late.

Mrs May *and* **Gilbert** *arrive on the scene, panting. She looks around her, conducts the proceedings like a military exercise.*

May   Take your boots and stockins off boy.

Gilbert   Eh?

She hitches her skirts and plunges her foot in the mud.

May   Plunge your foot in.

Gilbert   Eh?

May   Got 'ome twas rainin. Said to Stanly where's me bloomers? E said stoppin up the leak in the roof. I said proper job, cockles for tea. Plunge your foot in boy.

She plunges her other foot.

This is the spot. He'm down ere.

She feels about. No **Body**.

Damme e'm sunk.

Gilbert   Eh?

May   Take your trousers off boy.

Gilbert (*taking off his trousers*)   Eh?

May   E've gone deep. Ave to probe a bit.

Gilbert   Who's the policeman around ere.

May   *There* now.

Gilbert   What now?

May   That there body . . . 's vanished.

Gilbert   Gyat. Twad'n never there. Tis a figment.

May   Praise the Lord! E'm a Lazarus! E've took up his
bed an walked! Advance with me Gilbert! To the rector!

And she's gone. **Gilbert** *picks up his trousers and follows.*
Archie Gross, *pulling his handcart.*

Farmers (*sing*)
  With flying skirt
  And rolling lurch
  She forged a path
  Toward the church
  With Gilbert, close behind.
  Over hill
  And down the dip,
  Archie Gross
  Cracked his whip
  And galloped with his find.

Gross   Archie Gross, you'm a lucky man. You set out
this mornin with nothin more in mind 'n a handsome
bucket fulla cockles, and here y'are returnin 'ome with a
cartload a dead body! Hero a the parish! I'll have em
all yakkin. An Mrs May steamin like a silage pit for
lettin a dead body through her toes while jabbin for a
cockle beneath the iron bridge. She think she'm the big
I am, but who found the body!

The **Body** *slips off the back of the cart.*

Farmers (*sing*)
No sooner had he said those words,
He reached an incline in the road,
Steeper steeper climbed the cart,
And the body slipped off onto the path.

The church. The **Rector** *stands by the lychgate dressed as a Chinaman.* **Archie** *arrives with his empty cart.*

Archie   Rector! I see you're dressed as a Chinaman.

Rector   Observant Archie.

Archie   And the church seem somewhat altered.

Rector   On the outside.

Archie   Now thun.

Rector   The nave is exactly as you might remember it.

Archie   Got summin to show e.

Rector   You see Archie it started with the fund-raisin.

Archie   Twad'n me who stripped the lead off the steeple.

Rector   No twas the October gale.

Archie   I lost a dutch barn in that one . . . now look ere look, in the 'andcart . . .

Rector   I said to Jack Steeple the steeplejack that steeple, Jack, is leakin. Jack Steeple looked at me and then e eyed the steeple. Rector, said Jack, the leak in that steeple is gonna take some stoppin. That steeple's bent. I could erect a pagoda cheaper. A pagoda said I. Aye said Jack. A pagoda. I looked at Jack, then I eyed the steeple. All the while my 'and clasped the forty-seb'm an sixpence, the parish response to my appeal, includin bingo, and I said to meself, so Jack couldn 'ear, nuts. For all the attention I get on a Sunday mornin I might as well be a Chinaman, so here I am, pagoda, Chinese cassock wi dragons on, and pointed hat. And do you know Archie? You're the first bugger who's noticed.

Archie   Then Rector tis your lucky day. There's a body in the back a that cart!

Rector   Lead me to it!

Archie   Follow.

Archie *leads the* **Rector** *round to the back of the cart. The cart is empty.*

Archie   Aw. Aw my gor.

Rector   Dearodear.

Archie   I tell e Rector e was ere! Dead as a doormat, lyin in the back a the cart!

Rector   Come inside the pagoda Archie, an I'll relieve e of a sin or two, you'm clearly in need of spiritual aid.

Gross   Tis Mrs May. She'm a witch.

Rector   Mrs May is a stalwart of the parish.

Gross   She'll stop a pig bleedin a mile off, I seed er do it!

Rector   She has a shiny pew, through constant use Archie, I'm surprised you found your way here.

Gross   She spirited the bugger off the cart, set the parish yakkin!

Rector   Tis a sad state Archie when a man comes to blaspheme in the shadow of the house of er, God.

Gross   Tis a damn sorry state when a man can't go cocklin, find a dead body, an call the bugger is own!

He strides off. **Rector** *goes off.*

May *and* **Gilbert**, *striding sur place.*

May   Stride out Gilbert! We got a sensation on our hands! God look kindly upon they who shine his pews and I'm goin meet this Lazarus, in the flesh, wi blood pumpin through!

Archie Gross *striding towards them.*

Gross   Archie Gross, you'm a misunderstood man. If I could wrench the Rector away from is rice wine I could show'n a thing or two make is Chinese cassock curl.

May   Head for the church Gilbert! The steeple glowin with a strange an eerie light. E'm in there yarnin with the Rector more like.

Gilbert   With a gallon a rice wine.

Gross   This is a case for the p'lice. Gilbert got 'ear bout this.

May   That there Archie Gross, dun't knaw what e'm missin, milkin, I'll set the parish yakkin, shove'n out the limelight.

Gross   Mother May, blind as a badger, couldn see a dead body if e stood up an looked er in the face, got to resort to witchcraft get 'old of er dead bodies . . .

May   There's one or two points I want to raise with this Lazarus, 'bout Moses an the locusts.

Gross   That there Rector id'n no good. I was churchwarden there three years an e thought I was me brother.

May, **Gilbert** *and* **Gross** *all converge on the* **Body** *from different directions.*

May *(seeing the* **Body***)   There* now!

Gross   Hah! WHERE D'Y GET THAT BODY TO!

May   That there's MY BODY!

Gross   YOUR BODY IS IT! And WHAT make e so cocky on THAT ONE?

May   Cos I FOUND of er!

Gross   THEN WE HAVE A DISPUTE ON OUR HANDS!

May   Why's THAT?

Gross   Cos *I* found of er!

May   Milkin-cows?

Gross   I wad'n milkin no cow, so there's the first eye-opener!

May   Then you'm a dirty liard!

Gross   I'm a stalwart of the parish!

May   An I'm a pillar of the church!

Gross   Then go an 'old the roof up!

May   No roof left, lead you've pinched!

Gross   Well you'll always find a willin pair a bloomers, for to stop up the leaks!

May   That was Stanly! Gilbert! Arbitrate!

Gilbert   I'm gonna notify an authority.

Gross   Which authority?

Gilbert   Dunnaw. Water Board's nearest.

May   You idn' gonna notify no bugger till we got this body sorted out who it belongs to an I've ad me picture took with it on the parish 'all steps!

Archie   Who it belongs to is perfectly plain, who dug'n up and brung'n ere?

Gilbert   You did Arch.

May   Whose foot first found flesh!?

Gilbert   Yours Mrs May.

May   Then I demand the right, to be photographed, on the parish 'all steps, with this ere body propped up alongside, exclusive, black and white across the nation's news-stands!

Gross   Over my dead body!

May   Archie Gross you'm a greedy grabbin man. Defeat stands ere, starin y'in the face, and still your fingers spread and close like talons graspin air. No man hath less deserved notoriety and no man seeks it more. If this body could speak. If this mouth could utter but one sentence more before his passage through the endless night he would raise his bloodless hand, point to me, and say . . .

Gilbert   Thass goodbye to me dinner me brother's et it now.

May   . . . I belong to Mrs May. What further proof do e need.

Gross   You expect me to dribble? She've ad the whole parish dribblin before now but not me. Archie Gross dun't dribble!

Gilbert   Steak an kidney bloody puddin down me brother's gullet. E'm fatter'n a young shag and here's me thinner'n wind an 'ungry.

May   Dry mouths dun't dribble Archie Gross I knaw that. Snake's tongues flick and no saliva oils their jaw!

Gross   Well. Well. Now we knaw how far we'm prepared to go.

Gilbert   She got to callin y'a snake yet Archie?

Gross   Yes. That last one. Snake.

Gilbert   Right. That wraps it up. Satisfied Mrs May?

May   Archie Gross. Call this body mine.

Gilbert (*spreads his hands*)   No mercy.

Gross   Your foot found flesh first. My foot fell on tainted skin.

Gilbert   Nicely put Arch. Lost on the old bat but I could see the dignity in it. I'm arrestin this body.

May   What!?

Gross   Hell!

Gilbert (*to the* **Body**)   Anything you say will be taken down an used against you in evidence. I hope you gotta passport.

They all look at the **Body**. *It keeps its mouth shut.*

Unless anyone's prepared to raise bail . . .

They have no money about them.

I'll put me trousers on, go an get me Lambretta, an run'n down the lock-up.

May   Ad your dinner yet Gilbert?

Gilbert   No.

May   Then ere's a bucket a cockles.

Gilbert   Aw. Ta.

May   Bail.

Gilbert   Hell! I'm hungry. Hungry as a gap in the hedge. Bucket a cockles a go down well. Bloody job to keep a dead body upright on the back of a Lambretta . . .

May   Thass settled that thun.

Gross   Vanity and greed win the day.

May   I'll go an get me 'air done now. Phone Reuter, should get the world's press ere by four a clock.

She takes the **Body** *and makes for home, the* **Body** *across her* *shoulder.* **Gilbert** *pulls his trousers on. The* **Rector** *appears. He's been running.*

Rector   Ah. Caught up with e at last.

Gross   Too late, the bird ave flown.

Rector   I gather there's a body for me Gilbert.

Gross   This idiot ad the bugger under arrest. Some bloody p'liceman you are, let a dead body slip out your 'ands.

Gilbert   I'm that 'ungry I could eat these cockles raw. Shell's'n all. Oo are you?

Rector   Rector.

Gilbert   Whass this Chinese rigout?

Rector   Like it?

Gilbert   It make a splash.

Gross   Fower time she done the dirty on me. Clodploddin bastard farmers in this parish is near bankrupt tryin keep up wi me. She snatch a body from me an I'll snatch that body back an I'll paint my body black to get my body back cus that body's *my* body more'n tis anybody's, s'much as this body's my body so what better way to get a body eh?

Gilbert   Eh?

Rector   You talkin 'bout the body?

Gross   Yes.

Rector   That body deserve a Christian burial Archie. No plottin. I want that body clean an greased and laid out in the vestry before evensong.

Gross   I'll tell e summin Rector. I'm a key figure in this parish. King pin. I'm the man they look to, and after lookin, follow. I aren't used to bein shoved this way an that and bein made a damn fool of. You want that body you'll ave to stand in line, cus the battle id'n over yet!

He stalks off.

Rector Tell e summin Gilbert. I gotta feelin the clergy ab'm got the status in the parish no more. Worship seem to me to be very much a byline.

Gilbert Rector is it?

Rector There's few who bother to make the journey up the hill to the pagoda, and them as do dun't listen.

Gilbert Got your passport?

Rector And of course, that makes my life . . .

Gilbert Whass it like in China?

Rector . . . very, very, lonely.

*The **Rector** wanders off.*

Gilbert Hm.

He fishes a notebook from somewhere and writes a memo. Then he picks up the bucket and goes.

Farmers (*sing*)
  Back at home
  Grace had
  Waited
  Long enough
  For Kenneth to return.

Grace *sits at home.*

Grace Better go out lookin for im. I better tell em I miss'n. Cus I do. Though I can't be sure. If they say do you miss'n, course I a say yes. Dun't she lub'm? Course I lub'm. Well. I miss'n. I lub'm, cus e's there. But if I was honest, would I say I lub'm cus I miss'n, or I lub'm cus e's there, or what? I'm on me own see. If I'm on

me own I worry. In this 'ouse on this des'late farm in
the dark nights. Do I worry cus I lub'm? Or cus I'm on
me own? Then there's the dance. E's gotta be back for
that. I better go an look for'n.

She goes off.

Farmers (*sing*)
   A day, a night,
   And half another
   Passed
   Before she went
   And asked
   Her mother
   To offer
   Her advice.

Grace *on. Her* **Mother** *upstage, bending, taking eggy tart from
the oven, back to the audience.*

Mother   Dun't bother me.

Grace *walks down stage.* **Mother** *off.*

Gilbert *in the station. He eats a fairy cake.* **Grace** *walks in.*

Grace   Gilbert. Kenneth's missin.

Gilbert   One bloody fairy cake.

Grace   I asked Mother, and she was sympathetic, but
she said the first thing I should do is report it to you.

Gilbert   Whass she doin, Mother?

Grace   Smelt like eggy tart.

Gilbert *shuts up shop and puts his tunic on as* **Grace** *talks.*

Grace   He went out pickin mushrooms yesterday
mornin an e ab'm come back. I aren't sure what I'm
thinkin . . . You comin to look for'n?

Gilbert   I'm goin ave me bloody dinner.

Grace   Aw c'mon . . .

Gilbert   Dun't bother me . . .

He goes off. **Grace** *turns to the three* **Farmers**, *who are discussing in a circle.*

Grace   Excuse me . . .

Farmer One   Whose sheep was it?

Farmer Two   Mine.

Farmer Three   Whose field was it?

Farmer One   Mine.

Farmer Two   And whose fence was it?

Farmer Three   Mine.

Grace   Excuse me . . .

Farmers (*pointing at each other*)   So your sheep was in is field when e broke down your fence . . .

Grace   Er . . .

Farmers   Yup.

Grace   Oy!

Farmers   We are meeting to discuss.

Grace   Kenneth's missin.

Farmers   Dun't bother we . . .

Archie Gross *on.*

Farmers   So what we'm ere to debate, is who pay for the fence . . .

They notice **Archie Gross** *and stop talking. He approaches them and they ignore him, walk off. He glowers.*

Grace (*in tears*)   Archie, Kenneth went pickin mushrooms an e never come back. I dunno what I'm feeling. No one seem that concerned. I thought you, bein is father, thought you might juss worry with me, juss worry a li'l bit. E's disappeared, dun't you care? E's vanished! I knaw e's slow on the uptake Arch I knaw, an often I've 'eard you say e id'n worthy a the name a Gross, and indicated doubt at his ability to produce a progeny for to carry on the line but e got a sweet nature Arch, we a git there one day, we'll ave a li'l boy, li'l grandson for e, li'l, perky chap, but I gotta find im first! Please Arch, please . . .

Archie Gross, *who has been buried in thought, turns on* **Grace**.

Gross   Heed this Grace . . .

Grace   Yes?

Gross   Tomorrer night the name of Gross shall scorch its path across the sky and light this parish from Winnards Perch to Rumford with a neon power!

Grace   Oh . . .

Gross   And in a forgotten des'late field, neath a dark hedge shadow creepin, on her belly, shall Mother May slide, and eat grass. The taste of nettle sweet her tongue and revenge ride upon her back!

Grace   Please help me please . . .

Gross   Dun't bother me! (*He's off.*)

The **Farmers** *sing, in a dramatic, operatic way, with descant, as* **Mrs May** *makes her grand, sweeping entrance, the following aria:*

Farmers (*sing*)
  The very next day
  Mrs May
  Had her photo
  In the papers.
  The world's press

> On the parish hall steps
> Had snapped a legend
> In the making.
> Famous now, notorious,
> And Archie Gross was furious . . .

Mrs May *and* **Alice** *sit on the parish hall steps.* **Gross** *slinks on and glowers in the background.* **May** *and* **Alice** *have a pile of newspapers before them and are eagerly leafing through them. As the scene progresses,* **Farmers** *wander on and warmly greet* **Mrs May** *as if she's a celebrity, they maintain a discreet distance, at the same time interested in what is going on.*

May   See that there look?

Alice   Is that you?

May   No thass the body. I got me bonnet on.

Alice   They got a good angle there.

May   Thass the *Daily Mirror*. They took that from behind.

Farmer   Morning Mrs May.

May (*to* **Alice**)   First time e've spoke to me since nineteen forty-six. The best one's in the *Daily Telegraph* . . . (*Raising her voice a bit.*) Opposite the Court and Social. Captured me square on in the foreground with the sun behind and the body in sharp relief.

Alice   Oh yes, that's very plain. Very clear and sharp.

Farmer   Oho Mrs May . . .

May (*under her breath*)   Gittome.

The **Rector** *comes on. He notices* **May**, *and then* **Archie**. *He has in his hand a bible. He takes a stance on the steps.*

May   Tid'n too grainy. The body's come out nice. You can see tis a body, and you can see tis dead. There's no mistakin thass a dead body see?

Alice   Thass dead all right.

May   Queen'll see that photograph.

Alice   Will er?

Farmer   How do you do Mrs May?

May   That was Stanly. She look in the Court and Social and see what she'm doin for the day.

Alice   Hell. Where's the body to now?

May   Up 'ome. On the couch, in the parlour.

Alice   Dunne stink?

May   Couldn say. I aren't that nasal.

They bury themselves in their papers. The **Farmers** *slowly edge over and look over their shoulders without them noticing. The* **Rector** *starts to preach.*

Rector   Citizens! Congregation! I have come down, from my pagoda, on the hill, this afternoon, to preach a sermon in the forum, as it were. I speak, from the heart, of the parish! I have an important somethin to say to you all. Please, I beg your ears hear what your Rector has to say . . .

Farmer   Thass a very flatterin picture in *The Times* Mrs May, if I may venture my opinion.

Farmer   Definitely dead innit.

Rector   . . . An event has come to pass, which, bein Rector, of course I was one of the first informed. Now, as you probably all know, I'm talking about the body. This body has bin passed from pillar to post, shoved this way and that without so much as a prayer bein offered up in his presence. There are people in this parish, who are usin this ere body for their own ends. To further their own notoriety. Squabbles have broken out amongst respected members of the community over some poor chap who's dead. Even now I'm told he is lying on a couch in a private house! This is repugnant behaviour, thought of as lowly even by ants! I'm here this afternoon to uphold the standards laid down by the church, and ask those responsible for this appalling sin, to repent and bring the body to me!

Grace *comes on.*

Grace   Rector . . .

Rector   Aww what?

Grace   Y'ab'm seed Kenneth?

Rector   Oh, piss off . . .

Grace *wanders down and joins the poring crowd.*

Rector   People!

No one takes any notice of the **Rector**. *He starts to speak in Chinese. Slowly, as he speaks, people hear what he's saying and turn and listen. Towards the end of his speech, everybody is listening to the* **Rector** *speaking in Chinese, and* **Gilbert** *wanders on.*

Gilbert   Whass goin on?

Rector (*continues to speak in Chinese*)

Gilbert   Who is this man?

Alice (*vehemently*)   Bloody Chinaman, blind?

Gilbert   Now thun mister. Less see your passport!

Rector (*continues to speak in Chinese*)

Gilbert *takes the* **Rector** *roughly by the arm.*

Gilbert   Come on skipper. We got some cross examinin to be done . . .

Gilbert *manhandles the confused* **Rector** *off. The* **Farmers** *come forward to speak while* **Mrs May** *and* **Gross** *clear off,* **Alice** *remains seated on the step and* **Grace** *sits beside her, studying closely the paper that is left.*

Farmers (*speak*)
  We, the farmers of this parish,
  Uphold the moral standards
  Set down by the church.
  As rooted in the land
  As the sugar beet we nurture
  And unchanged by events
  That happen round us,
  We remain entrenched
  In the ditches of
  Our opinion.
  Nothing sways us.
  What we think is what we do,
  From market day to
  Milking time,
  What we see and who
  We meet are liable to
  The same fogbound horizons
  Framed by the seasons,
  And regular as the lessons
  Read from the bible.

The **Farmers** *move upstage whilst* **Alice** *speaks to* **Grace**.

Alice   I said to Gilbert why d'y wanna wear your
uniform to the dance? I said wear that tweed jacket you
wore to the hunt ball! E said e like wearin is uniform. I
said what is it to be your uniform or me? I aren't goin
no fuckin dance with a policeman. I wanna go dance wi
Gilbert . . .

Grace   . . . So y'ab'm seed'n thun.

Alice   . . . Gilbert said I am my uniform I said I'll go
dance wi Benny. E said Benny's a twit. I said not 'alf as
big a fuckin' twit as you. E said if you go dance wi
Benny I'll arrest the bugger. I said you arrest Benny I'll
smack y'in the fuckin mouth. E said you smack me in
the fuckin mouth. So I smacked'n in the mouth an e
arrested me an asked me for me passport so I said now

what you gonna do Mr fuckin Chief Constable . . . ?

Grace   This body id'n Kenneth, tis too square-shouldered.

Alice   . . . E said I'm gonna take e down the station an lock e up for the night. I said aww Mr Powerful I inna fraida you an your fuckin uniform. You take 'at uniform off, I said, an put your tweed jacket on see if you got the fuckin guts to lock me up . . .

Grace   You're sure you ab'm . . .

Alice   So off come the uniform and on go the tweed jacket an e's standin there lookin bloody sheepish rubbin is gob where I gib'm a smack an I says come on thun. E says where we goin? I said dance. E said aw all right thun. So off we went dancin, soon as we got there there was fuckin Mavis Rickeard all dolled up in er bandy legs'n mini skirt an e couldn keep is eyes off er so e danced wi she an I danced wi Benny . . .

Grace   And that was the end of that!

Exit **Grace** *and* **Alice**.

Archie Gross's *farm*. **Gross** *strips to his underpants in front of a fifty-gallon drum full of mud. Doves coo. At the back of the stage* **Gilbert** *enters on his Lambretta. A Pan Am bag is strapped on and from his belt dangles a menacing bunch of handcuffs.*

Gilbert   Oy!

Gross   What?

Gilbert   *indicates the pillion seat of the Lambretta.*

Gilbert   'Op on!

Gross   Uh?

Gilbert   Arrest. Passport?

Gross   For?

Gilbert   'Fficial!

Gross   Gittome!

Gilbert   C'mon!

Gross   I'm busy!

Gilbert   Same ere!

Gross   Then sling your 'ook!

Gilbert *alights from his Lambretta and approaches* **Gross**.

Gilbert   Come on Archie I got the 'ole parish to round up.

Gross   'Ole parish?

Gilbert   Yeah.

Gross   Why?

Gilbert   Can't divulge.

Gross   Why?

Gilbert   Tis official.

Gross   Body?

Gilbert   What body?

Gross   What body *the* body *my* body!

Gilbert   Dunnaw what you're talkin 'bout skipper.

Gross   Oh, course, tis official now. Ad a rocket up is ass an now e's in the shit. You piss off 'ome 'fore I tell your mother, I got business to conduct!

Gilbert   Aw dun't tell Mother for Chrissake.

Gross   Three days ago Gilbert, 'eads turned when I bid at market. Noses twitched an brains started tickin. When I strode forth with an empty bucket in me 'and speculation rose like steam from a fresh laid cowpat as to that bucket's fate. An I didn let em down. I found a dead body, cocklin. I swaggered back with it, proud man, but oh, how the mighty have fallen. For three days I've carried round in my head nothin more'n a janglin mix of humiliation and revenge. But I had a plan, and now that plan is goin into action, and no 'andcuff-danglin copper's gonna stop its glorious journey till once again this parish doffs its hat to me!

Gilbert   Bullshit! Doff your ass on the back a that Lambretta buster! Pronto!

Gross *leaps into the drum of mud and submerges himself completely. He emerges covered in mud.*

Gross   Do your business thun.

Gilbert *is taken aback.*

Gilbert   Hell.

Gross *re-submerges for another coat.* **Grace** *arrives.*

Gilbert   Ah!

Grace   What?

Gilbert   C'mon the Lambretta.

Grace   You id'n arrestin me I'm your bloody sister!

Gilbert   Aw please Gracy . . .

Grace   Gittout of it 'fore I tell Mother . . .

Gilbert   Aw, tch!

Grace   Where's Archie?

Gilbert   In there.

He indicates the drum and goes. **Gross** *re-emerges.*

Grace   That you Archie?

Gross   Ah. Grace. Give us 'and wi this . . .

Gross *trundles the drum off. The* **Farmers** *lurk, perhaps lend* *an unobtrusive hand.*

Grace   Archie. Kenneth's gone missin.

Gross   Gonna give Mother May the fright of er life . . .

Grace   Tis the Yank marines only normally as you know they only keep'n till dinnertime . . .

Gross   Need the parish there, bear witness . . .

Grace   Only e went off without greasin the combine, an I need 'elp, greasin it . . .

Gross   Outside er parlour window.

Grace   An I need to git that out the way Arch . . .

Gross *stops in his tracks.*

Gross   WHAT!

Grace   See?

Gross   Kenneth. E've gone you say?

Grace   E ab'm bin 'ome for three days . . .

Gross   AN E AB'M GREASED THE COMBINE!

Grace   No, but . . .

Gross   MY CHRIST ALMIGHTY! THAT BLOODY SON A MINE!

Grace   Eh?

Gross *(indicates the* **Farmers***)*   WHAT THE HELL ARE THE PEOPLE A THIS PARISH GONNA SAY WHEN THEY HEAR THAT KENNETH GROSS, SON OF ARCHIE, HAS BUGGERED OFF AND LEFT HIS WIFE GRACE TO GREASE THE COMBINE!

Grace   Well. Exactly.

Gross   HAVEN'T THEY DONE ENOUGH TO ME!

Grace I bin all round the parish an I've 'eard several innuendoes . . .

Farmers (*severally*) Innuendo innuendo innuendo . . .

Gross I'LL BET YOU HAVE!

Grace What we gonna do?

Gross Be outside Mother May's at eight o'clock tonight. Sit outside er parlour window and scream like a cat at exactly ten past.

Grace Eight.

Gross You got'n. Bring Gilbert if e've ad is dinner. Anyone else you can press-gang. After that we a go on a search for that bastard wayward son a mine. Teach the bugger to GREASE THE COMBINE . . . !

Grace Good job!

They go off, leaving the space empty.

Alice *sits doing her needlepoint.* **Gilbert** *enters.*

Alice What you come for? Slap or tickle?

Gilbert Now look ere. You're under arrest. Where's your passport?

Alice Aww, not that again . . .

Gilbert No this . . .

Alice Wouldn say boo to a goose in is tweed jacket an soon as e put is tunic on again e's back arrestin me . . .

Gilbert This is bloody serious this is . . .

Alice What is?

Gilbert Can't divulge . . .

Alice You was divulgin enough round the back a the parish all last night.

Gilbert Uh?

Alice Wi Mavis Rickeard. I was there when Benny switched is 'eadlights on, 'long with 'alf the district. You bin sid more round ere lately without trousers'n wid.

Gilbert Aw 'ell . . .

Alice Benny said e wished e ad is airgun wid'n e woulda popped e right'n the ass . . .

Gilbert Mother wad'n there was er?

Alice You woulda knawed soon enough.

Gilbert I dunnaw sometimes she keep these things secret an spring em on me at a later date. Ab'm told er have e?

Alice Bloody will if y'arrest me. Oo've e brung in so far?

Gilbert No one. 'Cept the Chinaman.

Alice Id'n doin too well then are e. Whass up, id'n they payin e enough?

Gilbert sits close to **Alice**, despondent. The handcuffs are between them so he places them on **Alice**'s lap.

Gilbert I got the feelin the constabulary ab'm got the status in the parish no more. There's too much afoot. There's ancient rivalries blowin' up an runnin amok amongst the morals a the place. There's the Chinaman runnin round, pervertin every bugger to Communism, there's the boys up the camp makin impossible demands, payin me all this money, an ere's me catched bang in the middle, tis like a whirlpool, an a course it go straight to me stomach . . .

Alice Come near me thun . . .

Gilbert I gotta Pan Am bag fulla dollar bills I gotta pay Mrs May for the body . . .

Alice   Pan Am bag you say?

Gilbert   Down the lock-up yeah . . .

Alice   Full you say?

Gilbert   Bulgin.

Alice   Thass 'ell of a lotta money.

Gilbert   Tis yeah . . .

Alice   Aww, Gilbert. Darlin . . .

Gilbert   I shouldna divulged it reely. Start with a
tweed jacket well a tweed jacket what the 'ell (*Close to
tears.*) twad'n my damn fault I weared a tweed jacket
thass what they'm there for, balls an parish 'all do's an
that, tweed jackets every bugger ad a tweed jacket an
where do it all lead to, arrest every bugger well thass a
damn sight easier'n it look mister with me sister near
distraction me mother lurkin with er threats an last
night's eggy tart thrust across the table . . . tis . . . tis . . .
if I could only git em all in one place . . . (*Sobbing now.*)
with their trousers down, all lined up with their 'ands
behind their backs I could snap snap snappetty snap em
all up but where's the chance a that? Tis too much to
ask Alice . . .

Alice   Aww, darlin.

Gilbert   All outside a winder, lookin in a room, thass
what I need . . .

Alice   Tis the respect innit, whass lost . . .

Gilbert   I'm like a reckless rat. All me body's
twitchin . . .

Alice   Respect an love an just a feelin a bein wanted.
Needed by people, like your mother see she was never
that maternal wi you an Grace, they all said that, she
was cold towards you when she was carryin Grace an tis
the rejection innit, aww, darlin. An I bin blind to it see.

Gilbert   Bloody blind.

Alice   Tis all, duty. No, dotage. Aww, darlin . . .

Gilbert   I'd love a li'l tickle.

Alice   Would e? Where?

Gilbert   Just ere. Below me two-way radio.

Alice   Aw dearest yes I give e li'l tickle . . .

Gilbert   Then I a carry on arrestin . . .

Alice   No 'urry sweet'eart . . .

Gilbert   I *gotta* do me duty see. Tis ingrained in me.

Alice   Forget your duty. Live a bit. Less ave a tickle, we a still be ere tomorrer, live for now darlin, forget tomorrer, tomorrer's another day . . .

Grace *tickles* **Gilbert** *and he laughs uncontrollably. They get to the point where it might develop into something else when* **Grace** *enters.*

Grace   GILBERT!

Gilbert *(hoisting his trousers up)*   Aw Christ dun't tell Mother . . .

Grace   Gilbert, Kenneth's run off an left me to grease the combine . . .

Gilbert   WHAT! Stay ere Alice this is a job for the p'lice . . .

Grace   An Archie's gone up Mother May's . . . needs the parish as witness . . .

Gilbert   Never mind that we gotta . . . (?) . . . what?

Grace   Gotta be outside er winder at eight o'clock.

Gilbert   That a do me. Foller!

They go off. The **Farmers** *of the parish conclude their debate.*

Farmers (*pointing to each other*)   So you pay half towards the fence, if you give me two thirds of the fleece.

Grace *rushes in.*

Grace   Kenneth's run off an left me to grease the combine!

Gilbert *and* **Alice** *follow.*

Grace   Follow me men!

Gilbert, **Alice**, **Grace** *and the* **Farmers** *of the parish walk in a line marchez sur place. They are in a hurry.*

Gilbert   I'm 'ungry. Oo gotta Nuttall's Minto?

Farmers   I ave.

They each take a Nuttall's Minto from their pockets and pass it up the line.

Alice   Can't see why you married a Gross Grace, they're none of em good.

Grace   Kenneth's all right. E's an open book thass all.

Farmers   What about the Rector? Oughta rope e in . . .

Gilbert   What rector?

Alice   Gilbert dun't go church.

Farmers   The one who dress like a Chinaman.

Gilbert   Thass a Chinaman.

Farmers   Where's e to?

Gilbert   Arrested. Under interrogation. Anyone ere speak Chinese?

Silence.

Aw.

Farmers   Where be us goin? Grease the combine?

Gilbert   Mother May's.

Farmers   Aw.

They go off.

Revealed is **Mother May***'s parlour. A settee and two armchairs, facing out, arranged around a television, with its back to the audience. A window at the back.* **May** *sits on an armchair, then there's the settee in the middle with the* **Body** *on it.* **Stanly** *is slouched in the other armchair, asleep with the cat on his lap. He wears a gasmask.*

May (*to the* **Body**)   This ere's my favourite programme. Comin up. Stanly! Stanly. Favourite programme Stanly. Damme Stanly wakey wakey. Darlinnn . . . Soon as e come 'ome e gather up the cat, fall in the chair an nod off. Ab'm wavered for forty year. I aren't gonna git up out me seat'n rouse'n. Dun't git thanked f'rit. 'Swhy tis so nice t'ave someone to talk to for a change. E a wake up, when tis all over, there a be ructions, I a stampede upstairs to bed an e a knock off back to sleep again till the cold wake'n up when the fire go out. An thass the way we d'go on. I dun't knit see. Aw. Kettle's boilin.

She goes off into the kitchen. The window opens and **Gross** *climbs through. He goes to the settee and removes the* **Body***. He takes it out the back, through another door, to the toilet and returns. He takes the cat from* **Stanly***'s knee and viciously wrings its neck. He replaces it on* **Stanly***'s knee. Then he sits on the settee where the* **Body** *was.* **Gilbert***'s and* **Alice***'s faces appear at the window.* **May** *returns with one cup of tea and a bun.*

May   Used to bring'n is tea in but the bugger never drunk it.

She places the tea and the bun on the sofa beside **Gross** *and leans forward to watch the favourite programme.* **Gross** *takes the bun and passes it back over the sofa to* **Gilbert** *whose hand is outstretched through the open window.* **Gilbert** *eats the bun.*

May, *glued to the telly, reaches over and feels for the bun. It isn't there. Puzzled, she goes to the kitchen for another bun.*

May   Hm.

She goes out. **Gross** *drinks her tea. She returns with another bun. Places it on the arm of the sofa.* **Stanly** *suddenly rises, pushes the cat off his lap.*

May   Aw.

The cat falls to the floor, dead. **Stanly** *runs his hand through his hair.*

May   Huh.

Stanly *grunts, then shambles off to the toilet.*

May (*calling after* **Stanly**)   Goin toilet are e? (*To the* **Body**.) E ab'm done that since 1962. E've bin toilet since 1962, several times, but e ab'm woke up, partway through our favourite programme, an chose to go at this particular time.

She notices the cat.

Hm. Cat's died now. Bloody funny. We've ad that cat fourteen years. Gone an died on us. Musta bin the shock a Stanly wakin up. Creatures of 'abit, cats. Good bit comin up now.

She takes her cup and leans forward to watch the telly. She drinks from it but there is no tea. She looks at the **Body**.

Hm.

She looks round. The heads duck from the window.

Stanly! You drunk my tea? You see? Who drunk my tea? Stanly? Where be e? Damme! Stanly!

Stanly *returns.*

Stanly   'S'at dead body doin in the toilet?

May   Another one?

Stanly   Sittin on the bloody seat.

May   Someone musta put it there. Is it dead?

Stanly   Course it is. Tis caked wi mud.

May   Still there?

Stanly   I aren't gonna shift'n. Ad to piddle on the crocuses.

May   Aw. (*She looks at her empty cup.*) Anyone out there?

Stanly (*matter of fact*)   'Alf the parish.

May   Hell.

Stanly   Gilbert got a wet trouserleg.

May   Cat's died.

Stanly   Aw.

He starts to shamble out. **May** *isn't too keen to be left alone. She rises and goes to the door after him. Calls after him.*

May   Where you goin?

Stanly (*off*)   Set traps for rats!

May   Why!?

Stanly (*off*)   Cat's died!

May *stands with her back to* **Gross**. *He checks the time but being naked he isn't wearing a watch. He looks at the clock and takes the cat up onto his lap.* **Grace** *screams loud like a cat.* **May**, *with an intake of breath, turns and sees the cat on the* **Body**'s *lap. She screams.*

May   Oo! Stanly! Stanly!

Stanly (*off*)   Now what?

May   Come back! Cat id'n dead! E juss screamed!

Stanly *comes back. He holds a rat trap, set. He goes to the front of the sofa. Puts the trap on the floor near* **Gross**'s *foot,* *and takes the cat off* **Gross**'s *knee. Shakes it, throws it back on the floor.*

Stanly   That cat's dead.

May   Ow d'e git on the body's knee?

Stanly   Rigor mortis.

May   Summin bloody fishy goin on ere Stanly.

Stanly   Is there?

May   Two dead bodies, dead cat screamin, missin bun, drunk tea . . .

Stanly *indicates bun on sofa arm.*

Stanly   Bun's there.

May   Thass another bun.

Stanly   Where's the other bun?

May   Tis missin!

Stanly *starts to shamble towards the kitchen.*

May   Where be goin?

Stanly   Git a bun.

May   There id'n another bun. This ere's the last one!

Stanly *makes for the kitchen.*

May   Stay ere!

Stanly *(off)*   Gonna make some tea!

May   Wait for me!

She runs off after him. **Gross** *stands and puts his foot in the rat trap. It snaps shut on his toe. He hops and screams in agony, all over the room, he manages to contain himself.* **Gilbert** *leaps through the window, steals the other bun and jumps out again, pocketing it as he goes.* **Gross** *sits back on the sofa but doesn't have time to remove the trap from his foot because* **May** *and*

Stanly *peer through the door.* **Gilbert** *and* **Alice** *peer in through the window.* **May** *and* **Stanly** *creep into the room and peer round.*

May   What was it Stanly? What was that noise?

Stanly   East wind.

He goes to the sofa to take the bun, which isn't there.

Aw.

He looks round for it but notices the TV.

Aw. Favourite programme.

He takes the cat and places it on his lap. Falls promptly back to sleep and starts to snore. **May** *returns tentatively to her seat, watches the TV, warily. She notices after a second or two the trap attached to* **Gross**'s *toe throbbing. She stands and circles it, trips on* **Stanly**'s *foot. Screams.*

Stanly   Uh?

May   Stanly. The rat trap.

Stanly   What?

May   Tis sprung shut. 'Cross the body's foot.

Stanly *(half asleep)*   Rigor mortis.

May   E got a throbbin toe. Tis swellin up blue. Stanly!

Stanly   Gonna make the tea.

May   Dead bodies dun't swell up blue Stanly. Throb?

Stanly   Do.

Exit **Stanly**.

May *(to the* **Body**)   Who are you? You bin sent to visit me? From a divine source? Are you a messenger from God? Speak to me Lord, for tonight you have touched me with your divinity, my heart is chastened, my soul pure, an my body strong, give me strength Lord, an I will do your biddin! If you ave chosen me to spread your message throughout the land . . .

Gross, *who can sense his triumph slipping out of his hands, leaps up and yells.*

Gross   COURSE E AB'M YOU BLOODY OLE BAT!

May *screams and faints into an armchair.* **Gross** *turns to the window. He points at* **May**.

Gross   See that! See that!

Gilbert *leaps through the window. He is handcuffed to* **Stanly**, *who is handcuffed to* **Alice**. *They naturally follow him in.*

Gilbert   Now thun. Whass goin on?

Gross   See that Gilbert?

Gilbert   You'm under arrest.

Gross   Whass up?

Gilbert   Breakin an enterin, causin Mrs May to faint, killin a domestic cat, an impersonatin a dead body.

Gross   I'm Archie Gross!

Gilbert   Thass another one.

Gross   What?

Gilbert   Impersonatin Archie Gross.

Gross   I *am* Archie Gross!

Gilbert   You're not Archie Gross. Archie Gross dun't land isself in the shit like iss. Archie Gross is a schemin, clever man. Archie Gross lead where others follow. Archie Gross is a respected member of the community. Buster. You id'n no Archie Gross. You'm an alien. Where's your passport?

He releases himself from the handcuffs and connects **Gross** *to the other two.*

Gross   Look at my face! Look! Underneath the mud! There's Archie Gross! Damme your sister's married to my son!

Gilbert   C'mon. In the toilet. I got business to
conduct.

He leads them out. **Gross** *limps.*

Gross (*as he goes*)   Any witch-hazel in the toilet Stanly?

Stanly   No.

Gross   Got a bad toe.

They are out. **May** *starts to come round.* **Gilbert** *returns with
the* **Body** *and the toilet key. He places the* **Body** *on the sofa
and climbs out through the window.* **May** *wakes up and stands.
She walks to the* **Body** *and peers into its face.*

May   Still ere are e? I got a damn good idea now
whass goin on and if you think you can get one up on
me Archie Gross tis a damn sight 'arde'n you think!

She twists the **Body**'s *ear. No response. Pinches its arm. No
response. Checks its toe. White, bloodless, not swollen. She screams
again and yells for* **Stanly.** *There's a muffled shout from the
toilet. She shouts for* **Stanly** *again and a Pan Am bag appears
at the window. At last she is struck dumb.* **Gilbert** *follows the
bag through the window. He dumps it on the settee and shows her
its contents.*

May   Whass this?

Gilbert   Pan Am bag. Under arrest.

May   Uh?

Gilbert   Where's your passport?

May *produces her passport as if by magic from her apron pocket.*

May   Ere.

Gilbert, *thrown by the fact that someone's actually got a
passport, feels he ought to check it, so he does.*

May   Tis all stamped an up-to-date.

Gilbert *pockets it.*

Gilbert   Hm.

May   Whass the money for? Good works?

Gilbert   The body.

May   You wanna buy it?

Gilbert   Thass my orders.

May   Hell.

Gilbert   So. You'm under arrest.

May   What for?

Gilbert   Er, harbourin a divine body, thass an offence for a start. You gotta turn over aliens for quarantine.

May   That body id'n divine. Tis dead.

Gilbert   E quoted the scriptures at ya! I 'eard'n.

May   That was Archie Gross!

Gilbert   Archie Gross is locked in the toilet missus, 'long wi Stanly an Alice.

May   What e arrested Stanly for?

Gilbert   Possession of a gasmask.

May   What about this money thun?

Gilbert   I'll have that.

He takes the money and handcuffs **May** *to the* **Body**.

Wait ere.

He goes out to the toilet. **May** *kneels before the* **Body** *and makes absolutely sure it's dead. The* **Farmers** *of the parish enter silently through the window and stand in a line behind the settee with their hands behind their backs. They study* **May** *examining the* **Body**. **Gilbert** *returns with the other three.* **May** *looks up.*

May   This body is dead y'know Stanly.

Stanly   Course tis bloody dead. Tis stinkin the place out! Why the 'ell d'you think I bin wearin a gasmask for three days!

Gilbert *releases* **May** *from the* **Body** *and handcuffs her to* **Stanly**. *The* **Farmers** *speak to the audience. While they speak* **Gilbert** *goes behind them and handcuffs them all together, and finally to* **Mrs May**.

Farmers
  We, the farmers of this parish,
  Have noticed
  Nothing much
  Amiss.
  Little to take our minds
  Off the ripening wheat
  Has come to pass.
  We were warned of chaos,
  Warned, we ignored it,
  Completely.
  United we stood
  As here we stand
  Before you.
  Depleted
  But wholesome.
  Shorn
  But uncontaminated.
  Worn down
  But self-contained.
  Pious, smug,
  Opinionated,
  Generally healthy.

They are all handcuffed. **Gilbert** *hustles everyone out. As he goes he jabs a finger at the* **Body**.

Gilbert (*to the* **Body**).   You stay ere.

They go out. The lights close up on the **Body** *and the dead cat* *on the floor. The* **Body** *slowly moves. It leans forward. Takes the cat up and places it on its lap, strokes it, looks at the audience and speaks.*

Body   I'd like to tell y'all a story. But before I begin, we have to go back, to the beginning . . .

The lights fade to blackout.

Act Two

*Early morning. A bright summer's day. A dead Marine lies centre stage. **Walt** stands guard by the fence. Larks sing. A jet takes off and flies overhead. Larks sing. The dead Marine sits up and tells a story to the audience.*

Body   When I was alive, towards the end of my life – by the way I'm dead right now, I died, close on five minutes ago – I had a fear of yawning. Got to figuring if I yawned too hard the skin round my lips, when they opened wide, would peel right back over my head and down my neck and turn me inside out. I started to yawn when I was sixteen, back home, when I was bored. I know that healthy guys when they hit sixteen start to do things other than yawn. But believe me where I came from there was little hope of that. And yawning was the next best thing. One day my paw caught me yawning. He said Son join the Marines. (*Here, as the* **Body** *talks,* **Walt** *starts humming to himself, 'The Star Spangled Banner'.*) I said Paw I'm bored. He said The Marines will sure kick the shit outa that. So. I enlisted. First thing they do is cut my hair off. Which kinda makes me uneasy cus by now I'd reached neurosis point about this skin-peeling business, and I figured the only thing which would stop the skin from shooting right back over the top of my skull when I yawned was the hair. Figured it might like hold it in check long enough for me to yank it all back into place. But on my first day . . . had my head shaved . . . believe me I kept my mouth tight shut. But, by the end of my training at boot camp on Parris Island I was a highly-tuned killing machine, prepared to be sent to any part of the world, get shot up and die protecting the free world from the onslaught of Communism. Paw was right. Sure kicked the shit outa yawning. I was ready to kill. Go over the top. I had a weapon in my hand and my finger itched to squeeze the trigger. Got to figure if it itched much more it'd drop off. I had visions of me, under fire, storming a treeline in a fire fight and comin up face-to-face with a big Soviet stormtrooper and there I am weapon in hand ready to blast the bastard to boot hill finger on the trigger and the damn thing's itchin so much it drops off. We were issued with ointment anyhow to relieve the ... er, but, what happens? I'm sent here. Guarding warheads. Sitting on top of that observation tower, which, thank Christ was made unsafe by the last gale, and walking up and down the fence guarding warheads against sheep! I started yawning again. Twice, three times a day. Then it hit me. We were trained to kill, and to die. Now I dunno whether any a you good people are dead, but if you are still alive, the one thing that bothers us about dying is what happens after. I only died five minutes ago but it strikes me being dead is much the same as being alive. It's boring. I think I've bin sent to hell. Don't die. I made a mistake. I erred. It's hell all right. So. I'm dead. And in hell.

He lies down again. Dead. The **Lieutenant** *walks on, he joins* **Walt** *and they continue, marche sur place, around the perimeter.*

Walt   Good day lieutenant.

Lieutenant   Oh hi, er, Walt. Hear the larks?

Walt   Sure can sir.

Body   This is my lieutenant, in charge of my platoon. I never thought we'd meet again so soon. And his promotion-hunting ass-lickin sergeant. These are the reasons I went!

Lieutenant   Have we developed a weapon yet Al, that's effective against larks?

Walt   Not to my knowledge sir.

Lieutenant   Hm. Goddam larks. Drive me crazy. Grates the nerves, the sound they make. Counted the sheep Walt?

Walt   Sir. All there.

Lieutenant   And the warheads?

Walt   Still here sir.

Lieutenant   Checked on the people?

Walt   They're going about their business.

Lieutenant   Fence OK?

Walt   No holes sir.

Lieutenant   What about this observation tower?

Walt   I spoke to Jack Steeple the steeplejack sir he says he happens to have a steeple he could build cheaper than a new tower. This steeple, strengthened, would withstand gales. It has a bell tower and spiral staircase.

Lieutenant   Some steeple . . .

Walt   So . . .

Lieutenant   Build it. Who's this?

The come upon the **Body**.

Walt   This is Bud sir.

Lieutenant   What is he doing? Lying, inert, on the grass?

Body   I'm dead.

Walt   He's dead sir.

Lieutenant   Before chow? How did he die?

Body   Boredom.

Walt   He was bored sir.

Lieutenant   Well let's move on and think about him after chow. I'm hungry.

Walt   Pardon me lieutenant I think it's more pressing than that.

Lieutenant   How's that Al?

Walt   He died of boredom sir.

Lieutenant   Hell.

Body   It sure is.

Walt   We gotta lotta marines here who think there's more to life than counting sheep, they are all bored. If they hear he has died of boredom, then boredom becomes a bona fide means of death. They'll start dropping like flies. I dunno. I might even die.

Body   Please Walt, no.

Lieutenant   Please Al, no.

Walt   Well sir.

Lieutenant   I get your angle Al. Oh here's Walt.

They come upon **Al**, *who's on guard duty.*

Walt   I'm Walt, this is Al.

Lieutenant   Oh. (*To* **Walt**.) Hi Walt, I was just saying to Al here . . .

Walt   You were saying it to me . . .

Lieutenant   Was I? What was I saying?

Al   These goddamn larks drive me crazy.

Lieutenant   That's right. (*To* **Walt**.) You're confusing me Al . . .

Walt   Walt!

Al (*to somebody, off*)   Halt!

Lieutenant   What's up Walt?

Al (*going off*)   Hey shitkicker, what the fuck d'you think y'doing?

Kenneth (*off*)   Pickin mushrooms.

Lieutenant   Better lie down Walt you never know . . .

He drops and hides behind the **Body**, *face to the ground, hands over head,* **Walt** *and* **Al** *go to the edge of the stage.*

Body   Soon as I die there's action.

Al (*to* **Kenneth**, *who is on the other side of the fence*)   You're standing thirty metres from a weapons store containing enough plutonium to devastate Moscow and you tell me you're picking mushrooms? Take a look at this Walt. Put your hands on your head.

Kenneth   I own this field.

Walt *ambles up.*

Al   Says he owns this field.

Kenneth   Look, I'm wearin bedroom slippers.

Walt   So what?

Kenneth   I'm not a spy.

Walt   Who said anything about spies?

Kenneth   I used to own the field you're in, before it was requisitioned.

Walt   Requisitioned . . .

Al   He was requisitioned.

Kenneth   I'm wearin bedroom slippers.

Al   Take em off.

Kenneth   There are thistles!

Walt *and* **Al**   Thistles!

They advance on him menacingly and stand, weapons levelled. He remains rigid.

Al   Come on.

Kenneth *shuffles forward.*

Walt   Take off your left slipper. Throw it over there. Now the right. Put your hands on your head and advance to the fence.

Kenneth *advances to the fence but with difficulty as his bare feet keep stepping on thistles.*

Walt   The warheads in that bin are medium range Thistle DX 43s. Where did you obtain this intelligence?

Kenneth   You juss tole me.

Al   This guy knows something.

He lifts the fence.

Al   *Entrez.*

Kenneth *crawls under the fence. They walk to the* **Lieutenant**. *He raises his head.*

Lieutenant   Oh it's Kenneth. Hi Kenneth.

Kenneth   Ullo.

Lieutenant (*rising*)   Well Kenneth, just a routine investigation, before chow.

They investigate **Kenneth** *as the* **Body** *speaks.*

Body   It's only Kenneth. Poor bastard. I dunno why they bring him in here. Plain as day he ain't no spy.

Walt   Sir I have a plan. It's a wild, crazy idea which might just work.

Lieutenant   What's that Walt?

Walt   Take your clothes off Kenneth.

Kenneth   Uh?

Walt   Do as I say turdbird!

He levels his weapon at **Kenneth**. **Kenneth** *strips to his underpants as they speak.*

Walt   Al, strip the body.

Al   Sure thing sarge.

Body   Oh, this could be interesting.

Lieutenant   What'n hell's going on?

Walt *takes the* **Lieutenant** *downstage.*

Walt   Sir Bud's death must be covered up. We cannot let it be known he died of boredom. In two months' time our battalion is gonna be posted, who knows where. If we can hold on, for two months, then Bud can be lost in the withdrawal. But right now he's gonna be missed. My plan is this: we substitute Bud, with Kenneth. The guys here are so bored they'll never notice the switch. But at least we'll have a Bud.

Lieutenant   Walt this plan stinks. Kenneth old buddy put your clothes back on.

Kenneth *starts to dress.* **Walt** *draws the* **Lieutenant** *further downstage.*

Walt   Sir, you're ambitious . . .

Lieutenant   Am I?

Walt   You hope to make general by the time you're forty-five.

Lieutenant   I do?

Walt   You have an imaginative, individual streak in you which makes your command special. You are iconoclastic. In this mass, conglomerate fusion of wills, which is the Marines, your will stands out, on elastic.

Lieutenant   Oh really?

Walt   It's the measure of a good peacetime command lieutenant that your men are seen to be happy and fulfilled. We are trained to die by the bullet sir, not by boredom.

Lieutenant   You have a point there Al. Kenneth take

your clothes off . . .

Kenneth *strips.*

Walt   I hope, sir, that when it comes to promotion you won't confuse me with Al.

Lieutenant   Oh I'm sure that right after I'm promoted names will come real easy.

He walks back to **Kenneth**.

Kenneth, er, Walt and me have bin chewing things over. How would you like to join the Marines? Spend a coupla months this side of the fence?

Kenneth   I got to grease the combine.

Lieutenant   Holy Toledo. Hear that Walt? Any other pressing engagements Kenneth?

Kenneth   Well there's the dance tomorrer night . . .

Lieutenant   Oh? Where?

Kenneth   Parish 'all. Me wife drag me off to these do's an we ave to prat about all night long. I aren't that keen on it reely.

Walt   Who's playing?

Kenneth   Manny Cockle and the Big Four Combo.

Lieutenant   Walt, I think we should take this in don't you?

Walt   I should say so, sir.

Lieutenant   Should I wear my uniform?

Walt   Well, lieutenant, there's Mavis Rickeard, who likes a man in uniform, but Alice . . .

Lieutenant   Oh, Alice . . .

Walt   I recall, Alice caught your eye last time, at the hunt ball.

Lieutenant   And how ... Alice ...

Walt   Well she's keen on a tweed jacket.

Lieutenant   This is the latest intelligence we have on Alice now Walt ...

Walt   This is intelligence gleaned from the most reliable source in the field, sir.

Lieutenant   Who's that Walt?

Walt   Gilbert the policeman sir.

Kenneth   Hah!

Lieutenant   He told you Alice falls for a guy in a tweed jacket?

Walt   No sir. I was listening outside the police station window when she and Gilbert were quarrelling on the subject.

Lieutenant   And this is recent intelligence?

Walt   This is tomorrow, sir.

Lieutenant   Hell. You mean to tell me that you have gathered intelligence, verifiable information, that hasn't happened yet?

Walt   The purest form of intelligence when you think about it sir. Impossible to deny, because it hasn't happened yet, and yet, confirmable, because international law states that a future event is verifiable up until it has taken place and been denied. In the event of a denial, of course it hasn't happened, in international law, even if it did.

Lieutenant   Did it?

Walt   Yes sir.

Lieutenant   When?

Walt   Tomorrow sir.

Lieutenant   Who's on guard duty tomorrow night Walt?

Walt   Bud sir.

Lieutenant   But he's dead.

Walt   Is he sir?

Lieutenant   That's his body.

Walt   That's yesterday's intelligence, sir. I see tomorrow's Bud standing here right before you. Full of life and bursting with energy.

Lieutenant   It works Walt.

Walt   He isn't keen on dancing sir.

Lieutenant   Is that correct?

Kenneth   Me? I aren't that keen no. Could live without it.

Lieutenant   He could live without it. He's alive.

Walt   What did I tell you sir?

Lieutenant   This is clairvoyance, Walt. So long as it happens. Then you don't mind standing guard duty whilst we go and dance?

Kenneth   I got to grease the bloody combine, mister! International!

Al   'S a fuckpig to grease . . .

Walt   Have a cigar Kenneth.

Kenneth   Aw. Thanks.

Walt   Beer? American. The best.

Kenneth   Wouldn say no.

Walt *lights* **Kenneth**'s *cigar and offers him a beer. They wander downstage.* **Kenneth** *in his socks and underpants.* **Walt** *speaks urgently to* **Kenneth**.

Walt Got a guy here died a boredom Kenneth. The
bear is sitting on your back doorstep, just waiting for the
chance to walk in. Boredom is a disease, which spreads.
Could wipe out a battalion inside a two months.
Imagine what havoc the pinkoes could wreak with that
kinda propaganda. Bud's death must not leak. I'm
offering you a chance to serve your country. And the
whole of western democracy. The freedom of Europe
and the free world lies in your hands. Sorta freedom
that allows you to enter a field a farmer and exit a
marine. Come brother. Be Bud.

Kenneth *ruminates. He puffs on his cigar and drinks his beer.
He swaggers a bit. As he speaks* **Al** *hums the tune of 'The Star-
Spangled Banner', absently, to himself.*

Kenneth Oft, while traversin a field, my stride
becomes a swagger. My round shoulders square up and
these brows knit against a scorching sun. Where a dutch
barn stood, a wagon rolls. Where bullocks grazed,
buffalo chew. A rabbit scampers, and an injun falls.
John Wayne comes to mind as I drawl a command to
the cavalry and rooks circle, like vultures, high above
the plain . . .

Lieutenant Welcome Bud.

Al Howdy.

Kenneth Howdy.

Body Nicely put Walt.

Walt (*to* **Kenneth**) Thanks Bud.

Lieutenant (*acidly*) Nicely done, Walt.

Al Mustard sarge.

Walt Thanks Al. What to do with the body, sir?

Lieutenant Ah. Well. You know the Marines treat
their dead comrades with the greatest respect, this is a
tradition we're proud to uphold . . .

Walt   We're mighty close to the cliff . . .

Body   Oh Christ bury me please. Dig a pit right here and cover me over . . .

Lieutenant   We could pitch him over the cliff . . .

Walt   Exactly how I read it, sir.

Lieutenant   Good. I'm glad I thought of it first. Pitch it over the cliff sergeant. Al help him out there. I'm gonna fix me some chow and dig out a tweed jacket. Kenneth slip into some pants willya an I'll lock y'in to the routine of things over chow and callisthenics.

Walt *and* **Al** *remove the* **Body** *and* **Kenneth** *picks over* **Bud***'s uniform. As the* **Body** *is carried out he waves to the audience.*

Body   Talk to you later.

The **Lieutenant** *sits while he waits for* **Kenneth***.*

Lieutenant   That Walt. He thinks of every goddam thing. For Chrissakes Bud who's the fucking lieutenant round here! Uh? I gotta think of something someday! I gotta teach that bastard smartassed sergeant a lesson! I'm iconoclastic Bud. In this mass conglomerate er, confusion of wills my will stands out on elastic. I hope to make general by the time I get to forty-five. I gotta see action to do that. I can't sit on my ass taking shit from a dumb turdbird sergeant who makes out he's some kinda guru! He makes things happen before they happen that's all! That's so simple it's stupid. It's so stupid I could think of something like that. Some day. But Walt has it coming to him. He's gonna get his.

The larks, which have been singing all through this scene, have reached prominence. The **Lieutenant** *notices them in the sky. He aims his weapon and fires a burst of automatic fire into the air.* **Kenneth***, now dressed in* **Bud***'s uniform, falls to the ground, terrified. A dead lark drops on his head. The* **Lieutenant** *picks the lark up and checks that it's dead.*

Lieutenant   Things are gonna happen so fast, Bud, Walt won't know which way to look.

Kenneth   How do I look?

Lieutenant   Oh you look smart, Bud. C'mon Buddy boy. Let's eat chow.

They go off.

The police station. **Gilbert** *stands behind the desk. He yawns.* **Walt** *enters. He carries a carton of popcorn and a wad of four hundred dollar bills.*

Walt   Good day Gilbert. Hard up?

Gilbert   'Ungry.

Walt   Here's a carton of popcorn.

He places the popcorn on the desk.

Gilbert   Aw. Ta.

Walt   And here's four hundred dollars that says you wear your uniform to the dance tonight.

Gilbert   Eh?

Walt   None of this tweed jacket crap.

Gilbert   I git four 'undred f'r an arrest.

Walt   We have an exacerbation up at the camp. Could repercuss. With me?

Gilbert   All right.

Walt   Talk to you later.

Walt *goes.* **Gilbert** *remains onstage but removes the popcorn and dollars from the desk and replaces them with a bucket which has a few cockles in the bottom. During the* **Farmers**' *speech he delves for a cockle and eats it raw. The* **Farmers** *of the parish, dressed immaculately in tweed jackets and grey slacks, invite us to* *the dance.*

Farmers
   We, the farmers of this parish,
   Care to inform you
   That tonight a dance
   Will take place
   In our hall.
   It gives our youth
   The chance
   To let its hair down.
   And all the day
   We look forward to it.
   People come from miles around –
   Rumford.
   And airbase personnel.
   Meticulous
   In our attire.
   Spruce.
   We prepare ourselves, well.

Gilbert *is down right, leaning on his desk.* **Grace** *sits down centre, applying make-up.* **Stanly** *stands in his undershorts stage left, ironing a voluminous dress. The* **Lieutenant** *stands up right shaving himself. He too is in his underwear. Near him, up left,* **Al** *stands, and on the other side of* **Al**, **Bud** *lies blindfolded, field-stripping and reassembling an M16.* **Grace** *wears a print dress.* **Stanly** *starts to sing 'Girls Were Made to Love and Kiss'. After a bar or two, the* **Lieutenant** *sings the same song, independently of* **Stanly**. *After a few bars* **Gilbert** *starts. It's sung as a round.*

Song

   Girls were made to love and kiss,
   And who am I to interfere with this?
   Is it well,
   Who can tell,
   I'm a man, and kiss them when I can.

When **Bud** *has reassembled the M16 the* **Lieutenant** *stops singing but* **Gilbert** *and* **Stanly** *carry on.*

Lieutenant   How's he doin Al?

Al   Ninety seconds sir.

Lieutenant   Good. Taken him through the small units tactics manual?

Al   Sir. Ambushes are murder – what are they?

Lieutenant *starts singing again.*

Bud   Ambushes are murder.

Al   And murder is fun.

Bud   And murder is fun.

Al   Didn't hear you shitkicker.

Bud   Ambushes are murder and murder is fun.

Al (*matter-of-fact*)   Hut two three four I love the Marine Corps.

Bud   Hut two three four I love the Marine Corps.

Al   Pray for war.

Bud   Pray for war.

Lieutenant   Callisthenics Al?

Al   Sir. Chinese pressups fingertips sacakashit nose only on the deck start up hut two faster fuckbird hut two faster . . .

Lieutenant   Liberty call's cancelled till I can look this man in the eye and see a Marine, DI.

Al   He's hacking it, sir.

Lieutenant   When you've finished here you can take him on a ten click hump round the perimeter with a seventy pack on his back and four 81 mortar shells hanging off his belt.

Al   I'll do that thing lieutenant.

Lieutenant (*matter-of-fact*)   United States Marines since 1775 the most invincible fighting force in the history of man gung ho gung ho gung ho, pray for war.

Bud *and* **Al** (*with only slightly raised voices*)   The United States Marines since 1775 the most invincible fighting force in the history of man gung ho gung ho gung ho pray for war . . .

Lieutenant   Oh Alice. I'm yours tonight.

Al   Saddle up motherfucker.

Bud *straps a seventy-pound pack onto his back and hitches a belt full of mortar shells round his waist. He and* **Al** *turn and are marching, marchez sur place. The* **Lieutenant** *splashes aftershave on, then smoothes his hair, what there is of it. Then he starts to dress, slowly and meticulously, in grey slacks and tweed jacket. Brushing his clothes before he puts them on with a clothes-brush his mother gave him. The whole operation takes him the entire scene to complete.* **Grace** *applies make-up,* **Stanly** *is ironing,* **Gilbert** *is chewing a cockle,* **Bud** *and* **Al** *are marching.*

Grace   Kenneth's bin gone a day and a half. I'm gettin worried now, 'bout the dance. No one seems that bothered that e's missin, but I gotta go the dance, else people a say where's Grace an Kenneth, they ad a tiff?

Bud *staggers.*

Al   Git up there move it out shitkicker . . .

They move off.

Lieutenant   I'll walk into that dance tonight and pull Alice not because I'm wearing a tweed jacket. No sir. But because I've bin told by wonderboy Walt that Alice goes for a man in a tweed jacket.

May *enters dressed in skirt, apron and corset. She goes to*

Stanly. **Alice** *enters the police station.* **Alice** *is dressed in a revealing get-up.*

Alice   Ready thun?

May   Where's the bucket?

Gilbert   What for?

Stanly   What for?

Alice   Dance.

May   Me bloomers.

Gilbert   I ab'm ad me dinner yet.

Stanly   Id'n in the bucket.

Alice   What e got for dinner?

May   I knaw. They'm in the roof. Stoppin up the leak.

Gilbert   Eggy tart I 'ope.

Stanly   Tid'n rainin.

Alice   Make sure you drink a glass a milk after you et it. Dun't wanne burpin egg up whilst we'm waltzin.

May   So what?

Lieutenant   That gives me a psychological edge over Gilbert, who . . .

Gilbert   Dun't burp.

Lieutenant   . . . will be wearin his uniform.

Stanly   Dun't need the bucket. If tid'n rainin.

Lieutenant   He'll wither at the sight of handsome me in a . . .

Alice   Put on that nice . . .

Lieutenant   . . . tweed jacket . . .

Alice   . . . tweed jacket you wore to the 'unt ball.

May   Where's the ladder?

Lieutenant   . . . and go sniff round Mavis Rickeard . . .

Gilbert   I dunnaw.

Lieutenant   . . . who likes a man . . .

Gilbert   Stick to me uniform . . .

Lieutenant   . . . in uniform . . .

Gilbert   . . . tonight, I think.

Stanly   What for?

Alice   Why?

Gilbert   Stick to me uniform.

Lieutenant   All I need is a psychological edge to . . .

May   Fetch me bloomers out the roof!

Alice   Bloody 'ell, why?

Stanly   What e want your bloomers for?

Gilbert   Cus I like wearin me uniform!

Lieutenant   . . . stimulate her animal instincts and . . .

May   Dance! Go dance in ya toad!

Lieutenant   . . . I'm irresistible.

Alice   I dun't wanna go dance wi no p'liceman I wanna go dance wi Gilbert!

Lieutenant   Alice is mine.

Stanly   Never wore your bloomers to the 'unt ball.

Gilbert   I am my uniform.

May   I've ad me picture took Stanly. People's gonna be scrutinisin me. Checkin, sayin, there's Mother May, ad er picture in the papers. She got er bloomers on?

Grace   On the other 'and and if I go on me own they

a say . . .

Alice   Right thun I'll go dance wi Benny.

Grace   . . . there's Grace, where's Kenneth?

Stanly   Aw.

Grace   They ad a tiff?

Gilbert   Benny's a twit.

Grace   When we ab'm ad a tiff.

Stanly   Ladder's in the sheep dip.

Grace   E've just gone. Missin.

May *goes off.*

Alice   Not 'alf as big a twit as you are.

Grace   But they a say we've ad a tiff.

Gilbert   You go dance wi Benny I'll arrest the bugger.

Alice   You arrest Benny I'll smack y'in the mouth.

Grace   If I say . . .

Gilbert   Come on thun, smack me in the mouth.

Grace   . . . e've gone, missin, they a say, aw, they've ad a tiff.

Alice *smacks* **Gilbert** *hard in the mouth.*

Gilbert   OUCH!

Grace   E've gone. Missin.

Gilbert *walks with purpose round the desk and confronts* **Alice**.

Gilbert   Right. You're under arrest. Where's your passport?

Grace   But we never *ad* a tiff! E've juss gone. Missin.

Alice   What you gonna do now Mr Chief Constable?

Gilbert   Lock e up.

Alice   Aww, Mr Powerful, I inna'fraid a you an your uniform you take at uniform off an put your tweed jacket on see if you got the guts ta lock me up.

Grace   If we *ad* a tiff e woulda greased the combine.

Stanly *has finished the ironing. He leaves the dress on the ironing board and starts to dress in a tweed jacket and grey slacks.* **Grace** *at the same time removes her print dress and dresses in a dress exactly identical to the one she took off.* **Gilbert** *undresses at the same time. The* **Lieutenant** *is completing his operation. When* **Stanly** *is dressed and* **Gilbert** *undressed,* **May** *enters with her bloomers on.* **Stanly** *takes the dress from the ironing board and* **Gilbert** *starts to dress in tweed jacket, grey slacks.* **Grace, Gilbert, May, Lieutenant** *all finish dressing at the same time.*

Stanly   There now!

Gilbert   Now what?

Grace   Wish we'd *ad* a tiff.

May   Come along Stanly.

Lieutenant (*pleased with his appearance*)   Right on your dying ass.

Alice   DANCE!

Lieutenant   Start swooning Alice.

Grace   If we'd *ad* a tiff . . .

Stanly *takes* **May**'s *arm and they start to go out.* **Stanly** *notices something and looks up.* **Gilbert**, *reluctant to go, transfers food from his uniform to his tweed jacket and slacks. Chocolate, fairy cakes, cheese sandwiches, cockles, all make the journey from pocket to pocket as* **Alice** *stands on and looks.*

Stanly   Hell.

May   Now what?

Grace   ... they could say what they like.

Gilbert   Got ave me dinner first.

Stanly   Started rainin.

Grace   And they'd be right!

Grace *goes off.*

Lieutenant   Ready for you now Alice.

Alice   'Urry up!

Stanly   Where's the bucket?

May   Gilbert got it.

Alice (*drumming her fingers on the desk, notices the bucket*)   Oose bucket?

Gilbert   Mrs May's.

Stanly (*a rare moment of power*)   Go git the bucket, or take they bloomers off.

May *crosses to the station desk.*

May   This my bucket?

Gilbert   Yeah.

She takes the bucket. As she goes out she notices **Gilbert**'*s tweed jacket and turns back.*

May (*with a glint in her eye*)   Smart Gilbert.

Gilbert (*doggy*)   'Kyou.

They all go off.

The dance. The parish hall. The **Farmers** *of the parish announce the band.*

Farmers   Ladies and gentlemen, fresh from his successful season down the Falmouth Dock an Rail Rock an Roll Club, Manny Cockle and the Big Four Combo!

Manny Cockle *and the Big Four Combo are wheeled on. He is an extraordinarily greasy prig of a classic macho mould, the Big Four Combo are all very short. He sings 'Once I had a Secret Cockle'. He croons it in a syrupy, sly, smiley way, calculated to make sensible women cringe and men jealous.* **Mrs May** *dances with* **Stanly**, **Archie Gross** *dances with* **Grace**. *Whenever* **Grace** *and* **Gross** *glide close they smile and scowl respectively at each other.* **Alice** *sits with her legs crossed, on the opposite side of the floor to* **Mavis Rickeard**, *who sits with her legs crossed. She is very tarty and all the men sneak glances at her. The* **Farmers** *of the parish all dance with themselves.* **Benny** *stands somewhere near* **Mavis** *and stares at her. The* **Lieutenant** *enters with* **Walt**. *The* **Lieutenant** *wears a tweed jacket, collar and tie, grey slacks.* **Walt** *is in uniform. His eyes find* **Mavis Rickeard** *who looks him up and down, uncrosses her legs and crosses them back the other way. The* **Lieutenant** *cups his hands and shouts in* **Walt**'s *ear.*

Lieutenant   Gilbert here yet!

Walt   Can't see him!

The **Lieutenant** *adjusts his tie and smoothes down his hair. He advances on* **Alice**, *offers her a dance, she reluctantly accepts and he sweeps her onto the floor.* **Gilbert** *enters in his tweed jacket. He eats a slice of apple strudel and rubs his jaw where* **Alice** *hit him. He sees* **Walt** *and shouts in his ear. The* **Lieutenant** *doesn't notice him as his face is buried in* **Alice**'s *hair.*

Gilbert   Bin a dead body washed up!

Walt *nods and takes a roll of dollar bills from his pocket. He hands them all to* **Gilbert**. *He doesn't notice* **Gilbert**'s *tweed jacket as his eyes are glued to* **Mavis**. **Gilbert** *pockets the money, along with the remains of the apple strudel, rubs the crumbs from his fingers and heads towards* **Alice**. *He taps the* **Lieutenant** *on the shoulder and elbows him out of the way, dances with* **Alice**. *The* **Lieutenant**, *cold-shouldered, registers alarm at* **Gilbert**'s *attire and heads for* **Walt**. *He shouts at him.*

Lieutenant   What in hell's going on here sergeant?!

Walt   Something wrong lieutenant?

Lieutenant   You bet!

The song comes to an end but the **Lieutenant** *doesn't notice. He keeps on shouting. Heads turn.*

THAT FUCKING POLICEMAN'S WEARING A TWEED JACKET!

Walt   Music's stopped sir.

Lieutenant   Where in hell do I stand now with this Alice!

Walt   . . . all make mistakes, sir . . .

Lieutenant   That all you have to say?!

Walt   There's bin a dead body washed up, sir . . .

Lieutenant   THE HELL THERE HAS!

Walt   I think we should discuss it . . .

Lieutenant   I say what we discuss round here and what we don't discuss! You're behaviour towards a senior officer, sergeant, is disgusting! I have it in mind to strip these stripes right off your arm! Right here and now! Right in front of these people here! Right where you stand!

He looks at **Walt**. **Walt** *looks at everybody else who are all looking at the* **Lieutenant**. *He is humiliated, he throws his hands to his face and buckles at the knee.*

Lieutenant   Oh Mother. Oh my God my God my God. Right. Er, (*Recovering.*) right. Er, strike up the band . . .

Manny Cockle (*sings*)   One two three o'clock four o'clock cockle, five six seven o'clock eight o'clock cockle, I'm gonna rock, around, the cockle tonight . . . *etc.*

Everybody starts to jive except the **Lieutenant**, **Walt** *heads for* **Mavis Rickeard**, *so does* **Gilbert**. **Benny** *heads for* **Alice**. **Gilbert** *arrives at* **Mavis** *before* **Walt** *and snatches her just in time.* **Grace** *collars* **Walt**.

Grace   Care to dance?

They dance. The **Farmers** *dance with each other,* **May** *with* **Stanly**. *The* **Lieutenant** *is caught in the middle of the floor and can't get out. They all jive round him.*

Lieutenant   I'll get my own back on you Walt! You haven't heard the last of this! I'll think of goddam something someday! I will! So help me I will!

He rips off his tweed jacket and stamps on it. **Manny Cockle** *chooses this moment to finish the song. Everyone stands and looks at the* **Lieutenant** *storm out. They then cast their eyes to the tweed jacket in the middle of the floor. A moment of stillness and silence. They all raise their eyebrows, then* **Stanly** *turns to* **Manny Cockle** *and requests a song.*

Stanly   'Kiss an Angel Good Mornin'?

Walt   'I've Got Everything I Need To Drive Me Crazy'.

Gilbert   'My Way'.

Gross   'Jezebel'!

Farmers   'Where Have All the Flowers Gone'.

May   'I Believe In Every Droppa Rain'!

To everyone's annoyance, **Manny Cockle** *strikes up 'I Believe'. They all shuffle about with their respective partners, unenthusiastically.* **Grace** *leads* **Walt** *downstage.*

Walt   Do I know you?

Grace   I'm Kenneth's wife.

Walt   Oh? Who's Kenneth?

Grace   No. Where's Kenneth?

Walt   How's that?

Grace   E left 'ome yesterday to grease the combine an e ab'm come back.

Walt   That's serious. What make of combine would that be?

Grace   International.

Walt   Wow. The grease nipples on an International . . .

Grace   Don't change the subject.

Walt   I'm afraid I don't know the whereabouts of your son.

Grace   Husband. I'll find im.

Walt *leads her to a corner. He sneaks a glance at the dance floor.* **Gilbert** *is dancing with* **Benny, May** *with* **Gross, Stanly** *with* **Mavis, Alice** *and the* **Farmers** *sit with their legs crossed.*

Walt   Let me say this lady. Kenneth is missing. I can't tell you where he is. You have an International needs greasing. We have an international situation to keep under control . . .

Grace   A man can't disappear without his wife askin where e's to mister. I'll churn the place up till I find im . . .

Walt   Whose side are you on lady?

Grace   I aren't at all sure. All I'm sayin is, the greasin bain't what matters most . . .

Walt   Lady we live in times when a simple squirt of grease from a gun, in anyone's hand could shift the delicate balance of things over the edge into the abyss and end in war, yes war. I'm a military man, an old timer, and believe me I've witnessed conflicts occasioned by less significant actions than that. Continue your search by all means, the people of this parish are less concerned about Kenneth than their combine, I know

that, but all I can say is one day Kenneth will return.
Go home and forget about him. I can't say more than
that.

He goes, leaving **Grace** *centre stage. Everyone is back dancing
with their partners again as* **Manny Cockle** *cranks to a close.
They all disperse, leaving* **Grace** *standing alone. A few stray
notes of music accompany her, as she says nothing, just thinks for
a while. She walks up and down, now and again looking as if she
might have something to say, but thinks better of it. In the end she
faces the audience.*

Grace   Hm.

She goes off.

*The Briefing Room. A large map of the area stands on the wall
side by side with a map of the British Isles. The* **Lieutenant**
stands with a pointer in front of the maps, facing **Bud**, **Al**, *and*
Walt, *who all sit. The* **Lieutenant** *is excited,* **Walt**
*disconsolate. There is a telephone somewhere, and a loudspeaker
tannoy.*

Lieutenant   It seems the body was washed up here.
(*He indicates on the map.*) Beneath the iron bridge. Now
luckily the body was covered with mud. But we know
that he's male, and white. This means he could come
from anywhere in the northern hemisphere. My theory
is this. He's a Russian.

Walt   Lieutenant . . .

Lieutenant   Not one word sergeant. This is my baby.
Let's look at the overall picture. We are here. Right on
the tip of Great Britain . . .

He indicates Cornwall on the map.

Now Britain is shaped like a funnel.

*He produces a funnel from somewhere, like magic. He holds it up
to the map to illustrate his point. The narrow end is Cornwall.*

If you were planning an insurgency operation. A propaganda mission aimed at the psychological overthrow of a nation, where would you land your agents? I wouldn't pour them in, at the top of the funnel. You'd need an army, no, I would *invert* my funnel, and have them enter, the nozzle. (*He points to the tip of the nozzle.*) Gentlemen we have here a nozzle situation, and goddam it, we are the nozzle.

Walt   Lieutenant this body . . .

Lieutenant   What is it Smartass?

Walt   Isn't it Bud?

Lieutenant   Bud is here.

Walt   No the real Bud. Our Buddy, who we threw over the cliff . . .

Lieutenant   Now I didn't hear you say that . . .

Walt   Lieutenant we all know about it here. It's our secret.

Lieutenant   That's how it's gotta stay.

Walt   But it's no use trying.

Lieutenant   Let me try something now Walt. Bud.

Bud   Sir?

Lieutenant   Stand up Bud.

Bud *stands.*

Lieutenant   What's your name Bud?

Bud   Bud.

Lieutenant (*to* **Walt**)   That's Bud.

Walt   OK. Now the guy, the villager, who's gone missing . . .

Lieutenant   Yup . . .

Walt   Kenneth . . .

Lieutenant   There must be a cell of at least five
agents here already. Maybe more. They've taken
Kenneth, he was a perfect shot to start on, round-
shouldered to denote passivity, impressionable, vague,
our file on Kenneth puts him out to be an ideal
specimen for brain-washing activities. He'll return in a
day or two a perfect pinko who will grease the combine,
convert his wife, and thus start the ball rolling . . .

Walt   But isn't he this guy here? Sitting next to me?

Lieutenant   Who Bud? Stand up Bud.

Bud *stands.*

Lieutenant   What's your name, Bud?

Bud   Bud.

Lieutenant (*to* **Walt**)   That's Bud.

Walt (*exasperated*)   But, he's just saying that. He's, he's
saying it . . .

Lieutenant   Stand up Walt.

Walt *stands.*

Lieutenant   What's your name Walt?

Walt   Walt!

Lieutenant   You just said it.

Walt   But I *am* Walt. I'm not Kenneth posing as Walt.
This is Kenneth, posing as Bud, I'm not dead, washed
up, I'm Walt.

Lieutenant   Seems to me you're displaying an
uncharacteristic lack of imagination this day sergeant.

Walt   I . . .

Lieutenant   Could it be you bin pooped? By a man in
a TWEED JACKET!?

Walt   Ohh this is bizarre . . .

Lieutenant   I dunno whether you know this Walt, but the bear is sittin on our back doortep, just waitin for the chance to walk in . . .

Walt   I told y'all this two days ago . . .

Lieutenant   Did you Walt? Ever occur to you that I might a known about it, BEFORE IT HAPPENED?!

Walt (*the light dawns*)   I see. You go right ahead lieutenant.

Lieutenant   What we have here is a pinko takeover of Great Britain. Not by force, but a brilliant, subtle, and blindingly simple, insidious psycho-subliminal saturation operation, wrought by experts so devious as to seem, at first sight, to be invincible.

Walt (*to Al*)   How can a dead body be invincible?

Lieutenant   Wrap it sergeant.

Walt   I'd like to register my opinion of this scenario as bullshit.

The telephone rings. The **Lieutenant** *picks it up.*

Lieutenant   Yuh? Yuh. Uh huh. Yeah? *Daily Telegraph.* Court and Social . . . wow. (*He takes his hat off.*) Uhh, yuh. WHAT!? MY GOD! Arrest him Gilbert, bring him up here, and fast!

He slams the phone down, glowers at **Walt**.

Bullshit huh? There's a Chinaman out there! Wandering around! Plain as day! Making out he's the fucking RECTOR!

Walt   Could be a simple explanation.

Lieutenant   So the Chinese are in on this. I suspected they would be. They are after all the experts when it comes to subliminal auto-suggestion. What I hadn't bargained for was when. We must act fast . . .

Walt   You're way ahead a me lieutenant.

Lieutenant   Then catch up. There's no time to take this higher. We must act on my own initiative.

On another part of the stage **Gilbert** *and the* **Rector** *walk, handcuffed together, marche sur place.*

Rector   Where be us goin?

Gilbert   Up the camp.

Rector   Ah.

Gilbert   Yuh.

Rector   Huh.

Gilbert   If I was a Chinaman I a make damn sure I ad a passport with me when I set forth in the parish.

Rector   I got a passport someplace, up the vestry.

Gilbert   Thass easy to say buster.

Rector   Twas only a li'l joke, this Chinese scat . . .

Gilbert   I'm a p'liceman. My jokes come in uniform. Blue one for a copper. Dog collar for a rector. Off duty tweed jackets is worn. Thass ow it was an always shall be. (*He rubs his jaw where* **Alice** *hit him.*) Bloody Alice.

Rector   What?

Gilbert   Smacked me in the gob.

They walk off, towards the camp.

We return to the Briefing Room.

Lieutenant   Counter-insurgency tactics. We round up anyone, I mean anyone, who has been acting strange, who might have been subjected to severe psychological disarray perpetrated by a Red agent. Now, how to go about this. Let's have it from the floor . . . Al.

Al   Lieutenant could I go play Space Invaders?

Lieutenant   What's up shithead?

Al   I just ah, I'll do anything you say, my head ain't together this day . . . What wi no liberty call'n all.

Lieutenant   OK you do anything I say, I say you suggest to me a counter-insurgency tactical concept.

Al   I think you should round up the whole village, get em in here, ask em if they're commies, if they say no they're lying so shoot em.

They all think about this.

Lieutenant   That's good.

Al   Can I go play Space Invaders now?

Lieutenant   Let's hear counters to that tactical concept put forward by Al.

Walt   It stinks.

Lieutenant   Ah, Sergeant Strategist has woken up.

Walt   It's a good tactical concept, it's what we're trained to do for Chrissakes, but I can see the parallels with Vietnam here. We went in to advise the ARVIN but it didn't work cus we didn teach em right. We blundered and used aggressive patrolling techniques which were not tailored to the geography or the social fabric of the country. I mean do we know what these people eat?

Lieutenant   Egg pie, cheese sandwich, fairy cakes, cockles.

Walt   Exactly. I think we should maintain a low profile, train a small guerrilla mission, taking into account their indigenous capabilities, and that way we come up on these bastards from behind.

Bud   Er ...

Lieutenant   What is it Bud?

Bud   Oo's what? You dunno oo's a pinko an oo id'n.

Al   Ask em! If they say no they're lyin, so shoot em.

Walt   Al I think you can go play Space Invaders now ... here's a dime ...

Lieutenant   No let im stay. He's warming to this ...

Walt   Could Gilbert be the hub of our guerrilla mission? We pay him well so he must be reliable ...

Bud   Hah!

Walt   Whaddayado with all these Joes once ya got em huh?

Al   Shoot em!

Bud   Tis brainwashin we'm talkin about innit? All the people a bin brainwashed into bein Joes, we gotta brainwash em back again.

Al   Listen turdbird, you're the guy who said he can't tell who from what. You get a guy in here you think is a commie who isn't, you brainwash him back again to what you think he isn't and he ends up what you don't want him to be and he goes back and starts over brainwashing people who are what you want em to be into being something you have to bring em back in here to brainwash em outa being ...

Bud   Ow dunnus just wait till they'm all brainwashed, then brainwash em all back again ...

Al   Just shoot em for Chrissake ... Go-od.

Lieutenant   I think, I can't be positive but I think, Al has a point.

Walt   Getting lost lieutenant? The ultimate decision is yours . . .

Lieutenant   Well Walt, in the past you've never been slow to advise me . . .

Walt   It strikes me we have two options. Shoot em, or train up Gilbert in counter-insurgency by stealth and reverse psychoanalytical subjection.

Bud   Gilbert?

Walt   Yah.

Bud   Shoot em.

Walt   He's capable of it, he draws a big salary . . .

Lieutenant   In that case, we'll leave it to Gilbert . . .

Gilbert *and the* **Rector** *arrive at the gate.*

Rector   How do we get in?

Gilbert   Ring the bell . . .

Gilbert *rings the bell. A bell rings in the Briefing Room.*

Lieutenant   Ah, that'll be Gilbert now.

Walt   I'll go get him . . .

Walt *goes out.*

Al   Can I go play Space Invaders now?

Lieutenant   Al, let me say something to you. At the end of all this we're gonna be heroes. Now my ambition is to make general by the time I'm forty-five. I'm iconoclastic. In this massed conglomerate, balloosion of wills, my will bobs out on elastic. And in the end, the reward isn't mine, it's ours. Cus I can't do it on my own. And we will (*Somewhere round here,* **Bud** *starts humming to himself the tune of 'The Star-Spangled Banner'.*) win Al, cus we are God's chosen people. Are you with me Al? No, don't answer, (*Close to tears.*) it was a rhetorical question, because I know, that deep down, you are with me, Al, and I know that Bud here is with me, and dear old Walt is with me. Because we are the chosen. So when next you think of Space Invaders Al, think instead of freedom, of God, his will, and put it out of your mind. I love you Al, I love Bud, and in the end I love dear ole Walt. I want you with me. You're coming along too.

Al   You got me lieutenant.

Lieutenant   That's just fine soldier.

Walt *arrives at the door. He greets* **Gilbert**.

Walt   Hi Gilbert. This the Chinaman?

Gilbert   Yeah.

Walt   Take the handcuffs off.

Gilbert   All right.

He releases the **Rector**. *The* **Rector** *rubs his wrist.* **Gilbert** *rubs his jaw.*

Walt   What the fuck you wear a tweed jacket to the dance for last night?

Gilbert   Alice smacked me in the gob . . .

Walt   Put me in the shit you know that?

Gilbert   Sorry.

Walt (*taking a wad of notes from his pocket*)   I'm gonna dock you ten dollars . . .

He hands **Gilbert** *the money bar one note.* **Gilbert** *places it in his back pocket.*

Walt   C'mon in.

He leads them in. As they go, **Gilbert** *takes from his top tunic pocket, from behind his two-way radio, a gingerbread man. He bites its head off.* **Walt** *enters the Briefing Room.* **Gilbert** *and the* **Rector** *follow.*

Lieutenant   What's your name?

Rector   Rector.

Lieutenant   Rector what?

Rector   People just call me Rector.

Lieutenant   People call me Lieutenant, but I have another name, which, for example, my wife calls me.

Rector   I aren't married.

Lieutenant   Are you a communist, Rector?

Rector   No, I'm a rector.

Lieutenant   A communist rector.

Rector   Church of England rector.

Lieutenant   Well Rector. Gilbert here tells me you're a Chinaman.

Walt   Unmarried sir, no dependents.

Lieutenant   You see you could easily be a Chinaman.

Rector   I'm a rector! I'm too tall to be a Chinaman!

Walt   Up in the North they grow to seven foot tall.

Lieutenant   Stand up.

Rector   I am!

Walt   If he was a rector he'd be kneeling sir.

Bud   Praying to get outa here.

Lieutenant   So he's an atheist Chinaman posing as a Church of England rector.

The **Rector** *kneels and turns his face to heaven.*

Rector   Please God get me outa here.

Walt   You see he's very short.

Rector   I'm kneelin down!

Lieutenant It's impossible to tell with that rigout on . . .

Al Shoot him.

Rector *stands, holds up his hands.*

Rector No!

Al Aggressive tactics when threatened. Trained in self-defence! If he was a real rector in the face of death he'd be counting his beads!

Lieutenant We got him!

Al Now shoot him!

Walt Aw go play Space Invaders!

Lieutenant Walt, let me say something to you. At the end of all this we're gonna be heroes. Now my ambition is to make general by the time I'm forty-five . . . In this mass, conglomerate gas station of wills . . .

Gilbert E was speakin Chinese on the parish 'all steps . . .

Lieutenant Jesus Christ!

Al The parish hall steps!

Lieutenant Who was there?

Gilbert Pretty well the whole parish.

Lieutenant Were they listening? Did they understand?

Gilbert There was a lot listenin to what e ad to say. Most I'd say.

Lieutenant How long does it take to learn Chinese Walt?

Walt (*resigned*) Five years sir.

Lieutenant My God they've all bin brainwashed!

Walt Looks like it sir.

Lieutenant   Gilbert. Go round em all up. Rector you stay here. Al, go draw some ammunition and patrol the bunkers. They could be planning a takeover of the weapons store.

Al   Sir.

He starts out.

Lieutenant   Al!

Al   Sir?

Lieutenant   Shoot on sight Al.

Al   Thank *you* lieutenant!

He runs out.

Lieutenant   Now then Rector, for such now I believe you to be. We have some brainwashing to be done.

*He leads the **Rector** out by the ear. **Bud** follows.*

Gilbert *and* **Walt** *are left behind,* **Walt** *is very disturbed.*

Walt   You and your fucking tweed jacket!

Gilbert   I . . .

Walt   That guy's psychotic, you know that? Means he suffers from abnormal emotional instability. Takes a tweed jacket to trigger off a bastard like that.

Gilbert   Sor-ry.

Walt   Some careers in public life Gilbert that's a smart quality to have. Gets you noticed. Wins votes. But in this scenario it's dynamite! Now where'n hell's that body?

Gilbert   Mrs May's.

Walt   Get it.

Gilbert   Now?

Walt   We need evidence. It's a fucking dangerous

ballgame Gilbert.

Gilbert   I might ave to buy it back.

Walt *takes a Pan Am bag bulging with dollar bills from under the table.*

Walt   Here's a Pan Am bag fulla dollar bills.

Gilbert*'s eyes stand out. He grabs the bag, takes it to the table, opens it and starts counting the money.*

Gilbert   My Christ almighty!

Walt *bites his thumbnail and thinks.*

Walt   I gotta brute this mess back into shape. Wire it down. I can't take it higher yet, Joint Chiefs'd laugh in my face . . .

Gilbert   Think I swapped the bugger for a bucket of cockles!

Walt   A lieutenant is a lieutenant until he's *proved* to be a psychotic. That's in the small units tactics manual. I must have a case. But proof. What is proof? When any action in this mad world is explicable. Untraceable back to its source. When you're working against a man who might do anything, and find a reason for doing that thing, and twist it to his advantage. Sanity is insanity blessed with authority. Evidence of insanity in that scenario is proof itself of – sanity. The chemistry alters and warps the mind and the minds of those around you till it is I who is insane and the mad one, the psychopath, sane.

Gilbert   Only get four 'undred for a live one . . .

Walt   Where to end it? If innocent people die it doesn't matter. I must walk when he walks. Run when he runs and jump . . . before he jumps. Gilbert.

Gilbert   Yes skip.

Walt   Do as the lieutenant says. Arrest everybody. Buy

the body back, then hide it. I'll send Al down to pick it up when we need it. If we live to tell the tale Gilbert there'll be a military hearing. If we don't, we'll be dead. With me?

Gilbert   Yup. Pronto.

Walt   Talk to you later.

Gilbert *starts out with the bag.*

Walt   Gilbert . . .

Gilbert   Yes skip?

Walt   Divulge none a this.

Gilbert *salutes and runs off.* **Walt** *goes in the opposite direction.*

Music, with a Chinese flavour. The **Rector** *sits, cross-legged centre stage. He smokes his pipe. His hands are crossed inside the voluminous sleeves of his Chinese cassock. The* **Lieutenant** *paces up and down behind him. We get the sense that the* **Rector** *is serene and things aren't quite going the* **Lieutenant**'s *way. After a while the music stops and the* **Lieutenant** *speaks.*

Lieutenant   You mean you're willing to be brainwashed?

The **Rector** *removes his pipe from his mouth, replaces his hand up his sleeve. The pipe goes too.*

Rector   I'm beggin to be brainwashed.

Lieutenant   Why Rector? Why?

Rector   Because I'm a tired man. I'm tired of sayin things to those who hear an dun't listen. I ask em when do your children first learn to kill? When you scat the bugger 'cross the ear to stop'n bawlin'? When you tell'n scat the bugger back who juss scat you? I say what do it

matter who got what? You take at I give e a scat. That
id'n the way to go on. Got to the point now where we
got iron out all that scat . . .

Lieutenant (*to himself*)   Sheeit. That's enigmatic.

Rector   I'm tired of seein things in a helpless light. I'm
juss tired a life. Perhaps if you brainwash me into bein
something I'm not, might give me fresh 'ope. Might
make me see things in a different way.

Lieutenant   The process of brainwashing is threefold
Rector. First, you break the victim down. Upset his
mental equilibrium, question his validity as a Chinaman.
Second, you convince him of the hopelessness of being a
Chinaman. You then build him up again, having infused
in him the advantages of being a rector. Seems to me
you're at a stage three already. But how in hell can I be
sure?

Rector   How can you be sure of anything?

Lieutenant   Sheeit. That's Confucian.

Rector   How can you be sure I'm a Chinaman? If you
brainwash me I might start out a rector. And end up a
Chinaman.

Lieutenant   I see now what Al was getting at.

Rector   And if I arrive at bein a Chinaman, how will
you tell?

Lieutenant   That's sure a simple one to answer!

Rector   Well?

Lieutenant   You *are* a Chinaman for Chrissakes!

Rector   Then brainwash me.

Lieutenant   Dammit Rector I sure as hell will!

Music. The path to the camp. **Gilbert** *strides, marche sur* *place. Behind him in a line, handcuffed together, are* **May**, **Stanly**, **Gross**, **Alice** *and three* **Farmers** *of the parish.* **Gross** *limps.*

Gross   Ease the pace Gilbert. Me toe's throbbin'.

Alice   Where be us goin?

Gilbert   Camp.

Alice   For?

Gilbert   Aren't divulgin.

Alice   *Musta* done *summin* wrong.

Gross   Where's Grace?

Alice   She scat when she 'eard the 'andcuffs clickin.

May   Tis the cat dyin what baffled me. Cats dun't die sudden. Cats start dyin the day they'm born. Dun't juss drop dead like at. They d'go all mangy and lose their whiskers. They go off their food an 'uddle. Bloody baffled me that cat.

Farmers   We, the farmers of this parish . . .

Alice   Belt up.

Gilbert *takes a bun from his pocket and starts eating it.*

Gross   Bloody toe's killin me!

Alice   Tch!

Stanly   Gilbert!

Gilbert   What!

Stanly   Where d'y git that BUN!

They all march off, to reveal the **Body** *sitting in his armchair, with the cat on his lap. He sings a song.*

Body (*sings*)
    I'm the only one left,
    It seems.

The rest are arrested
And gone.
And that is, perhaps,
As it should be,
When all is said and done.
We answer only
To the sun,
Who stands in heaven,
Hot and white.
Above God,
In my estimation.
On the day that sun
Is brought down to earth
To burn a hole
In our destination –
Will we,
On that day only,
Think again?

His song comes to an end. He stays in his armchair. He views the next scene from the armchair. From here to the end of the play he is never off, always insinuating himself into the action, being part but unseen. He keeps the cat with him.

*The brig. The **Rector** sits, as before, cross-legged centre stage, his hands in his sleeves. He is Buddha-like, in a trance. The **Lieutenant** leans on the wall, in shirtsleeves, sweating. He's exhausted after the brainwashing. **Bud**, **Walt**, **Gilbert** enter with the parish, all handcuffed.*

Gilbert   I arrested every bugger I could lay 'ands on. One's missin.

Lieutenant   Who's that?

Gilbert   Grace Gross.

May   Just 'appen to be is sister.

Gilbert   She runned off.

Alice 'Fraid a what is mother might say.

May Too fond of is stomach.

Stanly Whass goin on ere?

Farmers The farmers of this parish . . .

Lieutenant SILENCE! Seven. That'll do to start with. Time check Bud?

Bud *looks at his watch.* **Walt** *hands* **Gilbert** *a massive wad of dollar bills.* **Gilbert** *pockets them.*

Bud 22.08.

Lieutenant Good. Lock em in here with the Rector. Cool em off then we'll go into action after chow.

The **Lieutenant, Bud, Walt** *and* **Gilbert** *go off. The parish huddles round the* **Rector**. *Music. The* **Body** *sings a song. It is a fast rock number with a slow intro.*

Slow intro.

Body *(sings)*
    Now that I am dead,
    And my short life is through,
    I feel like a newborn child,
    Whose instincts are but two.
    To sleep and suck his mother's breast,
    I have no other yearning,
    To sleep and suck his mother's breast.
    All, the rest,
    Is learning . . .

Fast verse.

    My skin of protection
    Was more than complexion
    And something to wash in the morning.
    It covered my shame
    And my greed and my lies,
    It covered my pride

When I unzipped my flies,
It covered my hatred and fawning.
But now that I'm dead
My skin it has fled,
I'm free of my hang-ups,
I'm free of my dreads,
and I'm free of my fear –
Of yawning . . .

Yawn chorus. The musicians play the chorus and the **Body** *yawns an enormous yawn through it. Then he speaks to the parish.*

Body   That was the chorus . . . if you feel you can join in, without losing your skin . . . you're welcome . . .

He sings the verse once more and then yawns through the chorus. They all yawn with him, except the **Rector**, *who's in a trance, and* **Stanly**, *who wears a gasmask. At the end the* **Body** *melts into the background and the parish is still yawning.* **May** *emerges from her yawn and stands. She paces.*

May   Ow long they ad us in ere?

Stanly   Siddown.

May   Tis a disgrace. If I was on speakin terms with the mayor I a complain. Rector. Rector!

Alice   E's asleep.

May   Wake up Rector.

The **Body** *wakes the* **Rector**.

Rector   Uuuugghhhh. (*A long groan.*)

May   Uh?

Gross   Huh!

Stanly   Gyat.

Farmers   Er . . .

May   Yaddap!

Alice   Hah!

May (*to* **Alice**)   What?

Rector   Awww.

May   Sshh!

Alice   Tch!

Rector (*sings, weakly*)   Arise, ye starvelings from your slumbers . . .

May   E's singin.

Gross   'Ymn. Singin 'ymn.

Rector (*sings*)   Arise ye criminals of want . . .

May   Hmm.

Rector   For reason in revolt now thunders . . .

May   Sound like a Charles Wesley.

Gross   Tis definitely Methodist.

Rector   . . . and gone is the age of cant.

May   Thass early Methodist. Good strong tune.

Rector (*sings in Chinese*)

May   Damme e've reverted back to Chinese.

Stanly   I dun't like it.

May   None of us *like* it Stanly.

Gross   I never sung that when I was a Methodist.

May   Yaddap! Never was a Methodist.

Gross   Neither was e.

May   E'm a rector! They d'cross-fertilise!

Alice   So tis a Methodist 'ymn, so what.

May   Sing it again Rector. Rector!

Alice   E's asleep.

May   Wake up Rector.

The **Rector** *wakes up.*

Rector   Uh?

May   Sing it again, in English.

Rector (*sings*)   Arise ye starvelings from your
slumbers . . .

May   Stop! Stanly write it down. 'Arise ye starvelins
from your slumbers.'

Stanly   Oo got a pen?

All   I ab'm.

Farmers   We, the farmers of this parish, have a
cowlick.

One takes a cowlick from his pocket and hands it to **Gross**.

May   Cowlick. Use that. 'Arise ye starvelins from your
slumbers.'

Stanly   Oo got paper?

May   On the wall! Write it on the wall!

Gross *writes on the wall as the* **Rector** *sings the next line.*

Rector   Arise ye criminals of want . . .

May   Stop! 'Arise ye criminals of want.' Alice.
Remember that . . . Go on Rector.

Rector   For reason in revolt now thunders . . .

Alice   'Arise ye criminals of want.'

Gross   Tis old language see.

May   Yaddap! 'For reason in revolt now thunders.'
Stanly. Remember that.

Rector   And gone is the age of cant.

Alice Cant. Can't what?

Rector Can't ... go on ...

He slumps back into unconciousness.

May Go on, that was the next two words.

Gross Dun't want they do e?

May Thass the next line, start the next line. Go on, put em down, underneath. Go on.

Gross Go on.

May Yes, go on, go on ...

He writes it on the wall.

What we got thun?

They all stand back to look.

Alice Summin about revolt.

May 'Reason, in revolt, now thunders. Reason, in revolt, now thunders.' Thunder. Thunder. Thunder.

Gross That rhyme with slumber.

May Slumber. Slumber. Slumber.

Gross 'Arise ye starlins from your ... lumber ...' Thass it, tid'n slumber tis lumber. Tid'n starvelins tis starlins! Git up out the trees!

Alice What is starvelin anyhow.

Gross Zactly, tis a warnin ... e'm tellin we to bugger off ... We'm the starlins, arise, out the lumber, piss off 'ome e say, exit rapid through the winder!

Alice What winder?

Gross Damme through the door thun.

Alice Come on thun I dun't need tellin twice.

May Halt! Whas this 'criminals of want'. E'm tellin we

we done summin wrong, we gotta sort out what that is. We can run now but they a catch up wi we. We got unravel what we done!

Stanly   You knaw I got a feelin I've 'eard this ere 'ymn before. Next verse got cockles in it.

May   Cockles!

Stanly (*sings*)
  Go on, and bring home all the cockles,
  Carry them humble to the font . . .

May   Awww Stanly . . .

Stanly   Charlie Bate used to play it on is accordion, down the Ring O' Bells . . .

May   Tis a bloody 'ymn!

Alice   If we sing it, might make more sense . . .

May   Thass a damn good idea.

Gross   Which version, starlins?

May   Starvelins. Stanly give us a key.

Stanly   Mmmmmmmmm.

All   Mmmmmmmmmm.

May   Ready? And . . .

They start to sing the hymn. They sing it over and over.
Sometimes there's a pause when they get to the end when they try
to make sense of it, but always they start again. This can be
heard in the far distance during the next scene. It's too distant to
pick out the words, but the tune can be heard.

The Briefing Room. **Walt**, **Gilbert**, **Bud**, **Lieutenant**, *on*
another part of the stage.

Lieutenant   Now. We're all fully briefed, and fed.

Gilbert   Yes thank you.

Lieutenant   Time Bud?

Bud   22.30.

Lieutenant   Hm. Let's hear what they're saying to each other shall we? Before we go in?

He presses a button which activates a tannoy. The 'Internationale' can be heard through a tinny speaker. They strain to hear what's being sung.

My GOD! It's the 'Internationale'! The arrogant bastards! The communist anthem! On American soil! We got em!

Gilbert   Erm . . .

Lieutenant   What is it shithead?!

Gilbert   Juss like to say that in our circles an International is a make of combine . . .

Lieutenant *jabs his finger at the tannoy.*

Lieutenant   That's what we're all here for! THAT'S WHAT WE'LL ALL DIE FIGHTING! HEAR ME?!

Gilbert   All right all right . . .

Lieutenant   Er, Gilbert, let me say something, at the end of all this we're gonna be heroes . . .

Bud   Singin's stopped.

Lieutenant   Uh? Oh. Yeah.

Walt   So what are we gonna do about em lieutenant?

Lieutenant   We'll ask em if they're communists, if they say no, it's evident, with the information we've got, that they are lying. So we'll shoot em. Fall in.

They fall in.

Well, men this is the action we will all gain promotion for. I pray to God, that what we are about to do, is in the interest of democracy. Amen.

All   Amen.

Lieutenant   Let's do it.

They spring to attention, about turn, and are in the brig.

So, you even wrote it on the wall . . .

May   We ad to.

Lieutenant   Why?

May   Make out what it meant.

Lieutenant   The hell you didn't know . . .

May   Thass right we didn.

Stanly   Still dun't.

Lieutenant   Tie their hands behind their backs.

May   Now just 'ang on ere . . .

Lieutenant   One move and we shoot. Now get up. Put your hands behind your backs. Tie em up Walt.

Walt *starts to tie them up.*

Alice   Gilbert . . .

Gilbert   What?

Alice   We still engaged?

Gilbert   We're about to break it off.

Alice   They promoted you yet? To Chief Constable?

Gilbert   I'm retirin next week. Earned enough now t'open up a restaurant.

Alice   You was an agent thun.

Lieutenant   Cut the backchat willya?

Alice   I just wanna know why we'm ere!

Gilbert If Mother . . .

Lieutenant Wrap it Gilbert . . . You'll know soon enough.

Walt Tied up sir.

Lieutenant Now stand in line. One person moves, and Bud here has orders to shoot. He will shoot to maim. I don't want anyone dead until I've said what I have to say. OK Bud?

Bud Er, yuh.

Lieutenant Walt. What is the man doing with a gasmask on?

Walt They were issued them in the last war, sir. There was a scare they might be gassed and they got to carrying them wherever they went. It became a kinda security symbol sir, if you wore your gasmask everything would be OK. Some never kicked the habit.

Lieutenant After thirty-eight years?

Walt I sucked my thumb till I was seventeen, sir.

Lieutenant You sucked your thumb till you were seventeen?

Walt I had it beaten outa me at boot camp sir, back in Okinawa, it's a strange psychological phenomenon, Freud touched on it, sir. It has to do with change and the shifting of the individual's status. We have to have a constant in our lives. Something we can refer to as we experience an ongoing, altering situation. It's practically unheard of in New Guinea, where civilisation hasn't altered or progressed for thousands of years.

Gilbert I suck my tie when I'm 'ungry.

Lieutenant Do you Gilbert? And how old are you?

Gilbert Twenty-nine.

He takes the end of his tie and sucks it.

Lieutenant   Here, have a Nuttall's Minto.

He takes a Nuttall's Minto from his pocket and hands it to **Gilbert**, *who eats it.*

Lieutenant   Now see here. I'm gonna ask you a simple question, and how you answer will, to a certain degree, determine your fate. The question is this. And I'll spell it out, nice and clear . . . Are, you, communists?

All   NO!

Lieutenant   That's fine. Now Bud. Chamber a round, then shoot em. I think this will be messy, shall we walk out Walt, whilst Bud earns his stripe? In your own time Bud. See you for callisthenics . . .

He starts to walk out. **Bud** *chambers a round.*

Walt   Hold it Bud.

Lieutenant   Now what?

Walt   I'm relieving you of your command lieutenant.

The **Lieutenant** *stands down left, near the door, which is centre left.* **Walt** *is down right. The parishioners are ranged up centre with the* **Rector** *sitting in the middle,* **Bud** *is centre stage. He turns and faces downstage.* **Gilbert** *stands upstage of* **Walt**. *The* **Body** *is near the* **Lieutenant**.

Lieutenant   On what grounds?

Walt   Certifiable evidence. United States Marines Small Units Tactics Manual Paragraph D62 subsection 10a paragraph one . . .

Lieutenant   I know the manual.

Walt   If an officer, due to excessive duty, shell-shock, battle fatigue or boredom displays a tendency beyond reasonable doubt towards psychopathy, schizophrenia or any allied mental disarray it is in the sympathy of

supreme command for his under-rank to subsume
seniority and take over command. Subject to military
court proceedings at a later unnamed date.

Lieutenant   I KNOW THE FUCKING MANUAL!

Walt   Bud remove his insignia.

Lieutenant   Don't do it Bud.

Walt   Do it Bud!

Bud *does it.*

Walt   Now tie his hands behind his back and blindfold
him.

Bud *does this. They speak as he does it.*

Lieutenant   You're making a mistake Bud.

Walt   I have proof Bud. Just do it then I'll prove it to
you.

Lieutenant   He has no case Bud.

Walt   Tie him up Bud! Keep going!

The **Lieutenant** *is tied and blindfolded.*

Walt   Now gimme the weapon.

Lieutenant   Shoot him Bud.

Walt   Give it to me Bud.

Bud *walks towards* **Walt**, *hesitates centre stage as the*
Lieutenant *speaks.*

Lieutenant   He's wrong Bud I can have you court
martialled and shot it's in the manual he has no case
Bud shoot him Bud.

Walt   Don't listen to him.

Lieutenant   If there's any doubt in your mind Bud,
any question at all, stick with me Bud . . .

Walt   Gilbert . . .

Bud *alerts.*

Walt   Easy Bud. Just gimme a chance. Gilbert.

Gilbert   Yuh?

Walt   You hide the body?

Gilbert   Er, yes.

Walt   Where?

Gilbert   Tis down Mother May's.

Walt   Go find Al. He's patrolling the weapons bunker.
Have him run you down there in his Mitsubishi, pick up
the body, bring it back here fast Gilbert run! Let him go
Bud.

Lieutenant   Shoot him Bud!

Walt   This is evidence Bud.

Gilbert *goes.*

Lieutenant   What are you afraid of Bud? Sighta blood
make you queasy? Never guessed you'd crack Bud.
You're mustang material. Walt's cracked Bud but you
Bud, you can hack it. You're a soldier, you're a man. A
man, Bud, show us your skill, your training Bud, he's a
pinko Bud, he's the enemy, we gonna let him get away
with it Bud? Just you and me together Bud, there's no
one left, think of the glory, the promotion, they don't
promote you when you're dead Bud, you're a mustang.
Please Bud please, this guy's a sergeant, d'you think he's
told the half of it? Think he knows what I know? He
ain't so smart Bud, he's a dime-store philosopher Bud,
he's got it all wrong, he's wrong and he knows it. I bin,
I bin on the horn to Joint Chiefs Bud, they've bin
expecting this, monitoring it Bud, we're all behind you
Bud, the pogues, the heavies . . .

Walt   He's joshing you Bud, rear echelon know

nothing of this!

Lieutenant NO?

Walt No! Wait for the body Bud!

Lieutenant The whole of Europe's on a launch on warning did you know that Bud?

Walt He's kiddin ya!

Lieutenant We gotta act fast, there's no time, shoot him Bud!

Walt He's bullshittin Bud he's delirious!

Lieutenant Ignorant of this intelligence sergeant? You disappoint me.

Walt OK, where we got to then, NSC?

Lieutenant Beyond.

Walt We got DCL?

Lieutenant Negative. With SAC.

Walt Joint Chiefs?

Lieutenant On the horn to them.

Walt Then call for a dust off!

Lieutenant Too far down the pike sergeant.

Walt You mean we got CPOs out there punched BYPASS!

Lieutenant Tell me the time an I'll tell ya.

Walt 22.55.

Silence.

Gimme bypass time if you have it.

Lieutenant No dice.

Walt You have it.

Lieutenant   No dice.

Walt   If you have it how do you know it? If we ain't got DCL! See Bud he's fucking kidding, now gimme the weapon!

Lieutenant   That's Nebraska. We have DCL with Kneecap.

Walt (*resigned*)   OK, lieutenant let's brute it out. The world is about to blow up Bud and he's second-guessing me. Where will DCL take me?

Lieutenant   Joint Chiefs.

Walt   They on secure line?

Lieutenant   One way. After bypass time.

Walt   Then gimme bypass time.

Silence.

I gotta know bypass time for the right code.

Silence.

Lieutenant   Have yourself a sitdown sergeant. You're on rough turf. Is he sweatin Bud? Weasel outa this one Walt. Boy, did he think he had it all wired down but he's weaselling now, Bud, and I'm loving every minute. Every precious ticking minute.

Walt   You alerted Joint Chiefs?

Lieutenant   Uh-uh.

Walt   NSC?

Lieutenant   Nope?

Walt   JSTPS?

Lieutenant   Yup.

Walt   On the evidence of a dead body.

Lieutenant   And a tweed jacket.

Walt   You gotta be kidding lieutenant. You just gotta be kidding.

Lieutenant   There's no way a knowing Walt.

Walt   Bud.

Bud   Yuh?

Walt   You just let me put one call through to JSTPS. One call huh?

Lieutenant   Don't risk it, Bud.

Bud   I . . . I . . . dunnaw . . .

Walt   Bud. You're confused. You dunno who or what'n hell to believe. If I can prove to you Bud, just exactly ascertain who in hell you are, will you drop your weapon and allow me to make my call?

Lieutenant   What's your name Bud?

Bud   Bud.

Lieutenant   That's Bud.

Walt   Turn round Bud.

Bud *turns round. He's facing upstage, his back to the audience, facing the parish. They stare at him blankly.* **Walt** *moves up to* **Bud**'s *eyeline, remains stage right. The* **Body** *gives* **Mrs May** *her cat.*

Walt   We don't have any time. Now I'm gonna ask you all a simple question. How you answer will, to a certain degree, determine your fate. The question is this. I'll spell it out, nice and simple. Do – you – know – this – man?

All   NO!

Walt (*disbelief*)   Why do you say that? Why do you say it? Take your hat off Bud! Look at him! Look at him! (*Distraught.*) Drop your shoulders Bud! Look at him! Look at his face! Archie Gross for Chrissake! He's your fucking son!

Gross (*blankly*)   I aren't Archie Gross. Archie Gross wouldn land isself in the shit like iss. Archie Gross is a schemin, clever man. Archie Gross lead, where others follow. Archie Gross is a respected member of the community. Buster. I id'n no Archie Gross.

Walt   Mrs May! Look at him! Who is he?!

May   Archie Gross. You kill my cat? He killed my cat. So it seem to me. While I was out the room. Wrung the bugger's neck. Dishin up the tea.

Walt   Alice!

Alice   Twad'n my fault e wore a tweed jacket. Too scared a what is mother might say. Too fond of is stomach.

Walt   Stanly!

Stanly *is asleep*.

Walt (*points at the* **Farmers**)   YOU!

The following chorus occurs simultaneously with the ensuing dialogue, so **Walt** *speaks as soon as they start their rigmarole. They speak slowly and solemnly.*

Farmers
  We, the farmers of this parish,
  Smack our offspring
  When they misbehave.
  In the way our fathers taught us.
  Hit back, they said,
  And give as good as got.
  We came to no harm.
  And we acquiesced
  In all our fathers said.
  Our fathers were wise,
  And their fathers' eyes
  Though dead,

Were constantly upon them.
That way we keep
The generations steadfast.
We know what is right
Is right.
Because it happened
In the past.
We will never sway from that.

Walt   LOOK AT HIM! LOOK AT HIM! HE'S
KENNETH! HE'S KENNETH! LOOK AT HIM!

Lieutenant   It's no use sergeant.

Walt   He's your own fucking flesh and blood! He was
about to shoot you for . . .

He stops and realises what he's just said.

Sheeit.

*Al enters stage left. Behind the **Lieutenant**, opposite **Walt**.*

Walt   Al! Where's the body?

Al   What's goin on sarge?

Walt   WHERE'S THE BODY?!

Al   Right out here, you wannit?

Walt   Bring it in here for fucksake you hear? Lay it
out right there!

*He indicates downstage centre. **Al** goes out. **Walt** turns back to
the parish. The **Body** lies down where **Walt** indicated.*

Walt   Now. We have the body . . .

*He sneaks a look downstage and sees the **Body**. He turns back
and the **Body** gets up and returns to where he came from. As
Walt speaks, **Al** brings in **Grace** and lays her out downstage.
She is messy, covered in blood with one eye shot out.*

Walt   . . . I'm gonna ask Al to identify the body. He
will tell us that it is Bud, whom we pitched over the

cliff, and then I will ask Kenneth to tell us all who the fuck he is if that's Bud. Al tell us who the body is.

Al   I'm fucked if I know.

Walt *turns and sees* **Grace**. **Bud** *turns too. The* **Farmers** *stop speaking, silence.*

Walt   THAT'S THE WRONG FUCKING BODY! WHERE'S THE BODY?!

Bud *is studying* **Grace**, *recognition dawning.* **Al** *doesn't know what* **Walt***'s talking about.*

Walt   Where's Gilbert?

Al   That the cop?

Walt   For fucksake!

Al   He bought the ranch back there.

Walt (*incredulous*)   You zapped him!?

Bud, *who has been studying* **Grace**, *goes and kneels by her to take a closer look as they speak.*

Al   He's right out here you wannim brung in?

Walt   What you frag im for?

Al (*indicates* **Lieutenant**)   He tole me to. Shoot on sight. Place was crawlin with them.

Walt   Al . . .

Al   What's up with the looey? (*The* **Lieutenant**.)

Walt   He's cracked Al. Look we're busting heavies liberty call huh? Here's a dime, go play Space Invaders . . . gimme time to think, here's a dime, beat it!

He flicks **Al** *a dime and* **Al** *goes.* **Walt** *stands in the middle, confused. The* **Body** *unties the* **Lieutenant** *but doesn't remove his blindfold. Music. As he unties the* **Lieutenant**, *he speaks to* **Walt**, *reminding him of an earlier deliberation.*

Body The chemistry alters, warps the mind and the minds of those around you. Till it is I who is insane, and the mad one, the psychopath, sane.

Walt *emerges from his reverie.*

Walt Lieutenant. I was wrong. Down-rank me. Shoot all these people here. They are pinkoes. But please, we gotta call off bypass. Shoot em Bud, then we'll call off bypass. Is that a deal lieutenant?

Lieutenant What's the time Walt?

Walt 22.45.

Lieutenant It could be a deal Walt, if we act fast.

Bud 'Old on.

Walt What?

Bud This is Grace.

Walt So what the fuck who it is Bud, c'mon, shoot em!

Bud I'm not Bud. I'm Kenneth. This is Grace. My wife. Grace. What you shoot er for?

Walt You heard Al, she was caught blowing up a United States weapons store, she's a pinko guerrilla Bud!

Kenneth Look at er! Look at er!

He rises and walks to the **Lieutenant**, *who is still blindfolded. He screams in his face.*

LOOK AT HER!

The **Body** *removes the* **Lieutenant**'s *blindfold. The* **Lieutenant** *looks at his watch.*

Lieutenant We have two minutes.

Kenneth Don't move! Just tell me who I am. JUST TELL ME! Who I am! TELL ME! THAT'S MY WIFE! MY WIFE! TELL ME! WHO AM I! THAT'S

GRACE! TELL ME! PLEASE TELL ME! WHO AM
I?

Walt   You're Bud, Kenneth. Please, let me go.

Walt *makes for the door.*

Kenneth   DON'T MOVE!

Lieutenant   Bud, er, Kenneth, could we talk over this
a little more amicably? In the comfort of the De-brief
Room?

The **Lieutenant** *takes a tentative step forward.* **Kenneth** *is
shaking. He raises his weapon.*

Kenneth   Don't come any closer. Is this my wife? Or
is she a pinko guerrilla.

Walt (*quietly*)   She's whatever you want her to be Bud.
Need her to be. At any particular point in time.

Kenneth   What, what do I need her to be now? Tell
me. Tell me. I need to be told.

The **Lieutenant** *looks at his watch.*

Kenneth (*screams*)   DON'T MOVE!

Lieutenant   We have one minute Bud.

Kenneth   KENNETH!

Walt   Kenneth. She's no one you ever knew. She's no
one. She doesn't matter any more. To anybody. She is
dead. Forget her and think of those around you who are
alive.

The parish has walked down stage and are standing close.
Kenneth *looks around at them.*

Kenneth   Who is she? Do you know her?

They all look at **Grace** *and shake their heads.*

All   No.

Kenneth   Do you know me? Who am I?

They stare at him blankly. He stares back, at **Archie Gross** *naked and covered in mud,* **Stanly** *in his gasmask, the* **Rector** *dressed as a Chinaman,* **Mrs May** *holding her dead cat,* **Alice** *and the* **Farmers**.

The lights dim to blackout as **Walt** *walks through the door.*

Ting Tang Mine

Ting Tang Mine was first performed at the Cottesloe, National Theatre, London, on 23 September 1987 with the following cast:

Gonetta Bate	Lesley Sharp
Thomas May	Peter Halliday
Lisha Ball	Ralph Fiennes
Arthur May	Jay Villiers
Ysella	Caroline Wildi
Rutter	Antony Brown
Raw/Hoyle	Jim Millea
Ann Roscrow	Hazel Ellerby
Santo/Soames	Wayne Morris
Trefusis/Trice	Paul Kiernan
Hailsham	Leslie Sands
Jan May	Robert Glenister
Maude May	Di Langford
Betty Elder	Laura Calland
Gran	Joyce Grant
Colan	Craig Crosbie
Salathiel Trenannigan	Barbara Jefford
Preacher/Captain	Alan Towner
Blake/Moses Harvey	Paul Hastings
Martyn/Kitto	Grafton Radcliffe
Senara	Robin McCaffrey

Directed by Michael Rudman
Designed by Carl Toms
Music by Matthew Scott

This revised version was toured by Kneehigh Theatre Company in 1990 with the following cast:

Jan May	Giles King
Maude/Salathiel	Sue Hill
Gonetta/Gran	Anna Maria Murphy
Hailsham/Lisha	Mike Shepherd
Trefusis/Trice	Jim Carey
Rutter/Colan	Charles Barnecut
Thomas May	Dave Mynne
Roscrow/Betty	Mary Woodvine

Other parts were played by the cast

Directed and designed by Bill Mitchell
Music by Jim Carey

Act One

Summer 1815. **Gonetta Bate**, *a girl of indeterminate age, removes her shoes and socks by the side of the river, hitches her skirt and wades across, during:*

Song
> From Halifax to Hindustan,
> From Alpine peak to Baltic town,
> There's rivers deep, rivers wide,
> Rivers dammed and rivers dried.
>
> But this little river, duckfoot deep,
> This lazy trickle, half asleep,
> This teardrop on a mountain's cheek,
> Got all the other rivers beat.
>
> No Indus, Nile, Po or Rhine
> Cut so deep a boundary line
> As the one this river does define
> Twixt Brigan Bal and Ting Tang Mine.

Gonetta *climbs the hill overlooking Ting Tang and looks down at the count house, where Ting Tang* **Miners** *have gathered at the bottom of the steps.*

Gonetta Waterloo's won! Boney's crushed! Mr Prussia's on is knees! Britannia rules the ways!

Tom How far d'ya walk to tell us that?

Gonetta Brigan Mine!

Tom Oo sent ya, Shanks?!

Gonetta Coulda bin!

Tom Then tell im Mr Bonaparte stopped off ere on is journey down the south Atlantic for ounce a copper, but found none!

Gonetta No tin neither?

Lisha   No tin neither!

Gonetta   What e look like, Boney?

Arthur   Giant chap, wi two eads! Picked is teeth wi shovel 'ilts! Ad knees as big as Prussia's!

Rutter, *the mine captain, appears on the count house balcony at the same time as* **Gonetta** *is joined by a party of Brigan* **Miners**.

Arthur   We'll not work with these men Mr Rutter!

Lisha   Arm yourselves!

Ysella   Pick a rock to sling at em!

Rutter   Who're you?

Raw   Brigan men.

Gonetta   Sober, skilled, and lookin for work!

Ysella   Then emigrate!

Raw   We eard you ad a copper lode wide as the Ganges.

Gonetta   We eard today was count day!

Lisha   Send em off Rutter!

Gonetta   Go on thun!

Mrs Roscrow, *principal adventurer in Ting Tang, joins* **Rutter** *on the balcony. Her presence has a calming effect on the* **Miners**.

Roscrow   Who are these men?

Rutter   They're tributers from Brigan Mrs Roscrow, come to bid for work.

Arthur   We'll not work pitches with these people.

Tom   There's too many men chasing too little work. The prices will be set too low!

Ysella   We wun't ave em on this bal!

Tom   See em off!

Lisha   Break their heads!

Roscrow   Wait! We have a lode, the Great North Lode, which is at this time in bonanza. New shafts are to be sunk, and the set worked back along –

Arthur   Be worked out in a week!

Roscrow   That is a risk my fellow adventurers and I have decided to take.

Lisha   That lode wun't last.

Roscrow   It shows signs that it might.

Lisha   Who the hell advised y'on that one?

Roscrow   Good advice was sought –

Lisha   Rutter! Spale the bastard for tellin lies!

Arthur   Wide lode like that could stop dead in a fathom, ask any bloody tributer and e'll tell ya that!

Gonetta   Start the biddin!

Lisha   No!

Roscrow   Mr Rutter, would you auction one pitch?

Rutter   Jonas Hawken's pitch.

Roscrow   At what price did this pitch sell last month?

Rutter   One and eight.

Roscrow   Thank you.

A tense silence while **Rutter** *describes the pitch.*

Rutter   Jonas Hawken's pitch from the ladder winze so far as Halebeagle shaft from the thirty-fathom level so high as to join Amos Nicholl's pitch . . .

Lisha (*interrupting*)   Ten bob a ton!

Rutter   Too high Mr Ball. I've set this pitch at five shillin a ton.

Raw   Four'n six a ton!

Tom   Four bob.

Lisha   I'll dig it for three and nine.

Santo   Three bob.

Raw   Two'n nine!

Tom   Two and six!

Arthur   One and eight!

Raw   One shillin!

Lisha   Christ, 'ear that?

Santo   Sixpence!

Lisha   Fourpence!

Arthur   Thruppence!

Santo   Tuppence!

Tom   One penny a' penny!

Raw   Penny!

Lisha (*appealing to* **Roscrow**)   A penny bloody pitch!

Rutter (*calls up to* **Raw**)   What's your name son?

Raw   Raw.

Rutter *throws a pebble in the air. They all watch it drop to the ground. When it falls,* **Rutter** *says:*

Rutter   Raw. Taker.

Arthur   You can't dig ore at a penny a bloody ton!

Roscrow   If you don't like it you can bid again next month or go to another bal. You're free to come and go. These men are too.

Trefusis   We're different to these people Mrs Roscrow. We've never got on with em. We d'mix with the Polgooth crowd and they're more inclined to Trewhiddle.

Tom (*to the Brigan* **Miners**)   Will you people leave us to Ting Tang if we swear an oath?

Gonetta   Oath to what?

Tom   Oath that we will never cross the river into Brigan and bid against you if your mine start producin copper again.

Gonetta   On what will you swear this oath?

Tom   Book of Revelation.

Raw   Go on thun!

Roscrow *and* **Rutter** *return to the count house.*

Tom (*looking round*)   Didn't bring no militia with ya didya?

Gonetta   No.

Tom *swears on oath. As he does so, the* **Miners** *melt away until by the end* **Trefusis** *and* **Tom** *are the only two left.*

Tom   . . . and cast him into the bottomless pit, and shut him up, and set a seal on him that he shall deceive the nations no more till a thousand years be fulfilled.

Trefusis   Christ in hell thass some oath Tom. Thass an oath not to be broke Tom. Ezekiel woulda sent em off, or the Booka Job. Revelation? Thass a desperate oath Tom. Christ in hell Tom, thass some oath.

Tom *goes.*

Trefusis (*sings*)
 Thomas May and his son Arthur
 Dig cathedrals underground.
 They wield their cross and mitre
 Where copper can be found.

Their reward is not in heaven,
But closer down to hell,
Where night is everlasting
And the devil rings the bell.

Inside the count house, a long table is set with a white cloth on which are the remains of a sumptuous meal. Round the table sit the **Adventurers** *in Ting Tang. They drink brandy and smoke cigars.* **Roscrow** *enters the room with* **Rutter**, *who stays in the doorway.*

Roscrow   Continue the bidding now Captain.

Rutter *goes. A bell can be heard, off.* **Roscrow** *sits at the head of the table.* **Hailsham**, *an adventurer, speaks:*

Hailsham   What's goin on?

Roscrow   A disturbance Mr Hailsham. Some men from Brigan but they've gone now.

Hailsham   Good.

Roscrow   Mr Trice?

Trice *stands and opens a cost-book.*

Trice   Gentlemen and lady, Ting Tang Bal . . .

Hailsham   Mine.

Trice   I beg your pardon Mr Hailsham?

Hailsham   I adventure in a mine, not a bal. We'll have none of your vulgar slang here Mr Trice.

Trice   Ting Tang Mine is in bonanza. I'm pleased to tell you the Great North Lode is running rich and wide. Sadly we learned today that Brigan Mine, five miles distant, has ceased operation . . .

Hailsham   Come on, bugger Brigan.

Trice   Thank you Mr Hailsham.

Hailsham   And you can dispense with the
samplings . . .

Trice   That is out of order sir.

Hailsham   I'm a very busy man.

Trice *seeks approval from* **Mrs Roscrow**, *who nods
discreetly.*

Trice   I shall begin with the tribute miners.

Hailsham   Gross tribute.

Trice   Total tribute paid by us last month to the
miners was –

Hailsham   Quit the preamble.

Trice   Forty-one pounds, one shilling and no pence.

Hailsham *writes in a notebook.*

Hailsham   Highest?

Trice   Highest tribute paid was to Thomas May.

Hailsham   What weight did e raise?

Trice   One hundred tons from the twenty-fathom level.
(*To* **Roscrow**.) In order to raise this remarkable weight
of stuff Mr May worked no less than twelve . . . (*Consults
cost-book.*) forgive me, thirteen doublers.

Hailsham   What did we pay im?

Trice   Three pounds, ten shillings and no pence.

Hailsham   Oo got the least?

Trice   Lowest tribute paid was to Moses Harvey whose
pitch crossed Cauter Lode on thirty-two-fathom level
west –

Hailsham   Get to the point man!

Trice   He grossed one pound six shillin and no pence.

Hailsham   No pence no pence no pence here's a penny for ya!

Trice   Thank you sir.

Hailsham   How many ton of ore did e raise?

Trice   Thirty-two.

Hailsham   Damn slight.

Trice   Cauter Lode is slight sir, yes.

Hailsham   How many doubler did he work?

Trice   None sir.

Hailsham   Was e spaled for absence?

Trice (*calling*)   Mr Rutter!

Hailsham   Never mind Rutter I'm askin you.

Trice   Not that I know of Mr Hailsham.

Hailsham   Did e work full cores?

Trice   So far as the records for the month tell us, yes.

Hailsham   How d'you know he isn't leavin his best work behind and coverin it with deads on settin day?

Trice   Moses –

Hailsham   So when Captain Rutter re-sets his pitch at a higher rate of tribute up it all come to grass and Harvey Moses –

Trice   Moses Harvey –

Hailsham   Earns hisself a fortune! Bin done before.

Roscrow   Not here at Ting Tang Mr Hailsham.

Hailsham   How the hell d'you know?

Trice   Captain Rutter –

Hailsham   Captain Rutter id'n God Mr Trice. Mr

Rutter id'n Jesus. Mr Rutter, Mr Trice, knows not the
stations of the cross and Harvey is Moses in nothin
more than name –

Roscrow   Would you kindly make your point?

Hailsham   There's too many loopholes in the tribute
system. Money finds its way into the wrong pockets. I
move, whilst the Great North Lode is rich, we put the
tribute miners under contract and pay em by the day.

Roscrow   We don't work like that here.

Hailsham   Listen to me. You got Brigan Mine
exhausted. You got soldiers returnin from the wars, the
parish is rotten with idle men. Boney's defeat will knock
the market for six, prices will plunge madam!

Roscrow   Why don't you sell your share?

Hailsham   Eh?

Roscrow   A good speculator knows when to sell. By
your estimation the time is perfect.

Hailsham   By my estimation no bugger'd be daft
enough to buy.

Roscrow   I would.

Hailsham   What price?

Roscrow   Name one.

Hailsham   Four hundred pound.

Roscrow   I'm sorry Mr Hailsham. I can't offer you
more than three hundred and ninety-nine pounds
nineteen shillings and eleven pence.

Hailsham   Then I don't accept.

Trice   Here's a penny for you sir.

Trice *flips* **Hailsham***'s penny back to him.*

Hailsham   I'm a dangerous man to plot against.

Roscrow   I assure you sir, we're quite spontaneous.

Trefusis (*sings*)
 Now some say if a woman
 Cuts a foolish man to size,
 His fury clouds a narrow mind,
 He'll never more be wise . . .

Hailsham   I'll have my broker draw you up a
contract.

Hailsham *storms from the count house.*

Trice   Mrs Roscrow. That gives you a controlling
interest in the mine.

The **Adventurers** *clap and disperse.*

Trice (*sings*)
 And I say Mrs Roscrow
 Made Hailsham look a fool,
 He strode out pretty steamin
 And kicking like a mule.

Gonetta Bate *stands on the Brigan side of the river.*
Hailsham *approaches the Ting Tang bank.*

Hailsham   What's your name?

Gonetta   Not tellin.

Hailsham   Ere's a penny.

Gonetta   Gonetta Bate.

Hailsham *removes his shoes and socks.*

Hailsham   You from Brigan?

Gonetta *holds her hand out across the river.* **Hailsham** *flips
a coin across.*

Gonetta   Yes.

Hailsham   I heard the mine's shut down.

Gonetta   Why d'ya think I'm beggin?

Hailsham *wades through the river while* **Trefusis** *sings:*

Trefusis
No Indus, Nile, Po or Rhine
Cuts so deep a boundary line
As the one this river does define
Twixt Brigan Bal and Ting Tang Mine.

Hailsham *joins* **Gonetta** *on the Brigan side of the river.*

Hailsham   Wanna earn some cash?

Gonetta   No.

Hailsham   You don't?

Gonetta   I wanna stay poor and die young, starvin.

Hailsham   I eard Ting Tang and Brigan's deadly
rivals. See I gotta score to settle with Ting Tang, the
widow, know er? Roscrow.

Gonetta   Yep.

Hailsham   Reckon you could help me pull er down?
Wreck her little enterprise? Make her and Ting Tang
squeal?

Gonetta (*to audience*)   Don't ask much do e.

Hailsham   Take me to Brigan.

Gonetta *leads* **Hailsham** *off towards Brigan.* **Trefusis**
stays where he is.

The atmosphere changes. **Jan May** *appears as if from nowhere.
He is dressed in a bizarre mixture of exotic clothes, all slightly too
small for him. Loud check trousers, a military coat with gold braid
and huge epaulettes. A scarlet shirt with frills, multi-coloured
choker, a mis-shapen 'Napoleon' hat, and a bright yellow
handkerchief cascading from his pocket. He wears a riding boot on
one foot and a gentleman's walking boot on the other. He carries a
bulging carpet bag. He reaches the Brigan bank of the river, and
looks around him, as* **Trefusis** *sings:*

Trefusis
  Have you never bin to Egypt?
  It's a short day's walk that way.
  Have you never seen a Pharaoh king?
  Then set eyes on Jan May.

  Have you never seen a peacock?
  With its feathers in full fan?
  Then look across the river
  And set your eyes on Jan.

  Have you never seen a jackass?
  Or heard its empty bray?
  Don't look any further,
  E id'n far away . . .

Maude May, Jan's *mother, appears on the Ting Tang bank
of the river. She is dressed as drab as* **Jan** *is bright. She removes
her boots and hitches up her skirt as* **Trefusis** *sings:*

Trefusis
  And this extravaganza,
  Tis all about Jan May,
  Who crossed the parish border
  On his mother's back one day.

Maude *starts to cross the river.* **Jan** *notices her.*

Jan   Mother? That you Mother?

Maude *stops and looks up.*

Maude   Jan? Oh Jan! Aw, my darlin boy! My Jan!

Maude *crosses the river while* **Trefusis** *sings:*

Trefusis
  From Mexico to Jabalpore,
  With tired legs and feet so sore,
  He's staggered, sailed, rode and ran,
  All round the world and back again.

  But ere this prodigal tastes the lamb,
  Before e lays his body down,

This rolling stone won't gather moss,
There's one more bridgeless stream to cross.

Maude *has reached the other side and hugs* **Jan**. **Jan** *hops on* **Maude**'s *back and she wades in, transporting him back towards Ting Tang.*

Maude   There's bin plenty sightins of y'over the years Jan.

Jan   I bet there ave.

Maude   Lisha Ball said a man down Par said e saw you rowin a tuck boat for a seine net company.

Jan   Did did e?

Maude   That was eighteen eight. Lisha Ball said there was a man down Indian Queens told im you was married and sold your wife at Summercourt Fair for four shillin! E said you bought a pig!

Jan   Hah!

Maude   I said that id'n like Jan to do a thing like that, e never liked pig!

Jan   Hell! See that trout?

Maude   Hold still! I did not! Then last year, eighteen fourteen, Perrantide or Midsummer? Father was ome anyhow, Lisha Ball come round t'elp your father sink the well and I said g'day Lisha, any sightins? E said ab'm you eard? I said what e said Jan's dead! Your son's dead!

Jan   Hah!

Maude   I said e id'n dead!

Jan   How did I die?

Maude   I said now you listen ere Lisha Ball! I said boy Jan's runned off and we ab'm seed'n for nine year but that dun't mean e's come to any harm whatsoever!

Christ boy you'm some weight ... I said boy Jan's too
full of is own pride, too important to imself, to die
young. I said e's too damn pigheaded Lisha Ball! I said
e's safe inside some big house eatin butchers' meat and
tellin lies. Bugger id'n dead!

Jan   I arn't dead.

Maude   We eld a service for e anyhow, just in case.
Service of Remembrance. Just in case you *ad* died. Can't
recall oo twas oo, Primitive Methodists or Bible
Christians, aw I think twas the Thumpers, cus Betty
Elder's third usband, 'Arry, e got converted and runned
off. Joined the circuit, preachin. She never forgived you
for that, Betty Elder. Jan you've grawed big as a
bullock!

Jan   Bin eatin good butcher's meat Mother.

Maude   Where've e bin anyhow?

Jan   Bin round the world Mother.

Maude   Took e nine years? World id'n that big boy.

They are close to the opposite bank of the river.

Jan   I stopped off ere and there. And I was
shipwrecked three times.

Maude   WHAT?! You was SHIPWRECKED?!

Maude *drops* **Jan** *in the river.*

Jan   Aww, Mother!

Maude   You was shipwrecked? And y' ask me to carry
y' across the damn river?!

Jan *is drenched but he's managed to keep his carpet bag dry.*

Jan   Look at this! Look at it! Look at that! Aw Mother!
My best blasted rigout! Ruined! Thass my best suit! My
biggest hat! Look at it! Soaked! Colour's runnin, look at
it!

Maude *is sitting on the river bank, replacing her footwear.*

Maude   I suppose you wish to eat with us tonight.

Jan   My best damned rigout!

Maude   We got your grandmother still with us, your brother Colan's blind, your three sisters . . .

Jan   Three?

Maude   How many do e want?

Jan   Didn't ave any when I left.

Maude   They're out nestin, your father and brother Arthur's down bal workin doublers, I got food for four to feed ten then you show up out the blue.

Jan   I'll buy some butcher's meat.

Maude   You'll buy nothin! I got plenty ome without your charity.

Maude *and* **Jan** *have left the river behind,* **Maude** *striding out ahead with* **Jan** *waddling behind, arms and legs abroad. He suffers extreme discomfort with his wet clothes. He holds his bag at arm's length.* **Ann Roscrow** *approaches* **Maude** *from the opposite direction and* **Maude** *hails her.*

Maude   Oo! Mrs Roscrow! How's business?

Jan *arrives on the scene. He spies* **Roscrow** *and his jaw drops with infatuation.* **Roscrow** *stares at* **Jan** *with disbelief.*

Roscrow   Who's this?

Maude   My son Mrs Roscrow. Jan. E falled in the river.

Jan   I bin round the world.

Roscrow   Good grief!

Roscrow *wanders off, dumbstruck.*

Jan   Who was that?

Maude   Ann Roscrow. Er usband went to Jesus and left er oldin the fort.

Jan   Up Ting Tang?

Maude   Principal adventurer she is, shrewd as a cat. She once belonged to the Only-the-Sober Circle of Women but it was rumoured she elped er usband on is way to the hereafter so she left them after that . . .

Jan   Did you see the way she looked at me Mother? Did you see? Love! Love at first sight! In all the miles I've travelled round the world I've never set eyes on a woman half as beautiful as that. And she loves me!

Maude   There's a sinew of opinion, what ripple through the Tent Methodists, that she'm a witch . . .

Jan   Where does she live? How can I meet her?

Maude   Now the Bible Christians reckon she's a man dressed up as a woman and quote as proof the lack of children . . .

Jan   No children? Joy! Joy!

Maude   The Calvinists say tis er divine right to adventure in mines, and if er usband's gone before she'll more'n likely foller . . .

Jan   Imagine Mother, with your clothes all wet, clinging to your body, walking with your legs apart and your suit hangin heavy! Are these the conditions under which one falls in love?

Maude   I'd oped you might've altered in the last nine years Jan . . .

Jan   And she loves me!

Maude   . . . grown wiser.

Jan *and* **Maude** *have reached the top of the hill overlooking Ting Tang village. They look down on the scene below them.* **Trefusis** *sings a triumphal anthem to* **Jan**'s *homecoming.*

Trefusis
  Jan May! Traveller! Son of Ting Tang!
  None the wiser! Weary! And wet!
  World-wandered, love-struck man!
  Welcome home! Welcome home! Well met!

Betty Elder *washes her linen in the stream,* **Gran** *sits outside the* **Mays**' *house, with* **Colan, Jan**'s *blind brother, at her feet.* **Maude** *emits a blood-curdling yell.*

Maude   Look ere look! Look! Look oo's ome! Look! E's back!

Maude *rushes down into the village and* **Jan** *follows after.* **Betty Elder** *looks up from the stream,* **Gran** *and* **Colan** *don't show much interest.*

Maude   Look! Look! E's back!

The sight of **Jan** *in familiar surroundings is too much for her and she flings her arms around him and hugs him, sobbing.*

Gran   What the hell a you got on boy?

Jan   Tis soakin wet Gran.

Colan   What e got on Gran?

Gran   Three or four carpets.

Betty Elder *shouts from the river.*

Betty   You're supposed to be dead!

Jan   Ullo Betty!

Betty   We eld a service for you! Send y'on your way!

Maude *releases* **Jan** *and shows him off to the others.*

Jan   Colan, lost your eyes?

Colan   Lost em blastin.

Gran   Short fuse.

Colan   No I was tampin.

Gran   Rammin it ome too tight.

Colan   Twas a spark, from the bar, iron bar.

Gran   Too bloody lazy.

Colan   Christ in hell twas a spark, went up in me face!

Jan   Sorry to hear that Colan.

Gran   Where've e bin?

Jan   Bin round the world Gran.

Gran   Go Paraguay?

Jan   Paraguay? Oh yes.

Gran   Didya run into Dasher Smeely?

Jan   No I didn't. Just missed'n.

Gran   Bugger owe me money. Look'n out when you get back.

A distant bell sounds.

Maude   There! Thass the end a core and I ab'm thought about food!

Maude *runs into the house.* **Betty Elder** *approaches* **Jan**.

Betty   We eld a service for you! You're supposed to be dead! You're responsible for a conversion!

She pinches **Jan** *hard.*

Jan   Ouch! What the hell was that for?!

Betty   I arn't convinced.

Gran   She lost er usband cus a you.

Betty   E defied conversion. E was staunch against em all. Then we ad your memorial service, up Pasco Walters' barn . . .

Gran   No. Under a tree it was . . .

Betty   Twas a Thumper wannit? Preacher oo come round? Thumper.

Colan   Jumper.

Gran   Shaker.

Betty (*calls inside*)   Maude! You was a Thumper then wanne?!

Maude (*inside*)   When?!

Betty   When boy Jan died!

Maude (*inside*)   I left em after that!

Betty   Thumper. They're the worse of the lot.

Gran   Thump thump thump!

Betty (*to* **Gran**)   You dropped! (*To* **Jan**, *indicating* **Gran**.) She dropped! Dropped straight to er knees, soon as she got there! Straight to er knees . . .

Gran   I always drop. They dun't bother with e then. There's undreds claimed me for Jesus – Lutherans, Calvins, Primitives, Romans, drop straight to your knees at the lot and they think you'm one a them, but you gotta stay down. They get ya if ya git up.

Betty   Harry dropped, then e got up . . .

Jan (*to* **Colan**)   I thought er first usband was 'Arry . . .

Colan   They was all called 'Arry . . .

Gran   See?

Betty   All the while matey in the pulpit . . .

Gran   Under a tree it was . . .

Colan   Hot. June month . . .

Betty   His eyes was bulgin . . .

Colan   Whose?

Gran   Not yours . . .

Betty   E ad a luscious way a talkin . . .

Colan   Now then brethren, I'm gonna tell e a li'l bit 'safternoon 'bout eb'm!

Gran   . . . And a beard . . .

Colan   Heaven! Damme to Christ almighty in hellfire what do a crowda miserable sinners from Ting Tang knaw 'bout eb'm!

Betty   I knew Harry was gone when e got up off is knees and went up front, swayin . . .

Gran   E should never a got up!

Colan   Let's ask Abram! Abram bin up in eaven a brave while! (*Turns his face skywards and yells.*) ABRAM!

Betty   E was callin, swoonin, big man see, e ad tears streamin down is face, I was up the back there screamin 'Arry! Come back! Come back!

Colan   What sorta place is eb'm! Tell we down ere 'bout eb'm wille! (*Affecting a deep voice, looking down.*) Glory upon glories son! (*Looking up.*) That so? That so is a? I thought as much but these ere hellborn savages wouldn believe it!

Betty   E shoulda stayed where e was when e dropped!

Gran   She was there . . . screamin at im . . .

Betty   'Arry! 'Arry! Come back ere! 'Fore e lays 'ands on ya!

Colan   Come down! Thou great Jehovah! Bring thy stone ammer with e and scat the hard hearts of these wicked and perverse people! . . .

Gran   I said to'n, 'fore e got up, face flat in the dust, mouth fulla daisies, I said stick ere 'Arry, dun't let the bugger git old a ya!

Colan ... Oh grave! Where is thy victory! The day of vengeance is in my heart! Enter! Enter into the holiest! By the new and living way! Let the chains fall off your tongues!

Betty There was people stickin y'in the ribs, pokin about with their fingers ...

Colan Gimme Christ or else I die!

Betty Tearin the bark off trees ...

Gran Twas a sad day Betty ...

Colan Acquaint! Acquaint thyself with im and be at peace!

Betty Then e went ...

Gran Like a lamb in a trance ...

Colan Come out!! And let Sodom feel its doom!

Betty (*in tears*) Didn say goodbye or nothin ...

Colan Thou lewdly revellest in the bowels of God!

Gran Not a word. Not to any of us ...

Colan Where now is Lot?!

Betty Preacher chap got down off the pulpit ...

Gran Tree it was ...

Colan At Zoar safe! Where is his wife? Salt for pilchards!

Betty Took 'Arry by the hand ... and, and ...

Colan Great Og and Agog! Where are e?!

Betty Led im away into the yonder ...

Gran E's preachin imself now, under a tree.

Colan Followin Christ!

Betty All cus a you!

Betty *runs off in tears.* **Maude** *emerges from the house.*

Maude   Jan you want flesh or fish?

Jan   'Sorta fish?

Maude   Pilcher. Flesh is mutton . . .

Jan   Hah! Pilchard!

Maude *goes indoors.*

Gran   She's bin savin it up for ya, for when you returned.

Jan   Ave a?

Gran   Nine years she's ad that pilchard.

Jan (*calling indoors*)   I'll ave the flesh!

The men approach from the mine. A stream of tired miners, including **Tom**, **Lisha** *and* **Arthur**, *enter the village and make their way to their homes.* **Maude** *runs out with a plate of mutton for* **Jan**, *and scuttles back indoors.* **Gran** *moves* **Colan** *out of the way to make way for* **Tom** *and* **Arthur**, *who sit in chairs provided by* **Gran**. *They are too tired to notice* **Jan**. **Maude** *emerges with a bowl of mutton broth.* **Tom** *and* **Arthur** *put their heads back and open their mouths,* **Maude** *spoonfeeds them the broth. They are too tired to feed themselves.*

Jan   Ullo Father.

Gran   Dun't disturb im while e's eating.

Colan   Bin workin doublers.

Jan   Ah.

Gran   They gotta rich lode down bal.

Colan   Great North Lode. Go bal six in the morning, come ome six at night.

While **Tom** *and* **Arthur** *are being fed,* **Jan** *sits beside* **Colan**.

Jan   What do you do with yourself all day Colan?

Colan   Aw, sell sand, buy bones . . .

Gran   When e can get it . . .

Colan   I take ole donkey down, ole moyle, itch er up to the cart . . .

Gran   When the wheel dun't drop off . . .

Colan   Git the girls to lead me down there, down beach . . .

Gran   When they id'n raidin nests . . .

Colan   Thass nestin time Gran . . . Git the ole shovel . . .

Gran   When the 'ilt id'n split . . .

Colan   Dig up the sand . . .

Gran   If the tide appen to be out . . .

Colan   Load up the cart, and start knockin on doors.

Gran   When there's anyone ome.

Colan   I dun't get round to it that often.

Gran   When alligators swim in Mevagissey Bay.

Colan   There's too many snags reely . . .

Maude *has finished feeding* **Tom** *and* **Arthur**, *who are now asleep.*

Maude   Thomas. Tom. Wake up! See oo's ere! Tom!

Tom *wakes up.*

Tom   Whass for dinner?

Maude   You've *ad* your dinner!

Tom   What was it?

Maude   Boy Jan's back!

Tom   Jan?

Maude   Your long-lost son! Jan!

Tom   Jan!

Jan   Ullo Father . . .

Tom   Christ boy thass some outfit you got on . . .

Gran   Bal shag . . .

Jan   Tis soakin wet.

Tom   Where've e bin?

Jan   In the river.

Tom   In the river? 'Ear that Mother? Boy's bin in the river. What, on a boat in the river? Which river?

Jan   Mother dropped me in the river. Me suit's soaked. I bin round the world!

Tom   What e drop'n in the river for Maude?

Maude   Cus e was shipwrecked!

Maude *has piled up the dishes and is walking towards the stream.* **Lisha Ball** *runs up.*

Lisha   Maude! Maude!

Maude   Ullo Lisha . . .

Lisha   'Ear 'bout Jan?

Maude   What?

Lisha   E's dead now!

Maude   Is a?

Lisha   E got et be alligator in Paraguay.

Maude   Dear o dear.

Lisha   E'd bin round the world and e falled in a river they got out there and a big 'gator swimmed up and

swallered'n 'ole! E was sufferin discomfort before is
death on account e'd ad nothin to eat but monkey flesh
and soft fruit so tis best all round. Tis all over the
parish poor chap . . .

Jan What?!

Maude Jan wouldn get isself et be alligator!

Lisha E wouldn ave no say in the matter . . .

Gran E'd talk im out of it.

Jan Crikey!

Lisha (*indicates* **Jan**) Oo's this?

Maude That's Jan.

Lisha *is suspicious. He studies* **Jan** *and his suit.*

Lisha (*to* **Maude**) You sure?

Maude I'm is mother!

Lisha (*to* **Jan**) Whass your name?

Jan Jan!

Lisha Where d'y get this suit?

Jan Er, someplace, I forget.

Lisha Plymouth?

Maude E's bin round the world Lisha . . .

Lisha It's wet.

Tom E was shipwrecked.

Lisha I seen this outfit before.

Jan Where?

Lisha Someplace. I forget.

Jan Well ah, there's plenty more like it.

All (*disbelief*) Is there?

Jan   Oh, practically everywhere you go in the world every other man is wearing a suit identical to this . . .

Lisha   You buy it off a Frenchman?

Jan   Yes. Yes.

Lisha *sees* **Betty** *emerge from her house.*

Lisha   Ah! Betty!

Betty   What?

Lisha   There's bin a sighting of your beloved! E was last seen up Bugle with a bottle a gin in is 'and recitin to a flock a sheep 'bout the life ereafter . . .

Betty   Hah! What was is text?

Lisha   Summin 'bout the wicked gettin their just deserts. Gin bottle was half empty . . .

Lisha *goes.*

Betty (*to* **Jan**)   I ope you're satisfied with that!

She goes.

Jan   Christ in hellfire tis like I never bin away!

Maude   Oh we're all delighted you're back, arn't we Thomas? Arthur?

Tom   Arthur's still asleep.

Gran   Leave im be.

Jan *removes a selection of dry clothes from his bag. The clothes are just as gaudy as the ones he has on. He places the clothes in a pile on the bench, then tips the remaining contents of the bag out onto the ground before him. Ten thousand pounds in all denominations, notes, bonds, spill from the bag into a crisp, gleaming pile before his family, who watch silent whilst he does this. He leaves the money for them to ponder and he changes into his dry clothes as he speaks:*

Jan   That's what the world had to offer me. To you,

maybe, it look a fortune, but tis no more'n dust to my pocket. Cus the world's a brother to me now. I can stray out there and cross continents with ease. I've traversed whole countries without ever knowin I bin in em. I bin to places where they d'grow people to fit the mines and paint em black to save washin. I've spoke with men whose language I could never understand. Argued with princes, and popes. They tole me they was popes in a language I could never understand but who am I to question that? I debated with em and eld me ground, gambled with em and took their cash. Flirted with their mistresses! My Christ Mother what a vast and various herd is the human species and I tackled em all. I'm tired of adventure now. I've come ome to rest and share the fruits of my endeavour. Oh yes. Take it. Take it all. Do, take it.

Nobody moves.

Colan (*quietly, to* **Gran**) What is it?

Gran Nothin much.

Jan Ten? Fifteen? Twenty thousand pounds, I haven't bothered to count it. Notes, coins, deeds, dollars, francs, pesetos, pounds. Tis all yours . . .

Nobody moves. **Arthur** *is still asleep with his head flung back, mouth open, and snoring.*

Maude Shall I wake Arthur Jan? See if e want some?

Jan Aw Mother dear sweet Mother, bless you no there's no need for that . . . it id'n goin nowhere. If you're too proud to take it Father remember I'm your son too and I earned it just as hard as if I'd sweat down bal. Is it too much to comprehend? I can understand that. Think of it as a door Father. A door that's opened, and you can walk through that door. And on the other side is the Garden of Eden. Full of apples. Thass all it is Father. A door. Tidn money tis a door! A plain old oak wood door. With perhaps a big house in the grounds of this ere Garden of Eden Father, with exotic trees and peacocks!

Maude   Oh, peacocks . . .

Jan   Or has the fear of God and the dread of Mammon bin etched too deep in ya, by the Only-the-Sobers, the Methodists, the Enthusiasts, the Thumpers Mother, who say tis no one's right but theirs to taste the riches of this life and the poor will suffer till they die and fly to heaven? Well I tell'e I bin all round the bastard world and there's not one dead man I've met who's happy! There's no such thing as the life hereafter, you gotta take what you can in this! I didn't cross the Gobi Desert on faith Mother! I 'ired a camel! Thass the way the world go round!

Maude   Will you let your father go bed now Jan? E gotta core to work at six . . .

Jan   Don't you want it? Whass the matter with you all! Don't you want it? I'm givin it to ya!

Tom *rises and slowly walks indoors.* **Jan** *shouts after him:*

Jan   I couldn come ome wi nothin could I!

Gran   Why the hell not boy? If you couldn come back wi nothin, why come back at all?

Colan *rises and takes* **Gran**'s *hand.*

Gran   If you've bin dinin on fumigoes with the mightiest dons in Spain I wouldna thought this little lot woulda lasted ya more'n a week.

Gran *leads* **Colan** *indoors.* **Jan**, **Maude** *and* **Arthur**, *who is still asleep, remain.* **Jan** *is now changed into his dry clothes, which are even more preposterous than before. He folds his wet clothes and replaces them and his money in the carpet bag.*

Maude   See Father's got a sturt on now, with this Great North Lode. E bin workin doublers with Arthur. I run a tight ship, we got no credit nowhere and we

managed to save up thirty-seven shillin. Soon as e come
off doublers Father's gonna cut some stone and build on
two more rooms and a linney . . .

Jan A linney!

Maude We're gonna clear out the back, make room
for a pig, and me'n Gran're gonna grow vegetables. And
after that, your father ope to gain the post of Captain at
bal. And the girls a soon be big enough to work the
bellows and break ore, so you see boy, I think we dun't
altogether need it.

Jan's *bag is packed.*

Jan Goodbye Mother.

Maude (*tearful*) Goodbye boy . . .

Jan Where's the nearest inn, Brigan?

Maude Oh Jan, walk past Brigan. They're wicked
people up Brigan, they tear the limbs off Ting Tang
people and eat granite in their pies. Walk past
Brigan . . .

Jan I've bin round the world Mother! Brigan wun't
old no surprises for me! Brigan's five miles up the road!

Jan *starts to go.*

Maude You'll come back one day . . .

Jan One day, yeah.

Jan *goes.*

Maude Arthur. Come on son, wake up . . .

Arthur *wakes from a deep sleep and stretches.*

Arthur Gaw Christ. Mother I can't go on with this.
Bastard doublers. How does Father do it? Near
forty-four year old and ere am I, nineteen and half
dead with fatigue! What did I ave for me supper I
dunno what I ad for me supper ad summin for me

supper must ave . . .

Maude   Mutton broth.

Arthur   Mutton broth. Tis a poor life when a man can't enjoy is food, tis no life at all when e can't remember what e ad. Did I hear shoutin?

Maude   When?

Arthur   In me sleep.

Maude   Coulda bin Jan.

Arthur   Jan? Brother Jan?

Maude   E was ere.

Arthur   As e gone?

Maude   Yes, dear. E's bin and gone.

Arthur   And I missed'n?

Maude   You was asleep.

Arthur   Did no bugger think to wake me up?

Maude   It was discussed and Jan particularly said to leave you sleep.

Arthur   Why?!

Mother   I don't know boy, I don't know. If you want the answer to that one you must ask Jan . . .

Arthur   E id'n ere!

Maude   Then I shouldn bother with it.

Maude *has started to head for the house.*

Arthur   'As e altered much?

Maude   'Ardly at all.

Arthur   Whass e bin up to?

Maude   Oh, e ad argument with a pope . . .

Arthur With a pope?

Maude And I dropped im in the river . . .

Arthur Where's e gone to?

Maude Brigan.

Arthur Brigan? Brigan!

He follows **Maude** *indoors.* **Trefusis** *enters and sings a song.*

Trefusis
Jan May, son of Ting Tang,
Returned a wealthy man.
They welcomed him as best they could
And now he's gone again.

Jan May, in golden jacket,
Emptied out his pocket
And offered them a share of gold.
They turned their backs upon it.

Jan May has gone to Brigan.
There he'll find a welcome.
Our enemy will treat him like a god.
He'll not come here again.

Gonetta Bate *sits at a table in the Pick and Gad Inn,*
Brigan. **Salathiel Trenannigan** *stands with her back to*
Gonetta*, leaning on the bar, drinking a mug of gin.*

Gonetta This ere is the Pick and Gad Inn, Brigan.
Tis a pest 'ole. We're open but you wouldn know it.
She frightened em off. (*Indicates* **Salathiel**.) She achieved
in one proclamation what the Only-the-Sober Circle a
Women failed to do in a decade. She stopped Brigan
drinkin.

Salathiel *slams down her mug on the bar and turns towards*
Gonetta*. She walks across the room and stands over her. She is*
a large, predatory woman dressed as a man in clawhammer coat,
stovepipe hat and hobnailed boots. She sports a moustache. Her

waistcoat just meets across her belly, which she thrusts at
Gonetta.

Salathiel   Tell me the time Gonetta.

Gonetta *takes a watch from* **Salathiel**'s *waistcoat pocket and reads off the time:*

Gonetta   Nine o'clock.

Salathiel   Where's all the custom?

Gonetta   Ome.

Salathiel   Not drinkin? Thass unlike em!

Gonetta   They got no money, with the mine shut.

Salathiel   It id'n their money I'm askin for my gin
Gonetta.

Gonetta   No. Tis their bodies.

Salathiel   It seemed a watertight enough scheme to
me Gonetta, when I dreamed it up. I shut down Brigan
Bal, deprive the male population of its income. The
younger men can no longer pay cash for their gin so I
advertise terms contiguous to flesh! To the married men
of course I offer credit, but married men seldom drink
and single men, sadly, appear not to have took up the
gauntlet. How do you account for this sorry lack of
passion Gonetta? Is it my demeanour? My bearin? My
conduct? My mien?

Gonetta   I'd say twas your suit.

Salathiel   My suit!

Gonetta   Tis ardly conducive to romance.

Salathiel   And I say you should never judge a man by
the way e dress, cus there's always the chance there
might be a passionate woman underneath. Sadly God
has given me men's work to do on his fair earth and
this suit to do it in. God send me eccentric custom

Gonetta, or we die starvin and celibate.

Gonetta   Well it might just be that somewhere on this earth there's somebody who God in all his wisdom has dressed as daft as you, but I doubt it.

There is a loud knock at the door, and **Jan** *enters, dressed in his outrageous clothes and carrying his bag.* **Gonetta** *turns her eyes to heaven, then she shuts and locks the door.* **Salathiel** *and* **Jan** *look each other up and down.*

Salathiel   Thass a damn fine suit sir.

Jan   Thank you.

Salathiel   Damn fine. Where was that suit ah, assembled? I can't say knit, for that would denigrate the fine cut a the cloth. I can't say sewn together, for the same could be said of a sack. And in truth sir the suit you carry 'pon your broad back owe its pedigree more to a Boulton and Watt precision steam pumpin engine than shall we say a sack! No sir there's suits worn today that if you filled em fulla barley and stood em in a line you couldn tell they wad'n sacks. And I dare venture to observe if e took this suit along the butcher e a make a pretty profit from the top-grade meat e found inside . . .

Jan   Meat?

Gonetta *prods* **Jan**'*s body.*

Gonetta   Tis good'n ard.

Salathiel *smiles.*

Salathiel   So. Where d'e get this suit thun?

Jan   I forget. I bin round the world. I travelled all over.

Salathiel   A capital city. Thass a capital city suit sir. Rome. Madrid. St Petersburg. Sorta suit Mr Napoleon Bonaparte would be appy to be seen dead in. Christ in hell thass some suit.

Jan   I could say you was somewhat strikingly dressed yourself.

Salathiel   Thank you sir. Oh thank you. But yourself sir, who is he that cometh from Edom, dressed in the dyed fabrics of Bozrah?

Jan   My name is Jan May and I wish to purchase a room for the night.

Salathiel *offers* **Jan** *her hand by way of introduction.*

Salathiel   Salathiel Trenannigan.

Jan   Christ in hell, thass a man's name!

Salathiel   I do a man's job. I bin a kibble-lander years back. I own Brigan Mine now. Sure as hell own it. No sir, wouldn old for me to go be a name like Grace Briney.

Jan   You own Brigan Mine?

Salathiel   Yes sir. She's knacked, for want of capital. But what of that? I still got the Inn. No there's one area where I differ from a man and thass passion. And I'll tell e whass up with the world today and you'll bear me out, bein round it, and thass there's no passion left. Tis all enthusiasm. Now I can work up enthusiasm 'long with the rest of em, but I d'back it up wi passion. Take your fine suit sir. I've showed not a little enthusiasm for that suit tonight sir, no?

Jan (*uncertain*)   Yes?

Salathiel   But there's bin little rats nibblin away inside that first-class brain of yours posin the question where's the passion? Where's the passion in this woman? And runnin alongside that there li'l question, tryin ard to keep up, is the posture why, at half-past nine at night, with a knacked bal in the neighbourhood and a legion of idle men, is this inn empty?

Jan   It er, ad crossed my mind, yes.

Salathiel   Come sir, you've travelled round the world
from Akaba to Tregadillet, and there ab'm bin one inn
empty at alf-past nine at night . . . and the answer to
that one is plain as a bullock's tongue. They got less
stomick for *passion* these boys than they ave for cheap
gin! Now thun. You wanna bed for tonight.

Jan   Er, well . . .

Salathiel   Man who's travelled round the world you've
shared berths wi bigger men than me and I ave the
softest flesh. My when I hit the duckdown I can do a
woman's job. (*Fingers his jacket.*) I'll pick the cloth off your
back delicate.

Jan   But I'm in love! I can't break a vow of fidelity . . .

Salathiel   Tid'n love I'm askin of ya, tis passion . . .

Gonetta   E's bin took be the Methodists.

Jan   I got no fear of the afterlife!

Gonetta   Got too much fear in this.

Jan   I'm my own man!

Salathiel   No! You're lookin at me and the passion's
wellin up inside ya. But your fine suit and clean face
speak to me and say I'm a man Salathiel who has an
appearance in this world, all of it, bein round it, which I
wish my fellow men to take note of and respect. And
that appearance, in spite of the passion I feel for this
woman, does not encompass kissin a lady who wear for
example, a moustache upon er upper lip!

Jan   Yes! You hit upon the truth there!

Salathiel   Then I'll take it off!

Salathiel *removes her moustache. She stands back.*

Jan   Tis somewhat more'n the moustache.

Salathiel (*removing her clothes*)   The stovepipe hat? The clawhammer coat? The hobnailed boots?

Salathiel *is soon down to her undergarments.*

Jan   No! No!

Jan *looks round him. There's no escape.* **Gonetta** *guards the door with a pick handle.* **Jan** *drops to his knees and prays.*

Jan   Oh God!

Gonetta   E's on *our* side.

Jan *spills the contents of his bag across the floor.* **Salathiel** *and* **Gonetta** *stare in disbelief at his riches.*

Jan   What's this Brigan Bal? I'll buy it off ya.

Salathiel   Did I mention I was selling?

Jan   You said it was knacked.

Salathiel   Knacked sir? No sir. There's enough copper under Brigan to plate the whole of France. But tis best left under, till the price get yeasty. On the other 'and, for a man a means, for a capital city man with money to burn, you could afford to send an army down there and raise a thousand tons in one big dollop, flood the market and destroy the competition. After that the price is yours. Yes sir, for a man of means it got potential.

Jan   Well I'm nothing if not a man of means, and if you give me a single room for the night with a lock on the door I'll buy it off ya.

Salathiel   Let's hear an offer.

Jan   Shall we say five hundred?

Salathiel   Five hundred what?

Jan   Five undred pound.

Salathiel   That's without the pumpin engine.

Jan   Eh?

Salathiel   You dun't need no pumpin engine. Best off without a pumpin engine.

Gonetta *furnishes* **Jan** *with a mug of gin and tobacco.*

Jan   How much did we say?

Salathiel   Seven undred.

Jan   Will you take it in pesetos?

Salathiel   I'll take it in manure.

Jan   Thass two thousand pesetos, nearlybout.

Salathiel   Give us three and I'll throw in the pumpin engine.

Jan   Three with the pumpin engine.

Salathiel   Did I say three?

Jan   Three what?

Salathiel   Three thousand pound.

Jan   Three thousand pound?

Salathiel   Thass too much don't you think?

Jan   It's a bloody fortune!

Salathiel   I quite agree. We'll say four thousand.

Jan   Pounds?

Salathiel   Pesetos.

Jan   Thass near a thousand pound!

Salathiel   Thass more like it. Three's far too much.

Jan   Four thousand pesetos.

Salathiel   Thass without the pumpin engine.

Jan   With*out* the pumpin engine?

Salathiel   You want the pumpin engine?

Jan   For four thousands I *get* the pumpin engine!

Salathiel   That was three thousand pound you got the pumpin engine but we agreed three was too much.

Jan   We certainly did.

Salathiel   Then I'll drop to two with the pumpin engine.

Jan   Pesetos?

Salathiel   Pounds.

Jan   Two thousand pound?!

Salathiel   Thank you sir, that sound reasonable.

Salathiel *shakes* **Jan** *by the hand.*

Jan   With the pumpin engine.

Salathiel   Thass ten thousand pesetos.

Jan *starts to count out ten thousand pesetos.*

Salathiel   You didn come by this lot sinkin wells.

Jan   I did not.

Salathiel   Well I arn't surprised you're a wealthy man with a business head like yours . . .

Jan   You think so?

Salathiel   My Christ almighty tis twenty years since I struck a bargain like that one.

Jan   You're lookin at a man who's bankrupted sultans.

Salathiel   I arn't at all surprised.

Jan   And I got the pumpin engine!

Gonetta   I ope so.

Jan   Uh?

Salathiel *paces the floor.*

Salathiel   Y'know that was a capital city deal you struck there. I'm no capital city man Mr May, why you'd stretch my memory to the backs beyond if you was to ask me the last time I crossed the parish boundary. Forgive me. I rode to Plymouth a fortnight ago to see off Boney. But Plymouth? 'Ardly Madagascar! And before that? Doomsday! But often a knowledge of local affairs in business will take you a long way further in the world than shall we say intimacy with the value of the drachma against the Dutch noble . . .

Jan   Oh I'm intimate with that . . .

Salathiel   I thought you might be. On the other 'and, locally, a man with that kinda capital city knowledge on the tip of is tongue would cut a great deal of trust and admiration. Particularly amongst farmers.

Jan   Ah . . .

Gonetta   But which farmers?

Salathiel   Which, rich, farmers?

Gonetta   That require a knowledge altogether local.

Salathiel   Intimate.

Jan   There. Twelve thousand pesetos.

Salathiel *reaches into her bosom and withdraws a battered parchment.*

Salathiel   And here we have the deed.

Jan   Good. Now thun. My room.

Jan *takes the deed and places it in his bag. He scoops the remainder of the money into the bag and slings it across his shoulder.*

Salathiel   Mr May, you're a mineowner now.

Jan   Jan May. Mineowner. God in heaven.

Gonetta   She can do better than that Mr May . . .

Jan   Oh?

Gonetta   You've yet to talk of banks . . .

Jan   She owns a bank?

Salathiel   Thought of ownin a bank quicken the blood?

Jan   Christ in hell it got it pumpin bloody fast.

Gonetta   Jan May. Mineowner. Banker!

Jan   How could we go about it? Buyin a bank?

Salathiel   O thass pillow talk that is. I do all my bank business horizontal . . .

Jan   Jesus Christ! Jesus Christ in hellfire!

Salathiel *opens her arms to* **Jan**, *he drops his bag and leaps into her arms.*

Gonetta (*sings*)
I watched em through a crack in the floor,
I saw it with me own damned eyes.
When he flagged and drooped and she wanted more,
When the iron drained from his thighs,

One little word revived him
BANKER
One hot breath in his ear
BANKER
That paradigm got im pumpin
BANKER
Cranked im into gear!

They was at it through till the crowing cock,
Dawn couldn't quench their fire,
Like two wild pigs in an empty sack,
Each coupled to the other's desire.

A loud knock at the door. Enter **Hailsham**. **Gonetta** *gestures skywards.*

Gonetta   She sold the mine.

Hailsham   Who to?

Gonetta   A very wealthy man.

Salathiel *enters, brisk and businesslike.*

Salathiel   Aha! Mr Hailsham.

Hailsham   Good morning Mr Trenannigan.

Jan *enters. He is half-dressed, disorientated and shagged out.*

Salathiel   Mr Hailsham Mr May Mr May Mr
Hailsham.

Jan   How d'you do sir.

Hailsham   And you Mr May.

Salathiel   Gonetta, gin and fat cigars.

Gonetta   I can't abide an early mornin rush.

Salathiel   How's the market?

Hailsham   Tin's up, copper's static, lead's soft.

Jan   I'm relieved to hear that.

Hailsham   Slate's edgy. Granite's bottomed.

Salathiel   Kumpfernickel?

Hailsham   Firm.

Salathiel   Sounds volatile.

Hailsham   I don't like the look of it.

Salathiel   It's those damned Bolivians again.

Gonetta *slams a flagon of gin, a box of cigars and three glasses
on the table. She takes the cigars and hands them round.*

Salathiel   Gentlemen. Let us sit and talk of banks.

Salathiel *sits and leans back in her chair.* **Hailsham** *and*
Jan *do likewise.* **Gonetta** *lights their cigars and they puff on*

them in a satisfied way.

Gonetta (*to the audience*)   Bloody remarkable what a cigar does for em. Rolled up mass of stinkin weed, transports em to the golden palace of the Raj.

Jan   We should, we should open up a bank.

Hailsham   That's a proposal of vision if I may say sir.

Jan   Thank you Mr Hailsham. Thanks sir.

Hailsham   Shows a deep understanding of the market.

Jan   Well, see, I've bin to Bolivia.

Hailsham   You have?

Jan   Oh all over Europe . . .

Salathiel   We wanna no-nonsense, big-deposit bank, such as farmers favour.

Jan   A capital city bank.

Hailsham   A bank where they d'bring their cash in cartloads, and lodge it there to rot.

Salathiel   Naturally Mr May will be the President of this bank . . .

Jan   President . . .

Salathiel   A figurehead. Havin been outa the country for the last nine years, with his capital city wardrobe and European airs, he's exactly the sorta chap who'd command great authority in Truro, with farmers . . .

Jan   This is music to my ears . . .

Hailsham   Do we have sufficient cash to start this bank?

Salathiel   I can spare twelve thousand pesetos.

Jan   And I'm worth ten times that.

Hailsham   I see I'm in the company of giants.

Salathiel   But cash id'n all. We need securities Mr Hailsham.

Hailsham *smiles, but says nothing.* **Jan** *ventures a proposal.*

Jan   I'm prepared to put up Brigan Mine . . .

Hailsham *laughs.*

Hailsham   Brigan Mine is hardly a goin concern sir. I wouldn't stand Brigan Mine against a three-legged mule.

Jan   It'll be worth a fortune when I get it goin . . .

Hailsham   You intend to start it up again do ya?

Jan   Oh yes indeed, there's enough copper under Brigan to plate the whole Atlantic, now the cautious might say keep it underground till the price get yeasty, but I intend to send the army down there and raise ten thousand tons in one big . . .

Gonetta   Dollop.

Jan   . . . flood the market and decimate the competition! After that the price is mine Mr Hailsham. Ours.

Hailsham   Good. Well, I'll come in with you on this bank . . .

Salathiel   Thass mighty shrewd of ya . . .

Hailsham   On these terms. For a fifty per cent interest in Brigan Mine . . .

Jan   Eh?

Hailsham   I'll trade with you equal shares in my foundry down at Par, my smelting works in Fowey, my slate quarries in Delabole, my granite excavations in Withiel, my lime pits in Tregadillet, my lead interests in Tavistock, my engineering plant in Hayle, my porphyry in Roche, my Academy of Mining in Redruth, my coal in Porthmeor, my pilchard fleet in Padstow, my seining company in Polperro, my boatyard in Wadebridge, and my viaduct over Looe.

Gonetta   Half built.

Hailsham   Soon to be completed.

Jan *leaps from his seat.*

Jan   My Christ almighty!

Hailsham   That should give you all the securities you need to start a bank.

Jan   An empire! An empire at a stroke!

A rousing anthem is sung to **Jan***:*

Anthem
   Jan May! Emperor!
   President of Banks!
   Resurrector of Defunct Mines!
   Figurehead of Our Times!
   Let the gods be thanked!

   And so it was that this young man,
   Who could neither read nor write his name,
   In a matter not of years but hours,
   Scaled the highest peaks of power.

   Jan May! Emperor!
   Carved in stone!
   Alderman! Burgher! Man of Rank!
   Lord of his Domain!
   Let the gods be thanked!

Act Two

Ting Tang Mine. Underground. Darkness. Candles can be seen moving about. Men's faces are depicted beneath the candles. A kibble, a large metal container on wheels, is pushed towards a pile of rubble. The men light candles from each others' candles and set them about the place. **Lisha**, **Tom** *and* **Arthur** *inspect the rubble.* **Rutter** *is in the distance.* **Trefusis** *sits some way off, eating his crib.* **Lisha** *picks up stuff from the rubble and slings it in the kibble.* **Tom** *inspects the face,* **Arthur** *sorts through the rubble.* **Rutter** *approaches.*

Rutter This your pitch Thomas May?

Tom Yes.

Rutter What's it lookin like?

Arthur Rich.

Rutter Much stuff?

Tom See for yourself.

Rutter *moves to the face and inspects it with* **Tom**. **Arthur** *picks up a huge lump of rubble and carries it to the kibble.*

Arthur Look at that Mr Rutter. Solid ore.

Arthur *slings the rock in the kibble and goes back for another.*

Rutter I gotta re-set this pitch.

Tom Tid'n no richer'n last month.

Rutter I know that.

Lisha Bin runnin like this since Lent.

Trefusis (*from a distance*) Before Lent!

Rutter I know that.

Lisha 'Long as you know that.

Rutter We can't offer you more'n three farthin a ton

this month.

At this, everyone stops what they're doing and looks at **Rutter**. **Trefusis** *stops eating.*

Lisha   Say that again?

Rutter   Three farthin.

Tom   Outa the question.

Arthur   We'll be diggin two ton a farthin after biddin.

Tom   We can't raise ore at that price. Christ, we're thirty fathoms down.

Rutter   There's nothin I can do about that.

Lisha   Oo's given ya that thun?

Rutter   Trice. E came back from the smelters with a big hole in is pocket.

Tom   Three farthin a ton? We can't touch the stuff at that price.

Rutter   Thass up to you mister.

Rutter *makes off.*

Lisha (*calls after him*)   You can't walk away like that Captain Rutter! If we can't dig it the mine will shut down, then where will you be?

Rutter *turns and calls back.*

Rutter   Where will I be? Y'ask where will I be? Huh! I'll be at Brigan! Where will you be?

Trefusis   Never shoulda sworn that oath. Revelation is a portentous book.

Rutter   They gotta whole disbanded regiment under contract diggin ore at Brigan. Dozens and dozens of new shafts bein sunk. Place is like a ruddy sieve. We can't compete with that.

Tom   A regiment you say?

Rutter   They march em in from Fraddon every day.

Arthur   Fraddon?

Rutter   There's Dolcoath Mine shut down, Binney's, Great Consols is layin men off, they've all gone to Brigan. Tis like a ruddy ants' nest.

Tom   You mean to say there's militia down there, diggin ore? With tributers?

Rutter   All musclin in together, under contract.

Rutter *wanders off.*

Trefusis   On the day we swore that oath Jan May fetched ome after nine years in the wildnerness bearin great wealth. You shunned that wealth and Jan May went on to Egypt. Egypt was locked in famine but Egypt took im to its bosom, and the famine ceased in Egypt.

Trefusis *nods at* **Tom** *and wanders off.*

Lisha   My pitch is nothin like as rich as this. Lode I'm workin is barren. Tis all quartz. I pick and scrape in search of ore. I offer up a prayer and lo! there's a fingernail of copper. I ask five shillin a ton for this copper. Thass a prayer that's never answered. The transaction of cash is a man-made invention, left by the gods for men to sort out amongst themselves. Like a pumpin engine. Have you ever noticed if you pray for a broken pumpin engine to work the gods wun't touch it? They'll flood the mine for ya but they'll never pump it out. Thass cus a pumpin engine never grew out the ground, or swam in the sea, or flew in the air. They look down on we and say what the hell are those bastards down there doin with a pumpin engine? We never made one a them in six days! Split the beam with a shaft of lightnin! Bang. The beam's gone. Mine floods. Knacked. All thanks to they selfish bastard gods. And if we defy em? More lightnin. Split again. Head to toe.

Entrails angin out. Food for dogs and kites. Dead if you're lucky. So. There's nothin left to do but pray.

Tom and **Arthur** *have filled a kibble.*

Lisha   I've never seen a kibble fill so fast.

Arthur   Tid'n worth a bloody farthin.

Arthur and **Tom** *push the kibble towards the winze. When its momentum is up,* **Tom** *leaves it to* **Arthur** *and walks back to pick up tools.*

Lisha   I often pray to a god to make me appy. Burn an animal, sacrifice a rabbit to Apollo or Artemis before I go bed. But I d'still wake up bloody un'appy. I go work un'appy, I work un'appy, go ome un'appy, trap a rabbit un'appy, burn it un'appy, and go bed un'appy.

Tom   You'd be a damn sight appier if you et the rabbit.

Rutter *approaches.*

Rutter   Mr May.

Tom   That you Rutter?

Rutter   When I'm gone to Brigan they're gonna be short of a bal captain ere.

Tom   Whass the point? Bloody bal's dead, whass the point?

Rutter   They'll need a strong man up front to wind it down.

Tom   Aw, hell.

Rutter   There's valuable machinery to be raised to grass.

Tom   You tellin me this? I was the bugger oo put it down there!

Rutter   I'm offerin to recommend ya. Whaddaya say?

Tom   Ab'm got no choice ave I. No choice.

Rutter *goes.* **Arthur** *wanders up.*

Arthur   What did e want?

Tom   He promoted me. To bal captain.

Lisha   Tonight when I sacrifice I shall ask the gods to make me angry.

They go.

Trefusis (*sings*)
    Have you never bin to Egypt?
    Tis a short day's walk that way.
    There's tons of corn in Egypt
    And tons more every day.

Roscrow *stands on the count house steps.* **Trice** *is behind her with the cost-book in his hands.*

One by one the **Miners** *come to grass.*

Roscrow   Last night my fellow adventurers and I held a board meeting. We discussed the market price of copper and concluded that under the prevailing circumstances Ting Tang is no longer viable as a working mine. The adventurers have therefore instructed me to inform the tributers that we have no other option but to close down –

Lisha (*interrupting*)   What about the deal with Sir Richard Crabbe?

Roscrow   That deal is off. The Nanphysic mineral rights have been sold.

Lisha   Oo to?

Roscrow *turns to* **Trice**.

Roscrow   Er –

Lisha   How much?

Trice   Twenty-three pounds.

Lisha   Twenty-three pounds!

Roscrow   With that money it was agreed we should keep Newbolt Shaft pumped dry –

Lisha   Take a damn sight more'n twenty-three pounds!

Roscrow   That's all –

Lisha   Where's it gone?

Trice   It's all down here Mr Ball, in the cost-book.

Lisha   Two months ago this mine was rich. Where's it all gone?

Trice (*offering* **Lisha** *cost-book*)   Would you care to see for –

Lisha *skips up the steps and grabs the cost-book.*

Lisha (*tearing pages out*)   Dividends! Thass where it's gone! Dividends! All leeched out! Bastard dividends!

Trice   Mr Ball, this is a legal record of –

Lisha   That wun't help us eat! We shall have to break an oath to eat! And where will that land us! Hades! Thass where! Hell!

Roscrow   That depends on the strength of your religious beliefs.

Tom   We can't break an oath –

Lisha   Blasphemy!

Trice   Mr Ball –

Lisha   I'll cull my food! I'll go up on Goss Moor and kill for it!

Roscrow   For God's sake, go and work at Brigan!

Lisha   I'd like to see you swear an oath and bloody break it!

Arthur   That wun't do no good she's agnostic.

Tom   She'm a witch!

Lisha   She butchered er usband, shut down Ting Tang and now she's gonna make off with the money!

Roscrow (*incensed, to* **Trice**)   Fetch me a bible!

Trice   Er . . .

Lisha   You wanna bible?

Lisha *conjures a bible and thrusts it at* **Roscrow**.

Roscrow   As a true Christian I make a solemn pledge by all the books herein –

Lisha   That include Revelation –

Roscrow   All the books, damn you!

This outburst silences the **Miners**, *and* **Mrs Roscrow** *swears her oath in a quiet, cold voice.*

Roscrow   . . . that I shall do everything I can to keep Newbolt Shaft pumped dry so that one day we mine copper here again.

She hands the bible back to **Lisha**. **Lisha** *hands the cost-book back to* **Trice**.

Ting Tang village. **Gran**, **Betty** *and* **Colan** *are hunched in a secret conversation.*

Gran   There's a consignment of green bananas, from a West Indies ship went down off Phoebe's Point. Close tag's bein kept and these bananas is headin inland in a sealed wood crate on the back of a mule. A source close to the mule tells me there's a buyer for these bananas in St Wenn. But progress is slow. By the first mornin these bananas ad'n got no further'n Boscoppa Downs. Next mornin they'd reached Carclaze. On my estimation these bananas should be ripe by the time they get to Stenalees, so tis a dash to St Wenn after that t'avoid em turnin mushy. Possibly transferrin to orse'n cart round Coldvreath. This is where they bananas will be at their most vulnerable. I propose an ambush at 'Ensbarrer tomorrer night . . . well?

Betty   I don't have the stomach for a fight.

Gran   A mule! Thass all it is! A mule!

Betty   They'll ave the militia guardin em.

Gran   Bananas?

Colan   Militia ride wi more'n meat now.

Betty   I saw three militia ridin with a Spaniard oo wad'n carryin nothin more'n a bunch of onions.

Gran   Gittout!

Colan   Sure put the kybosh on bananas that do Gran.

Gran   They're food! They're fibre! They're fillin!

Betty   There'll be half Bodmin after they bananas. There'll be limbs torn off and several deaths.

Gran   Bodmin wouldn kill for bananas!

Colan   They will if they'm ungry. And they'll eat more'n bananas.

Betty   Thass my vision of hell, walkin round Bodmin inside a somebody's gut.

Gran   Well!

Arthur *and* **Tom** *arrive.*

Arthur   Where's Mother?

Gran   Off.

Tom   On the scavenge?

Gran   Gatherin limpets.

Arthur   Aw Christ.

Colan   'Samatter wi limpets?

Arthur   They're damn tough and salty.

Colan   All right in a pie.

Arthur   Gotta filla pie with a sight more'n limpets to get ridda the salt.

Gran   She'll pick uppa coupla slugs on the way back.

Gran *has several sparrows in her lap which she is plucking.*

Colan   Sparrers. Got several sparrers.

Gran   We in't puttin these in a pie.

Arthur   Why not?

Gran   I like sparrer burned to a crisp in a hot oven I do. Pop em in your mouth and crunch em up. Only way I'll eat em.

Arthur   Puttem in a pie, wun't make no damn difference. There id'n no pastry, stack em on top they a still burn.

Gran   I arn't eatin sparrers bin on toppa limpets. The salt permeate up.

Colan   Listen to that. I gotta put up with that all day.

Gran   You wait till you get to my age.

Colan   Yes yes yes.

Gran   I gotta delicate stomach, wun't take too much salt.

Colan   If you didn't ave a gut like an iron foundry you a be dead by now.

Gran   Hah! See? Dead! See? It never take long for the conversation to wander round to that!

Colan   Be one less mouth to feed.

Gran   Did you all hear that?

Arthur   E's right. You shoulda died bloody years ago.

They all ponder what life would be like without **Gran***.*

Colan   What about Jan?

Tom   What about im?

Colan   It's bin my opinion Arthur should make a pilgrimage to Truro and talk to Jan.

Gran   You should do what e did, go out and tackle the world.

Tom   I'm too old for that.

Gran   Too old? You're forty-four! You're a captain now, you'd make a damn fortune. They're cryin out for mine captains in the Americas.

Arthur   If Jan can do it so can we. Think what he was like before e left . . .

Gran   E was weak.

Arthur   And yet e lived through three shipwrecks.

Colan   Book a passage. Sail across the Atlantic.

Gran   Send the money back.

Lisha   I know where to go. Michigan. They gotta copper belt there wide as Europe.

Arthur   What about it?

Tom   Well, if Jan can do it, so can we.

Gran   Exactly!

Arthur   Yes!

Falmouth Harbour. **Arthur***,* **Tom** *and* **Lisha** *wander through the crowds.* **Maude** *and* **Betty** *in attendance.* **Trefusis** *sings while* **Maude** *bids her farewells:*

Trefusis
 Have you never bin to Michigan?
 It's a short walk up a plank,
 Nothin more, nothin less,
 We're going to meet the Yank!

 Have you never crossed an ocean?
 Tis a sit out on the deck,
 Nothing more, nothing less,
 We won't break our neck!

 Have you never ambled far from home?
 It's an amble in the breeze,
 Nothin more, nothin less,
 A skate across the seas.

 And when we get to Michigan
 We're going to break the bank,
 Nothing more, nothing less,
 We're going to meet the Yank!

The sound and bustle of a busy embarcation can be seen and heard. **Betty** *is very emotional, mopping her tears up with a handkerchief, consoled by* **Lisha**.

Arthur   Goodbye Mother.

Maude   Goodbye boy.

Maude *hugs* **Arthur**.

Arthur   C'mon Mother.

Maude *leaves* **Arthur** *and hugs* **Tom**.

Maude   Goodbye Tom.

Arthur   Goodbye Maude.

Maude *clings to* **Tom**.

Arthur   C'mon Father.

Tom   C'mon Maude.

Maude   Goodbye dear.

Tom *gently parts from* **Maude** *and* **Arthur** *prizes* **Betty** *from* **Lisha**. **Tom**, **Arthur** *and* **Lisha** *wave to* **Maude** *and* **Betty** *as they walk up the gangplank and depart.* **Maude** *and* **Betty** *are left alone.*

Betty   Tis your damn son oo's done this. Jan May. Im and is bank. And is Brigan. I knew when e come ome e was up to mischief.

Maude   Stop bein so damn miserable.

Betty   Look, there's men ere from all round the district, bein shoved off to sea by your son Jan . . .

Exit **Maude** *and* **Betty**. *An anthem is sung.*

Anthem
  The Worshipful Jan May Esquire!
  Lord High Sheriff of the Shire!
  Honoured Guest at Public Functions!
  Top of the table at Civic Functions!
  Chief Executive of Justice!
  Loved by all but sadly, loveless!

The boardroom of Brigan Consolidated Bank. The room is vast. **Salathiel** *sits one end drinking gin.* **Hailsham** *sits the other end perusing a petition.* **Jan** *is in the middle, dressed in an outrageously foppish pink and purple suit, preening himself in front of a mirror.* **Gonetta** *is the only one working. She is run ragged.*

Gonetta (*to audience*)   This ere is the Brigan Consolidated Bank Number One Lemon Street Trura. I'm the only bugger oo can add up.

Salathiel   Gonetta! More gin!

Gonetta *runs for gin* . . .

Hailsham   Tell me the time Gonetta!

She finds a watch . . .

Gonetta   Five o'clock!

Jan   Fill me a bath!

She fills a bath.

Hailsham   Gonetta! Pack me a case!

And packs a case.

Salathiel   Where's e goin?

Gonetta   London.

Salathiel   What for?

Jan   Read my engagements Gonetta!

Gonetta   Tonight you're the Guest of Honour at the Loyal Friends of Freedom's Anniversary Celebration of the Fall of the Systematic Engines of Corruption and Disorder at the Public Rooms.

Hailsham (*checking strongbox*)   No cash?

Gonetta   None left.

Hailsham   Then gimme promissories!

Gonetta (*to audience*)   Bloody remarkable how much quicker tis possible to spend other people's money than your own.

Hailsham (*to* **Gonetta**)   Run Rabbit!

Gonetta *runs.*

Gonetta (*as she runs*)   I got im (**Salathiel**.) drinkin the profits, im (**Jan**.) spendin em and im (**Hailsham**.) givin em away left right and centre to any Whig or Tory who swear to stamp out the Labour Protection Bill.

Hailsham   I shall be residing at the Saracen's Head, Westminster.

Salathiel   Why?!

Hailsham   To petition Mr Castlereagh and Lord Liverpool about their buggerin Labour Protection Bill.

Gonetta (*to audience*)   Lashin em with his dogfish tongue.

Jan   That should do some good.

Hailsham   Damned Protection Bill. Tis we oo need protectin!

Jan   From agitators.

Gonetta   From farmers, when they ask for their deposits back.

Hailsham   Thass enough Gonetta!

Gonetta   Bath's full.

She unfolds an exotic Chinese screen around the bath. **Jan** *disappears behind the screen and* **Salathiel** *follows, rolling her sleeves as she goes. Clothes appear draped over the screen as* **Jan**, *behind it, is undressed.*

Jan (*behind screen*)   It's my opinion agitators should be shot!

Salathiel   Bravo.

Jan   That's my opinion. And I've let it be known to the Bench.

Hailsham   If we ad'n called in the militia down at Withiel there woulda bin mayhem.

Jan   Lumpsa granite flyin through windows, quarriers rampagin through the streets but no, we brung in the militia, one man was shot and peace reigned.

Hailsham   You should make it the centrepiece of your speech tonight Mr May. The Labour Protection Bill, where will it end? Its effect on the creation and distribution of wealth. The role of the militia. The defence of the pocket.

Jan (*behind screen*)   Yes, O yes! 'My Lord Ladies and Gentlemen! Loyal Friends of Freedom! The defence of the pocket!'

Hailsham   That's the ticket.

There's a knock at the front door. **Hailsham** *cowers, scuttles to the back door and lets himself out. Unknown to* **Jan** *and* **Salathiel**, **Gonetta** *answers the door and admits a visitor during* **Jan***'s speech.*

Jan   'My power is in my pocket. My trousers bulge with it. I can take it out whenever I like and disseminate it across the county. On the other hand I can keep it where it is and watch it grow. This is freedom, Loyal Friends. We'll not be blackmailed by those who see it as their right to plunge their hands into my pocket! And take whatever they like when they like!'

Roscrow *stands listening to* **Jan***'s speech.*

Jan   Whaddaya make a that?

Gonetta (*to* **Roscrow**)   Well?

Roscrow   I'm sure the Loyal Friends will applaud it to the rafters.

Jan   Who's that, that you Gonetta?

Gonetta   No.

Roscrow (*to* **Gonetta**)   Have I come at a difficult time?

Gonetta   No.

Jan (*behind screen*)   What?

Gonetta   I said no!

Jan   How d'ya mean, no!

Gonetta   No she ab'm come at a difficult time!

Jan   Who?

Gonetta   Ann Roscrow!

A giant splash behind the screen and **Jan**'s *naked torso appears over the top.*

Jan   Aw my God! Jesus Christ in hellfire!

Roscrow   I think I should go.

Jan (*to* **Gonetta**)   Get riddofer!

Roscrow   I'll go. I'll come back. I'll make an appointment.

Gonetta   E's that busy you're lucky to a catched im in the bath without Hailsham.

Roscrow   Well, there's that. I'll stay.

Salathiel *appears from behind the screen. She glowers at* **Roscrow** *and crosses to her desk.* **Jan** *appears. His clothes are soaked and he is covered with wet promissory notes.*

Jan   Mrs Roscrow . . .

He crosses to greet her.

Roscrow   God evening Mr May.

Jan   Huh! Why is it every time we meet I'm leakin wet?

Roscrow   I won't stay long.

Jan (*to* **Gonetta**)   Gimme a gin. Give er a gin.

Roscrow   Thank you I don't drink.

Jan *sits uncomfortably in his seat.* **Gonetta** *furnishes him with a gin and replenishes* **Salathiel**'s *glass. She finds a chair for* **Roscrow**.

Gonetta   Y'allowed to siddown?

Roscrow   Thank you.

She sits.

Jan   State your business Mrs Roscrow.

Roscrow   I've come to ask you for a loan.

Jan   A loan?

Roscrow   Ting Tang is in desperate trouble.

Jan   I didn't know that.

Roscrow   I'm sure you didn't.

Salathiel   We id'n a lending bank madam, we'm a depositary.

Roscrow (*confidentially, to* **Jan**)   You don't understand Mr May. I ask it as a special request. A personal favour. From your own pocket.

Jan   I'm very flattered Mrs Roscrow. Very taken. Tis only the second time I've met you and here you are, askin me personal favours.

Salathiel   If e went round dishin out cash to every tinpot bal owner e'd met twice e'd be bankrupt madam.

Jan   This is a special, a personal request.

Salathiel   They all say that.

Jan   You don't understand . . .

Roscrow   I considered that under the circumstances . . .

Jan   See there's circumstances . . .

Jan *waddles over to* **Salathiel**.

We love each other.

Salathiel   Who?

Jan   Me and er.

Salathiel   Roscrow?

Jan   Yes.

Salathiel   She loves you?

Jan   We fell in love the first time ever we set eyes on each other.

Salathiel   And she got the bald audacity to come in ere and beg you to bail er out cus you love each other? That id'n circumstances Mr May, thass blackmail!

Jan   Blackmail?

Salathiel   Call er bluff.

Jan   How?

Salathiel   Offer to marry er.

Jan   You think I should?

Salathiel   Marry er and you get Ting Tang by default without parting with a penny piece.

Jan   O Zeus! Two dead birds wi one stone!

Salathiel   After all you're a man of passion, you've met er twice, tis 'igh time you got wed.

Jan *takes up his glass and returns to* **Roscrow**. *On his way he passes* **Gonetta** *who hands him a cigar.*

Jan   Mrs Roscrow.

Roscrow   Yes?

Jan   Ann.

Roscrow   Yes?

Jan   Will you marry me?

Roscrow   I beg your pardon?

Jan   Marry me, Ann.

Roscrow (*staggered*)   I need a glass of gin.

Gonetta *rustles up a glass of gin.* **Jan** *follows her as she scuttles to and fro.*

Jan   What's the matter with er?

Gonetta   I can't imagine.

Jan   We fell in love. Good God a day asn't passed when I haven't dreamed of marriage to the woman half a dozen times.

Gonetta   The vanity of the man.

Jan   Vanity? Vanity?

Roscrow *drains her gin and stands.*

Roscrow   Did it never cross your mind the circumstances I spoke of might have been the hardship of your mother and your sisters, your grandmother and blind brother?

Salathiel   Bugger them . . .

Jan   They wouldn't take my money. They wouldn't take it d'you hear? They turned their stupid ignorant backs upon it. That's the truth!

Roscrow   They didn't know what to do with it, just like you Mr May.

Gonetta   Your father ad a linney to build. Thirty-seb'm shillin saved, that was his fortune, that was his great achievement . . .

Salathiel   Gonetta!

Jan   Look, I'm a busy man –

Gonetta   E loaf about all day.

Salathiel   Stuck ere in Trura.

Jan   Here in the bank.

Salathiel   Guest of honour ere and there tis a different damn world!

Jan   How d'ya expect me to follow their every damn move?

Salathiel   They didn't want is money, you eard im.

Jan   I'm different to them I'm a man of the world . . .

Salathiel   They're ignorant, little people . . .

Jan   Yes!

Salathiel   E's a successful proud man. E offered it to em once and they scorned im like the ingrate, broad-horizons narrow-minded hard-hearted granite-headed bastards they've always bin down Ting Tang. He's a Brigan man now, pure and simple, and Brigan people dun't talk to Ting Tang people, Brigan people dun't meddle with their affairs cus Brigan people's better'n Ting Tang people, cus Ting Tang people's the meanest, leastest people who ever crawled on their bellies across God's earth!

Salathiel, *the worst for gin, falls asleep.* **Gonetta** *crosses and inspects her.*

Gonetta   She's gin-distant.

Roscrow   I swore an oath on every book in the bible that I would do everything I could to keep Ting Tang open. If I refuse your offer of marriage I break the oath. Well that doesn't trouble me. I don't believe for one minute that I shall rot in hell, but there are people in Ting Tang who do, and they've taken great risks because of it. And those who are left will suffer far more than I will if I marry another man I don't love. Another ridiculous man.

Jan (*to* **Gonetta**)   What does she mean? She gonna marry me? What does she mean?

Gonetta   You don't ave to marry im.

Jan   O yes she does. Now you shuttup Gonetta, you done enough damage. Leave er be . . .

Gonetta   Just tell im about his father and brother . . .

Jan   Eh?

Gonetta   Tell im where they've gone.

Jan   What? Where?

Roscrow   They've gone to the world.

Jan   Oh no.

Gonetta   But you don't want to hear about them, the meanest, leastest people who ever crawled on their bellies across God's earth . . .

Jan   Tell me, where've they gone?

Gonetta   Plenty a time for them when you're married and dishin out your frozen charity . . .

Jan   Tell me!

The sound of a hymn can be heard. The atmosphere changes. A **Preacher** *can be seen standing under a tree, a gin bottle hidden behind him.* **Maude, Gran, Betty Elder** *and* **Colan** *kneel before the* **Preacher**. *He speaks as the hymn is sung.*

Hymn
  Sing from the chamber to the grave,
  I hear the dying miner say,
  A sound of melody I crave,
  Upon my burial day.

  Sing sweetly as you travel on,
  And keep the funeral slow,
  The angels sing where I am gone,
  And you shall sing below.

  Then bear me gently to the grave,
  And as you pass along,
  Remember twas my wish to have
  A pleasant funeral song.

The **Preacher***'s sermon can be heard during the hymn.*

Preacher   Great Og and Agog, where are e? Where now is Lot! At Zoar safe? And his wife? A pillar! Salt for pilchards! Come down! Come down thou great

Jehovah! Scat the granite hearts of these hellborn savages!

Jan   Where are we?

Gonetta   Goss Moor.

Jan   Who's dead? Who's died? Tell me.

Gonetta   This is a service of remembrance.

Jan   Who for?

Gonetta   Your father. Tom. He met his death in Michigan.

The service is over. **Maude** *and* **Betty** *start their journey home.* **Betty** *is in floods of tears and* **Maude** *comforts her.*

Maude   Tom id'n dead! E ad'n died! Jan didn die di' e! They all said Jan was dead and I said e wad'n. Tom id'n dead. E a turn up one day, out the blue, just like Jan.

Jan   Aw Christ e's dead Mother! E's dead! Don't you understand e's dead! Listen to me!

Gonetta   She can't 'ear ya. You id'n ere.

Maude *stands alone on a headland looking out to sea.*

Jan   Why don't somebody tell er Thomas is dead! Why can't somebody tell er I never left these shores!

Gonetta   Of course you was shipwrecked.

Jan   No!

Gonetta   You told er that. You told er you survived three shipwrecks.

Jan   I witnessed one. I never left these shores!

Jan *tells the story to* **Maude**, *who doesn't hear.* **Gonetta** *and* **Roscrow** *look on.*

Jan   I'd bin up Plymouth, the big do they ad up there

when Bonaparte was anchored in the Sound? I was
rough as rats. I ad'n et for three days. I was sleepin in
hedges. I resolved to walk home back along the coast to
see what I could pick up off the beaches ... I got some
way down and fetched up at Ropehaven one night. You
know Ropehaven?

Gonetta   No.

Roscrow   I do.

Jan   I walked straight through the place and bedded
down behind a hedge at a remote place called Fox
Cove. On the edge of a cliff. When I woke it was thick
fog. Early mornin. There was a breeze blowin onshore
and the fog hung over the water round the cliff. Did I
say I was alone?

Gonetta   No?

Jan   Well, I wasn't. I thought I was, but I wasn't.

A voice can be heard through the fog. It is the voice of **Blake**, *a
member of a ship's crew. He speaks quietly, without fuss.*

Blake   She's paying off sir.

Captain   Let her wind round on her heels.

Blake   Hard over.

Jan *is now apart from* **Gonetta** *and* **Roscrow**, *next to*
Maude, *on his belly, looking over the cliff.*

Jan   There was no panic in their voices. Commands
were spoken. Voices carry far across water.

Captain   Let go the peak halyard.

Jan   I could see nothin.

Captain   Take a sounding by the bow.

Hoyle   Four fathom sir. We're finding rock.

Captain   Sound aft.

Blake   She's veering.

Captain   Bring the wind aft.

Blake   Hard to starb'd.

Martyn   Three fathoms aft!

Hoyle   Rocks on the larb'd quarter!

Soames   Rocks to starb'd!

Captain   Let go anchors! Both bowyers! Keep her apeak! Tackle up the sheet and let go aft! Reef the t'gallants!

Jan   The anchors splashed, and the sails slatted the masts. All this I was able to hear quite clearly. The breeze had freshened and the fog begun to lift. Suddenly I was able to see a brig schooner, lyin uneasily about a mile offshore, smack between two rocks.

Captain   Weigh anchors! Set the stays'ls! Set the t'gallants! We'll wear her out Mr Blake!

Blake   Brace the yards!

Jan   Close-hauled, she managed to sail more or less straight out to sea. I nearly lost sight of er, but by now the wind was blowin a near gale, and in less time she took to wear the two miles out to sea, the wind blew her back again!

Blake   Furl the t'gallants! Haul it to the yard!

Hoyle   Buntline's parted!

Soames   Foretack's parted!

Captain   Heave her to!

Blake   Clew up the main tops'l! She's slattin! Put down the wheel! Head her! Head her!

Martyn   Stays'l's parted!

By now the sound of wind and sea are very loud, the voices are desperate shouts.

Captain   We must cut away the foremast! It's the only way to head her! Mr Blake! Cut the weather shrouds!

Blake   Down from the rigging! Topmen! Down from the rigging there!

Hoyle   The rudder's dismounted! She's took the sternframe to bits!

Captain   Jury-rig it best you can!

Blake   Come down topmen!

Captain   Martyn! Hoyle!! Soames! Help Mr Blake there! Look out!

Blake   Let go the port boryer!

Jan   Her anchor dragged! They couldn't save her!

Hoyle   Make sternway!

Captain   Let go the starb'd boryer!

Hoyle   That's no bastard good!

Soames   We're stoked in the bilges!

Blake   She's splittin open!

Jan   She was back on the rocks!

Captain   Sling over the boats!

Jan   The ship broke up!

The storm dies down.

It was nearly dark but I could see bodies and debris washin in. Cargo, luggage, utensils, tangled rope, everything you could name. Poultry, dogs, the boats capsized, men were flung this way and that, broken bodies were washed up and I made my way down the cliff to the beach.

He walks on the beach, surrounded by bodies and debris.

I was still alone. Huge breakers crashed and pulled.
Bodies bent backwards over double were tossed and
shaken like straw.

*He walks among the bodies. He checks to see if they're dead. He
finds a carpet bag and a trunk full of clothes, uniforms,
neckerchiefs and boots. He is terrified. He hears a sound. He finds
the body from which it emanates. He looks up at* **Gonetta**.

Jan   God in heaven forgive me for what I did next.
Jesus don't turn your back on me.

*The man who made the sound crawls towards a box which is
sealed and watertight. He falls across the box.* **Jan** *rolls him off
the box and finding a stone, breaks it open. The box is full of
money. The man weakly attempts to clutch at the box.* **Jan** *raises
the stone and brings it down on the man's head.*

Roscrow   You killed him?

Gonetta   'Course e did. How d'ya think people get
wealthy, hard work?

Roscrow (*half to herself*)   So it was murder.

Gonetta   E woulda died anyhow. E couldn save im. E
helped im on is way. Put im out of is misery. E's appier
where e is in the ereafter.

Jan *throws the rock in the sea and shovels the contents of the box
into the carpet bag. He squeezes clothes into the bag and changes
into those which are left. He climbs wearily up the cliff.*

Jan   I cut away from the coast and journeyed across
Goss Moor.

Jan *and* **Maude** *stand opposite each other, far away from each
other.*

Jan   The first person I met, the first living person I
met, was my mother.

Maude *sits on the bank and removes her boots.* **Roscrow** *has
left the bank but* **Salathiel** *is still slumped across her desk.*

Gonetta *sits on the edge of the desk, swinging her legs and drinking gin.* **Hailsham** *bursts through the door.*

Hailsham   Gonetta!

Gonetta   Welcome back.

Hailsham (*indicates* **Salathiel**)   Wake im up!

Gonetta   Bad news?

Hailsham   Labour Protection Bill's bin voted through! We got riots in the lime pits, Tavistock's under siege, they've gone on strike in Brigan, the pilchard fleet's sunk and the viaduct's collapsed over Looe!

Gonetta   Disaster!

Hailsham   There's worse! The potato crop's failed! There's a thousand farmers marching this way demanding back their cash!

Hailsham *is desperately searching for cash.*

Gonetta   You've ad it now.

Hailsham   There's not a penny in the place!

A loud knocking on the front door. The roar of a thousand **Farmers** *without.*

Gonetta   The farmers are here!

Hailsham   Where can I hide?

Gonetta   There's only one place.

Hailsham (*gibbering*)   Help me Gonetta, save me!

Gonetta   The strongroom!

Hailsham   Oo got the key?

Gonetta (*indicates* **Salathiel**)   She keep it down er bosom.

Hailsham *panics.*

Gonetta (*to audience*)   Sad choice, poor chap, face the farmers or take the plunge, tis enough to make you pity im.

Hailsham *decides on the* **Farmers** *but the roar intensifies and the front door bulges on its hinges.* **Hailsham** *picks up* **Salathiel**, *slings her over his shoulder and makes for the strongroom.*

Gonetta (*to audience*)   That should wake er up!

Gonetta *flings open the front door. The* **Farmers** *fall silent.*

Gonetta (*to* **Farmers**)   If you're lookin for your cash Jan May took it Bolivia and bought up all of Kumpfernickel, lead's gone ard again and slate's edged up on granite's bottom so y'can all bugger off ome and celebrate!

She slams the door shut.

(*To audience.*) Tid'n only farmers oo's mesmerised be jargon. If ya wanna tell a lie tell it fancy and fast.

The knocking starts again and the roar intensifies. **Gonetta** *runs.*

Jan *calls across the river:*

Jan   Mother? That you Mother?

Maude   Jan?

Jan   I'm comin ome Mother, for good!

Maude   Why dear, whatever for?

Jan   I've eard all about Ting Tang and I intend to make sure it never happen again.

Maude   But Jan, it id'n likely to.

Jan   Well the bank's gone bust and I ain't got no money so there's nowhere else to go.

Maude   I suppose you want ferryin?

Jan (*wading into river*)   Bless you Mother no. Clamber on my back, I'll see you across.

She climbs on his back and he starts to wade across.

Maude   We got news your father died.

Jan   I heard that.

Maude   Well there's no truth in it. E's too good. God gived im life and e'll die natural when is age come up. E's too damn good to die young.

Jan   Christ Mother you'm some weight.

Maude   Arn't that heavy boy.

Jan   I can't hardly lift ya.

Maude   Aw. (*Pats a bag she's carrying.*) Must be the gold.

Jan   What gold? What, gold? What? Gold!

He drops **Maude** *in the river and grabs for the gold.*

Maude   You stupid wilful boy!

They splash about mid-stream, fighting over the gold.

Jan   Where d'ya get this?

Maude   Your brother Arthur sent it from Michigan put it down! Get me up!

Jan   Now thun Mother I'll do good business with this gold. Tis all I need to get back on me feet again –

Maude   Leave go!

Gran *and* **Colan** *arrive at the river bank.*

Colan   Whass goin on Gran?

Gran   Nothin much, your brother's robbin your mother thass all.

Colan   Oo got the gold?

Gran   E ave.

Colan   Give it back!

Jan   I know exactly where to invest it –

Maude   I got me own plans!

Jan   Madagascar, tother side a Plymouth –

Maude *struggles to her feet and snatches the gold.*

Maude   I don't need no advice.

Jan   What y'gonna do with it?

Maude   Book a passage and join your father in Michigan.

Jan   You can't do that!

Maude   Yes I can.

Colan   Let er go!

Jan   Tom's dead!

Maude   No e id'n.

Jan   Wake up Mother! Face the truth!

Gran   Leave er hope.

Maude   E's only after the gold.

Jan   Don't go!

Maude   See?

Gran   Take im with ya?

Colan   Oo?

Gran   Not you.

Maude *and* **Gran** *look at* **Jan**, *expectant.*

Jan   Me? No! See . . .

Gran   Why?

Jan   I can't. I never went round the world.

Colan You never?

Jan I never left these shores.

Gran Well now's your chance.

Jan *considers the awesome prospect of sailing scross the Atlantic.*

Jan I'm too busy.

Gran O dear.

Colan E goin Gran?

Gran 'Fraid not.

Jan See I'm still chairman of this and that and I got engagements.

Gran Thass too bad.

Jan Tomorrow I'm judgin pies for the Only-the-Sober Circle of Women's fundraising at the Jesuit seminary.

Maude Thass no good. I'll be halfway to Michigan by then.

Jan Mother!

Maude (*to* **Gran**) Jan's come ome. For good.

Gran Why?

Maude Don't ask me, ask Jan.

Exit **Maude**.

Trefusis (*sings*)
Have you never bin to Michigan?
It's a short walk up a plank,
Nothin more, nothin less,
We're going to meet the Yank!

Jan (*in despair*) What have I done? What have I done?

Colan Whass e done Gran?

Gran Gone bust. Got wet.

Hailsham *and* **Salathiel** *arrive at the Brigan side of the river.* **Salathiel** *is dressed in a colourful fetching dress with matching bonnet.* **Hailsham** *is gaunt, a shadow of his former self.*

Hailsham Mr May!

Colan Oo's that?

Gran Arn't sure.

Jan Hailsham? That you? Where've e bin?

Hailsham We was locked in the strongroom.

Jan For three days?

Hailsham We intend to get wed.

Jan Who?

Hailsham Me and um, er . . .

He motions towards **Salathiel**, *then hitches her on his back to cross the river.*

Hailsham See I'm a changed man and she's a changed er, um, and we eard you'd struck gold up Ting Tang and so we said, didn't we dear, wake up blast ya, now's the time to heal the rift and –

Gran I know you.

Hailsham Uh?

Gran Dasher! Dasher Smeely!

Hailsham Aw my gor!

Gran Thirty years I bin untin you!

She hops on **Colan**'s *back.*

Colan Which way?

Gran Fordward! Where's that money y'owe me! Come back ere!

Exit **Hailsham** *and* **Salathiel**, *pursued by* **Gran** *and* **Colan**.

Jan, *alone, sits in the river. He spies* **Mrs Roscrow**.

Jan   Mrs Roscrow! Ann!

He kneels mid-stream.

You see before you a humble, contrite man with nothin more in the world than the suit I stand up in. I gotta big heart though and underneath it all I arn't bad to look at. Won't you marry me now?

Roscrow   It's well known that my last marriage was unhappy and ill-matched Mr May.

Jan   O I accept you're difficult to live with Mrs Roscrow –

Roscrow   After my husband died I emerged from a brief period of mourning to hear the story going round that I'd killed him.

Jan   I can defend myself!

Roscrow   The Bible Christians reckoned me a man and quoted as proof the lack of children.

Jan   Show me how to do it and I'll prove em wrong!

Roscrow   I did nothing to deny it because I was too busy reviving my fortunes. My husband only left me his share in Ting Tang. His money perished with him.

Jan   Perished?

Roscrow   His skull had been shattered by a rock. The storm was so complete that we assumed the cause of death to have been the force of nature.

Gonetta *has arrived. She sits on the river bank, listening.*

Roscrow   He was a brutal man. His death was quite fitting. And the freedom it brought has filled me with a profound love of life Mr May. And I have no one to thank more than you.

Exit **Roscrow**.

Jan (*to* **Gonetta**)   What does she mean? She gonna marry me? Well is she?

Gonetta   You don't love Ann Roscrow.

Jan   Don't I? I love some bugger, must do. Who?

Gonetta   Me.

Jan   You? Gonetta?

Gonetta   Look at ya. Wet through, soaked to the skin, on your knees mid-stream in the river, are these the conditions under which one falls in love?

Jan   No.

Gonetta   Well thass too bad.

Jan   How d'ya mean?

Gonetta (*going*)   You've had your chance.

Jan   What?

Gonetta (*to audience*)   First thing ya do is plant the notion in is ead then y'turn the bugger down and watch im scramble.

Exit **Gonetta**.

Jan   Gonetta?

An anthem is sung:

Anthem
    Jan May! Traveller! Son of Ting Tang!
    None the wiser! Worthless! And wet!
    Fortune's come and fortune's gone!
    Welcome home! Welcome home! Well met!

CPSIA information can be obtained at www.ICGtesting.com
Printed in the USA
LVOW08s0721120813

347437LV00001B/7/P